Textbook of
MEDICAL ETHICS

Textbook of
MEDICAL ETHICS

Erich H. Loewy, M.D.

University of Illinois College of Medicine at Peoria
Peoria, Illinois
and University of Illinois at Chicago
Chicago, Illinois

Plenum Medical Book Company • New York and London

ISBN 0-306-43280-3

This book is dedicated to my
students—past, present, and future

Acknowledgments

It is impossible to single out all the persons who have contributed to this book. Special thanks go to my chief, Dr. A. William Holmes, not only for the opportunity to write this book but especially for creating within our Department of Medicine an atmosphere conducive to such efforts. His insights, encouragements, and criticisms were crucial for moving this work along.

Likewise, very special thanks must go to Dr. David C. Thomasma and Dr. Larry R. Churchill for their criticisms, comments, and seminal suggestions as well as, and above all, for their friendship. Without them this work would have been impossible.

I especially want to thank my students whose continued help and encouragement were so vital. Among the many, I especially want to thank Dr. Kurt Hopfensperger (currently doing his residency at the University of Kansas), Ms. Sally Rigler (about to be Dr. Rigler and also about to go to the University of Kansas), and Mr. Joel Diamant (a new Senior and my James scholar). These three waded through preliminary drafts, criticized, commented, and encouraged. Their special contributions were, and continue to be, invaluable.

Lastly, and most certainly not least, I want to thank my wife. As a philosopher, her insights were essential; as a person, her support was of immeasurable importance. If this work does not fall "dead born from the presses," it is largely thanks to her.

Preface

When physicians in training enter their clinical years and first begin to become involved in clinical decision making, they soon find that more than the technical data they had so carefully learned is involved. Prior to that time, of course, they were aware that more than technology was involved in practicing medicine, but here, for the first time, the reality is forcefully brought home. It may be on the medical ward, when a patient or a patient's relatives ask that no further treatment be given and that the patient be allowed to die; it may be in ob/gyn, when a 4- or 5-month pregnant lady with two other children and just deserted by her husband pleads for an abortion; it may be in the outpatient setting, where patients unable to afford enough to eat cannot afford to buy antibiotics for their sick child or provide him or her with the recommended diet. Whatever the setting, students soon find themselves confronted with problems in which an answer is not given by the technical possibilities alone; indeed, students may have to face situations in which, all things considered, the use of these technical possibilities seems ill-advised. But choices need to be made.

Some of us may choose to hide behind a mastery of technology. Trained in a complicated endeavor and fully occupied keeping up with changes in our field, we may choose not to use our precious time thinking about the moral implications of our task. When medicine allows its practitioners to pay attention only to technology and, by this, forces them to shortchange other things, it necessarily reduces professionals to technicians who must act under another's direction.

Medical ethics applies the principles and rules of everyday morality to the medical context.[1] It is, therefore, not an esoteric discipline dealing with matters tangential to medical practice but is central to it.[2] The medical context is both charged with intense emotion and problematic because of the complexity of its subject material and options.[1] It shapes our ethical thought, forces it to adapt, and necessitates a supple interpretation and reconstruction of everyday morality so that it can be sensibly applied.

Medicine as a profession requires an enormous amount of technical information and skill. Schools of medicine, therefore, justly require that its graduates acquire a minimal basis of technical information and skill and, above all, that students develop a habit of learning and of scholarly analysis. Such habits allow an orderly acquisition of new material and knowledge and prepare students to integrate such material into the basic core taught at school. In that fashion, colleges of medicine, as do all other institutions of higher learning, undertake a community responsibility. Communities support such institutions to safeguard their own future. They trust that graduates of such institutions will be at least minimally informed and skilled in the profession of their choice. Colleges, as do all other institutionalized organs of a community, thus bear a moral responsibility to the community as well as to their own members. In the initial charge given to the institution by the community, a moral presupposition is implied.

There are two broad ways of ethical thinking: in one, there are those who believe that absolute "truth" exists and that it is accessible to man; in the other, there are those who either disbelieve the concept of absolute "truth" or who, while they may believe in its existence, hold that such truth is not accessible to man in the human condition. Absolutists usually draw the obvious conclusion: knowing the absolute truth necessitates that others must be forced to share the absolutists' view if only for their own good. The nonabsolutist, on the other hand, knows "truth" in an only tentative way and is loath to force such tenuous conclusions on others by force. The gulf that divides these two basic attitudes is unbreachable for neither side can convince the other. A pluralist society obviously can remain peaceful only as long as respect for other points of view is tacitly and explicitly acknowledged.

Ethics is not simply "doing the right thing" or "feeling the right way." Rather, ethics gropes for what the "right" thing to do is. In a pluralist world, the "right" thing becomes very problematic, and religious ethics loses general appeal. What is "right" in a religious ethic is "right" within a specific belief group and is justified by appeal to that group's belief system. Such an appeal remains uniquely unpersuasive to others who do not happen to share in the same belief system.

Secular ethics, therefore, seeks to find a common bond among men. The problem, as Engelhardt so aptly puts it, is "how to fashion an ethic for biomedical problems that can speak with rational authority across the great diversity of moral viewpoints."3 This, of course, is hardly a problem unique to biomedical ethics. It is true not only for the biomedical sciences but for virtually all activities that engage more than one belief group. In secular ethics, we attempt to appeal our judgments to reason. The way we think about situations derives from our views of ethical theory (everyone, in fact, has an ethical theory, however inchoate it may be) as well as from our emotions, aesthetic feelings, experiences, and background. Such a variety of underpinnings to our thinking eventuate in the broad principles to which we tailor our daily rules, from which we derive our specific judgments, and with which we ultimately guide our lives. Medicine, in its ethics, obviously is an example of this.

Ethics can be done on two levels: one can do ethics on a preprofessional or on a professional level. Either one can look at ethics as an exchange of pleasantries and feelings or one can conduct a disciplined inquiry into the "rightness" or "wrongness" of certain things. It is somewhat analogous to using sugar. Sugar can be used by a nice grandmother to bake wonderful cookies. She knows that sugar is sweet, and she knows approximately how many tablespoons to use, seasoning as she goes. Or sugar can be used in the way that a professional person would use it. To do this, sugar must be known to have a certain biochemical structure, to be metabolized in certain ways, and to yield a certain amount of calories. Exchanging pleasantries about the rightness or wrongness of, say, abortion or the maintaining of vegetative persons is a far different issue than a disciplined investigation of what it is about killing people that we hold to be wrong and then addressing a clinical problem in that way. If we approach ethics in the grandmother's model, we have a "bull session": valuable, even enjoyable, but of not much lasting professional value. "Bull sessions" are to be encouraged and can be learned from, but they are most valuable when grounded in disciplined knowledge of a topic. The preprofessional or grandmother approach to ethics, furthermore, cannot help reconcile differing visions of what is and what is not sweet or what is and what is not "right."

Why should physicians have to bother about ethics? Their task is to promote health and cure disease, and that of the student physician is to acquire the knowledge and the techniques to do this. Surely, health and the curing of disease is a moral task about which few would quibble, and those who would would surely not seek out physicians. Or would they? People define health, disease, and cure in vastly different ways not only within our "time slice" but historically. Is masturbation a disease?4 Is abortion a cure? What do we mean when we use these terms? There are no value-free activities, and there is no absolute way of adjudicating differences in values.[3]

Plato, who distinguished between an "art" and a "craft," held medicine to be an art.[5] An art, according to Plato, used technical means to subserve a moral end (seeking the patient's "good"); a craft used technical means to bring about a technical end (a pair of shoes or the normalization of blood gases as an end in itself). In being a profession, medicine (today as always) must be, in that sense, an art.

According to Pellegrino,[6] the act of profession seeks "to bring about a good act of healing in the face of illness." This "good act of healing" is more than the restitution of "numbers" or the normalization of "blood gases." Central to medicine, no matter what the field or mode of practice, stands the "good" of the patient. In a pluralist society, the definition of the "good" and the arbitration of different conceptions of the "good" therefore form a necessary element of medical practice.[7,8]

To profess "a good act of healing in the face of illness," then, requires a notion of the moral end that our technology must subserve. If physicians are to function as knowing professionals instead of as technicians taught only a very narrow understanding of their craft (if, in other words, they are to be men and women of discernment who can make and not only carry out choices and options) they must understand the underpinnings of medicine, be it pathophysiology, pharmacology, or ethics. It is my contention that ethics is as intrinsic to medical decision making as are more technical matters.

Physicians and basic scientists who wish to contribute to medicine share a common enterprise. Physicians must understand basic facts of physiology or pharmacology in order to function intelligently; medical physiologists, on the other hand, need to understand the needs of practitioners. A body of cognitive knowledge common to both enables their joint enterprise. Ethicists and physicians likewise share this mutual need for a comprehended body of cognitive knowledge.

The realization that physicians and other health professionals all too often have confronted ethical problems ill equipped to think out reasonable options has motivated the teaching of ethics in an ever-larger number of American medical and allied colleges today. Ethics does not pretend to supply answers that can be applied in a "cookie-cutter" fashion to problems. Instead, it aims to impart a core of knowledge so that it can be applied to the problem at hand and, after that, to provide practice in manipulating this knowledge and to use analytic skills in the context of actual cases. It is not the aim of teaching ethics to make students more moral any more than it is the aim of teaching medicine to make students healthier.[2] It is hoped that teaching ethics will help reconnect the student with the nonmedical world and will foster sensitivity, the first and the most essential step in dealing with ethical problems.[9]

REFERENCES

1. Clouser, K.D., What is medical ethics? Ann. Intern. Med. 80(4):657–660, 1974.
2. Loewy, E.H., Teaching ethics to medical students, J. Med. Educ. 61(8):661–665, 1986.
3. Engelhardt, H.T., The Foundations of Bioethics, Oxford University Press, New York, 1986.
4. Engelhardt, H.T., The disease of masturbation: Values and the concept of disease, Bull. Hist. Med. 48:234–248, 1974.
5. Plato, Gorgias, in: Plato: The Collected Dialogues (E. Hamilton and C. Huntington, ed.), Princeton University Press, Princeton, NJ, 1978, pp. 229–307.
6. Pellegrino, E.D., Toward a reconstruction of medical morality: The primacy of the act of profession and the fact of illness, J. Med. Phil. 4(1):32–55, 1979.
7. Loewy, E.H., Physicians and patients: Moral agency in a pluralist world, J. Med. Humanities Bioethics 7(1):57–68, 1986.
8. Pellegrino, E.D., and Thomasma, D.C., For the Patient's Good: The Restoration of Beneficence to Health Care, Oxford University Press, New York, 1988.
9. Clouser, K.D., Teaching Bioethics: Strategies, Problems and Resources, Hastings Center, Hastings-on-Hudson, NY, 1980.

Contents

CHAPTER 1

Historical Introduction

This chapter gives a brief overview of the historical forces that have tended to condition the way we look at medical ethics today.

INTRODUCTION

Medical ethics in one sense does and in another does not differ from ethics in general. In a qualitative sense, the principles of action that underwrite all moral choice underwrite the choices here; in another, more quantitative sense, medical ethics differs because of the complexity and often puzzling nature of its subject material and because of the intense emotions accompanying many of its choices.[1]

Ethics in general (and applied ethics in particular) if it is to accomplish its avowed goal of helping people to live the good life, relies for its deliberations and judgments on a rich background of philosophy, psychology, anthropology, sociology, history, and the arts; applied ethics, in addition, requires an understanding of the matter to which it is to be applied, an understanding that includes emotive and experiential considerations rather than cognitive material alone. Some would deny this. They feel that ethical analysis can take place away from the context in which the problem is embedded and from the moral actors who eventually must act, that it need only be conversant with the cognitive material under immediate considerations and that such analysis then constitutes the sufficient condition for action.

This book assumes that medical ethics cannot make a judgment about problems unless it considers their context as well as the moral actors involved. A dispassionate analysis of encapsulated problems

1

unmindful of their context may help clarify some aspects, but it cannot, in a practical sense, provide equitable solutions.[2,3] Problems taken out of their context, divorced from the moral actors who must act, and uninformed by history are changed problems. Analyzing them in such an encapsulated fashion can be helpful in providing more dispassionate insights; but such insights, if they are to fulfill a meaningful role, must be carefully fitted into particular contexts and must be mindful of the moral actors involved.

When physicians first learn about disease, they do so outside the context of specific patients or situations. Only after they have mastered pneumonia as a concept, only after they understand a disease's pathophysiological underpinnings, can they turn to the specific problem of pneumonia in Mr. Tintfeather. Mr. Tintfeather may, in addition, have a variety of underlying pathological conditions, live in a specific social setting, and have other features that alter both diagnostic and therapeutic considerations. Mr. Tintfeather may be an active college professor, an alcoholic living on the street, or he may be brain dead. He has pneumonia in that he meets certain necessary and sufficient criteria for such a diagnosis, but his particular pneumonia can be understood and dealt with only within his own peculiar circumstances. Likewise, Ms. Swidalski, who wants an abortion, cannot be dealt with outside the realization that she is, perhaps, a 15-year-old who was raped by a psychotic madman carrying a dominant gene for insanity or a 25-year-old woman who wants an abortion so as to fit into her new spring dress. Analyzing the diagnosis and treatment of pneumonia away from Mr. Tintfeather, or the problem of abortion apart from the persons involved is perhaps helpful; but it is helpful only up to a point. It is a sterile exercise unless the results of analysis are carefully, thoughtfully, and compassionately applied to the locus of the actual problem.

Primitive Medicine

Medical ethics is an integral part of the fabric of medical decision making and has undoubtedly always been an important consideration in medical practice. Medicine, philosophy, and religious practices had their origins in the mass of primitive beliefs and taboos that early man used to try to understand and manipulate his world. Tribes of hunter/gatherers roamed the earth without much specialization and with little regard for individual talents or skills. No doubt it was soon evident that some were less adept at hunting and perhaps had a special knack for making flints or tools. They produced tangible material objects and were supported by their tribe in return. Specialization, if indeed it ever did not exist, was born.[4]

Men have always feared the unknown and have always stood in terror of forces beyond their comprehension. Understanding these forces and dealing with them (even if "understanding" and "dealing" were, to our way of thinking, purely illusory) allowed man to cope with terror. The same activity goes on today. We label a constellation of findings and call it a disease (or we attribute causality on shaky grounds), and, having so labeled it (or attributed causality), we now feel better about it. Primitive man constructed a series of stories and created a myriad of myths to explain these forces and consequently made them appear less terrorizing. The world and its objects swarmed with spirits, many malevolent and all needing to be appeased. No doubt, some men were temperamentally better equipped to deal with these mysteries. They soon developed a series of elaborate rites and customs to propitiate the unseen powers. Such men, the medicine man or shaman found in all tribes, were seen as skillful. They were the first intellectuals: men supported by their compatriots not to produce material objects but to deal with abstractions. Philosophy, religion, and medicine have common roots in dealing with these forces. Magic was their tool.

Primitive man in dealing with his fellows and with the forces about him was necessarily, even if often unconsciously, concerned with ethics. Propitiating the unknown and mediating between it and his charges, the shaman had to make judgments based on a system of values and had to evolve a set of rules eventually expressed in ritual. Such behavior, in turn, was in need of justification by an appeal to higher values or principles.

Shamans were not frauds. They believed as intensely and as passionately in their capacities as we believe in penicillin or open heart surgery today. In treating their patients, therefore, they were faced with a set of moral problems even if these were not labeled as such. Ethical dilemmas in treatment do not depend on the technical "rightness" or "wrongness" of such treatment; what is "right" today may well be proven "wrong" tomorrow. Such dilemmas depend on the application of a treatment sincerely believed to be the "right" thing for a patient to that patient and on the relationship between professional and patient. If, in the shaman's sincere belief, a certain rite can propitiate the evil spirits that cause the patient to burn and shake, the decision to use such a rite becomes a moral decision. The fact that rites rarely cure malaria is irrelevant to the issue.[5]

PRE-HIPPOCRATIC

Our knowledge of ethics in the pre-Hippocratic world is fragmentary.[6] Amundsen's claim that "ethics . . . is even less apt to be borrowed . . . than are medical theory and concomitant technique"[6] is undoubtedly true but does not negate the influence that the philosophy of one has upon the philosophy of another culture. It is now firmly established that there was widespread communication between the various cultures flourishing in the known ancient world; to believe that diverse beliefs were entirely without influence on each other would be a naive notion.

And yet, there were vast differences between the rigid rules that governed the practice of medicine in Hammurabi's Babylonia or in ancient Egypt and the freedom with which medicine was practiced in ancient Greece. In Babylonia, the *Code of Hammurabi* (1727 B.C.E.) represents the first attempt to regulate medicine and to protect patients from incompetent (or unlucky) doctors. In Egypt, too, medical practice was rigidly fixed by law: in the Hermetic *Book of Toth*, Egyptian physicians are enjoined not to deviate from the rigidly prescribed regimen under fear of death.[7] Aristotle, however, states that physicians were allowed to alter treatment if, after the fourth day, the traditional approach had been found useless.[8] Persian medical ethics was "modern" in speaking not only of the cognitive but also of the characterological attributes of the good physician.[9] In Greece and in most of the later Hellenistic and Roman world, no strict laws applied.

THE ANCIENT WORLD

The fabric of ethics, like a woven cloth, has always consisted of a large number of strands combining various ground views. Does ethics seek to benefit patients, physicians, the profession, or the community and its particular institutions? When we look at these various forms of ethics, some very obvious differences exist. The Hippocratic corpus, extending as it apparently does over several centuries and authors, is not all of one piece. Nevertheless, its main thrust is to prescribe a certain standard of decorum, "a certain etiquette, mainly to uphold a certain standard of performance, and serves to distinguish the expert from the charlatan."[10] Greek physicians, unlike their Babylonian or Egyptian colleagues, were quite unfettered by state regulations. They were itinerant craftsmen. To the Hippocratic physician the sole purpose of medicine was the application of knowledge to the treatment of disease, and his ethics consisted of doing this well. It is, as Edelstein repeatedly points out, "an ethic of outer achievement rather than one of inner intention."[10] The injunctions and enjoinders given to physicians in the Hippocratic corpus are intended to safeguard the art and guard the reputation of the profession and its practitioners. Hippocratic physicians, furthermore, were neither the only nor the most common medical practitioners in ancient Greece. The Asclepiads and many other models coexisted and, at times, freely exchanged patients with the Hippocratics.[11]

One cannot understand the medical ethics of ancient times unless one acknowledges that they were informed by a wide variety of philosophical persuasions. There was a wide variation between Homeric beliefs, which, for example, viewed chthonic personal immortality as being that of shadows in the underworld, and the beliefs of the Pythagoreans, who initiated a belief in divine personal immortality otherwise alien to Greek thought.[9] Greek philosophy as well as Greek medical ethics is not a monolithic point of view. Rather, it is composed of diverse strands forming a rich fabric that imperceptibly merges into the later Roman and early Christian practices.

The depth of the Pythagorean influence on the Hippocratic Oath is debatable.[9,11] Whatever its extent, a significant influence is probably beyond doubt. The Pythagoreans in many respects presaged some of the later Christian doctrines: personal immortality and an essentially life ethic, to name but two. The Hippocratic Oath, when seen in its original form, prescribes the relations of student to teacher, establishes the duty to transmit knowledge as well as fixing those to whom it is and those to whom it is not to be transmitted, and sets standards of medical function and decorum. Interpreted by our light, it provides a framework of medical behavior and, perhaps, ethics to which we can relate even though we may not be able to agree with it in its entirety; viewed in the light of Greco-Roman culture, it emerges as a powerful tool seeking to safeguard the reputation of medicine and that of its practitioners rather than, in the main, seeking to promote the patients' good for its own sake. Clearly it is a document of outward, rather than one of inward, intention. What matters most to the Hippocratics is how the physician's behavior is perceived.

THE HELLENISTIC AND ROMAN WORLDS

The Hellenistic world spread Greek culture, modified by local custom, throughout the known world. It provided a bridge to the Roman world and to the Christian era beyond. The philosophy, the science, and the medical ethics of those times are composed of the many strands of early Western culture and, in addition, show a strong influence from the Persians and other more Eastern nations. Pythagorean views, undoubtedly of substantial influence on Platonic ideas and ideals and to a greater or lesser extent influencing the ethics central to the writing of the Hippocratic corpus, contrasted with those of the Stoa (starting with Zeno ca. 300 B.C.E.) and of the Epicureans (ca. 200 B.C.E.). These, in contrast to the Pythagoreans and to Plato who believed in personal immortality, believed in natural personal dissolution without after-life and without heaven or hell. The purpose of life was to be fulfilled on earth. They strove for "phronesis" or practical wisdom. The belief in the unity of all rational beings and in the fundamental equality of all men, is central to Stoic and Epicurean beliefs. Panaetius (190–109 B.C.E.), as later represented by Cicero in On Duties, speaks about professional ethics. On Duties became "the manual of all later humanism, ancient and Christian, secular and religious alike."[10]

These different threads and views must have found expression in the late Hellenistic and early Roman world. The first expression of what we today would consider truly medical ethics is recorded in the writing of Scribonius Largus (2–52 C.E.).[10,12,13] Intriguingly, Scribonius speaks of what we today would consider to be medical humanism not as something to be argued for but rather as something "quite self-evident to himself and his readers."[13] Influenced profoundly by the Stoa and interpreting the Hippocratic corpus in their light, Scribonius sees medicine as a "profession" and, therefore, in the view of the time, as necessarily containing a fundamental core of ethics. He introduces a textbook of pharmacology in which he argues for the use of drugs in treating patients (not by any means an established thesis then) by a chapter on what we today would clearly call "medical ethics."[12,13] Scribonius carefully deals with the question of what a physician is (not an easy one in the days before universities, licensing boards or, in Greco-Roman times, state control) and what the duties of physicians are vis-à-vis patients. Humaneness, friendliness, and philanthropy, as Scribonius sees them, are not merely minor social virtues meant to enlarge medicine's reputation (as they largely were seen to be in the Hippocratic corpus)[10] but are the special obligation of the physician.

Ethics, in Scribonius' view, is intrinsic to medicine, not extrinsic to it. With Scribonius we have advanced from an ethic of outward performance to one of inner intention. Among other things, Scribonius grapples with the duty of physicians toward their patients and toward the state. When in state service (Scribonius served as physician with the Roman legions), physicians may fight against the enemy as soldiers but, as physicians, they must harm no one and treat friend and foe alike. "Medicine," Scribonius says, "is the knowledge of healing not of hurting." Physicians are remiss in their duty if they do not know all that they ought to know, make use of that knowledge for the benefit of (all) the sick, and, especially, if they fail to fulfill their ethical obligations.[10]

MEDIEVAL MEDICINE

Scribonius' rather progressive and, to contemporary ears, pleasing perspective (one that in its outline and humane views resembles much of Ramsey's work in this century[14]) did not directly manage to perpetuate itself. Although Galen (131–201 C.E.) felt that a true physician optimally should himself become a philosopher and practice medicine out of love of humanity, he saw nothing inconsistent with other motives (love of money, love of status, etc.) underwriting the physician's function. The matter of motive, to Galen and others, is one of personal choice and has no intrinsic connections with the practice of medicine.[10] From the point of view of medicine, the physician's "specific morality is incidental rather than essential."[10] A physician is expected to be an expert in medicine—all else is supererogatory. Once again, and less than 100 years after Scribonius, we are back to an ethic of outward performance; inner intention is a desirable decoration but little else.

The influence of Galen permeates the medieval period. His views, adopted early on by the Church, became near-dogma to be learned, not to be challenged. Attitudes toward health and disease profoundly affected ethical positions. In one view, God sent disease as punishment (a just affliction sent in retribution for some sin) or as a test: in either case, the problem is outside man's province and jurisdiction. If we are to follow the Sermon on the Mount, are we not like the "fowl of the air" or the "lilies of the field," cared for without our efforts by our Father?[15] Such problems had been argued in the Talmud and had been clearly adjudicated in favor of healing: God intended physicians to heal just as He expected farmers to till the soil. God no more intended the earth to lie fallow and men to starve than He did disease to go untreated. In Some Christian circles, an ambivalence toward medicine (the physician as opposing God's will or the physician as instrument of God in opposing disease, pain, and death) has persisted until this day.[25]

The emphasis on Christian charity, however, worked toward the institutionalization of care for the sick. Despite the existence of hospitals in ancient Egypt and the Asclepiad temples of Greece (in which patients underwent "incubation"), hospitals in the Western world first began to emerge at the beginning of the fourth century. Such "hospitals," however, were not hospitals in any modern sense. Rather, they involved a conglomerate of charitable institutions and included foundling homes, orphanages, old-age homes, hostelries for the traveler, and infirmaries. Administration was largely in the hands of the clergy. Physicians were often priests, and the duties of physicians were, first of all, largely defined in religious terms. Healing the soul was not distinctly separated or separable from healing the body, and healing the soul had priority. Physicians were enjoined to make sure that their patients' spiritual needs had been met both because "many illnesses originate on account of sin" and because the safety of the soul was the main issue. The Lateran Council of 1225 advised that physicians admonish patients to see a priest, and Pius V in 1566 asserted that after 3 days physicians cannot continue to treat patients who had not confessed. Violators of this rule were to be disbarred from further practice.[16] Institutions granting medical licensure required graduates to take an oath promising to abide by this rule. The physician not rarely was crowded from the bedside by the priest, in part, it is said, in order to extract payments for relics, masses, holy candles, or appeals to the Saints.[17]

Medical regulations and licensure began largely during the medieval period. In the 12th century, Roger II of Sicily decreed that all potential practitioners of medicine had to appear before judges and officers of the crown to be examined before being licensed to practice. Roger's grandson Frederick II of Hohenstaufen, who was the Holy Roman Emperor, confirmed and extended this decree by insisting that all those who were to be licensed must first be examined by the medical faculty of the medical college at Salerno. Before the examination could take place, candidates were required to show proof that they had undergone a rigorous course of study for a total of 8 years and had then spent an additional year (an internship of sorts) working under the direction of an experienced physician. This attempt to institute a secular license was, of course, part of the ongoing struggle between the papacy and the Holy Roman Empire: the Guelfs and the Ghibellins.[18]

Medicine, furthermore, was hardly a cohesive whole; as it emerged in the later Middle Ages it was a pyramid. At the top stood university-trained physicians with a reputation for learning. Until after the 14th century, unfortunately, such learning largely consisted of circular memorization and scholastic quibbling. It was largely useless. Next, in a hierarchical line, came the surgeon (united with the physicians and becoming university trained only after the 14th century). Surgeons had less training but frequently were more likely to help. Barber surgeons, a large step down from "surgeons," practiced phlebotomy and cautery, sometimes on their own but much of the time at the direction of physicians or surgeons. More often than not, barber surgeons were illiterate. Apothecaries mixed often useless "Galenicals," and a host of untrained quacks pretending to things medical completed the "health-care team" of that day.[19]

Physicians were expected to be charitable and competent. The definition of this, of course, was in the framework of the time. Euthanasia and abortion (after "animation" or "ensoulment" at any rate) were considered unethical. (This is elaborated in later chapters.) As with most other aspects of life, medical ethics was determined and directly or indirectly enforced by the Church and by its secular agents in accordance with the church's particular agenda.

THE PLAGUE

The Medieval Plague (1348–1352) and the subsequent series of plagues that struck Europe had a profound influence on every aspect of life. The role and duties of physicians vis-à-vis their patients was severely tested.[19] It is amply clear that while some physicians abandoned their patients, most stayed (see also Chapter 8 on risk-taking). Available documents indicate that physicians who stayed were "motivated by compassion, charity, and a sense of duty."[17] The Black Death of 1348 gave rise to what was then called (and is still called in many eastern European countries today) "medical deontology": medical ethics done to examine the ethics of the profession.[21-24]

POST-PLAGUE

After the plague swept Europe in the 14th century, physicians more and more began to see themselves as bound by moral duties beyond those imposed by the Church. Furthermore, the formation of guilds had their influence on medicine. In institutionalizing medicine and the colleges, in keeping qualifications and licensure predominantly within medical hands, medicine shared in the medieval idea of keeping the function as well as the production of professionals within professional control. Peer-review, licensure, board certification, and other aspects of modern medicine are directly derived from this. The frequent preoccupation with medical etiquette, as distinct from medical ethics, can be traced to the prevailing desire to safeguard medicine's reputation (we would call it "image" today). The ethic of outward performance, then as now, still played a predominant role.

As ideas of science progressed, the role of medicine changed. Francis Bacon (1561–1626) divided medicine's function into the preservation of health, the cure of disease, and the prolongation of life. The prolongation of life was seen as a new task—it had, as Amundsen has pointed out, "no classical (and also few medieval) roots."[26] The care of the "incurable," heretofore not a part of the ethical practice of medicine, now became important, initially in order to learn how to treat diseases previously held incurable and, after the 17th century, for other reasons as well. Prolonging life was shortly to be seen as medicine's prime function, and keeping people alive—not necessarily the same thing—was shortly to become almost an obsession.

From the early 17th century onward, works of medical ethics (as distinct from medical etiquette) began to appear. Rodericus à Castro (1546–1627),[25] overlapping Francis Bacon, published one of the very first works of medical ethics: *The Responsible Physician or the Duties of the Physician towards the Public*. A later work by Johannes Bohn of Leipzig (1640–1718) deals both with the obligation of physicians toward their patients and with the physician's civic responsibilities.[25] The literature of the day, still largely rooted in Church attitudes, started to involve itself with the physician/patient relationship as well as with medicine's civic responsibilities in more modern terms.

THE ENLIGHTENMENT TO MODERN TIMES

The Enlightenment of the 17th and 18th centuries and its emphasis on human reason as well as its goals of knowledge and freedom propelled medieval thought into the modern era. Newton (1643–1727), emphasizing the application of scientific principles to the solution of problems, presages medicine's later preoccupation with science. Medicine began to view itself as a largely dispassionate scientific enterprise. Philosophers of that era, furthermore, had a profound influence on the evolution of medical ethics. Hume (1711–1776), with his emphasis on moral sentiments (the physician's character, as it were), Kant (1724–1804) examining concepts of duty and the relationships of categories of thought and later Mill (1806–1873) and his examination of the role of utility left a stamp on ethical thinking in medicine which is reflected in much of our thinking today. In addition, the French revolution (1791) changed the relationship of men to each other: individual dignity and individual rights, class differences notwithstanding, began to be emphasized and subtly affected the relationship patients and physicians had with each other. Daring to ask questions of those in power was no longer unthinkable.

Physicians and physician-scientists continued to be schooled in the areas of humanism that a classical education favored. They continued to pursue moral ends by ever more complicated technical means. Applying these means to their patients in a more and more "Newtonian" fashion, medicine lost some of the warmer social aspects of its previous function. Traditionally paternalistic, seeking the patient's "good" on terms defined by the doctor, medicine evolved into the 19th and early 20th century model of "scientific" medicine. Scientific medicine, of course, had enormous benefits: it allowed many to escape disease, many to be cured, many to live without pain. It allowed physicians to understand disease process rather than conflating symptom and disease. Unfortunately, it also allowed a new confusion: symptom no longer was held to be disease, but the patient and the social context in which disease took place were often forgotten. A military metaphor[27,28] in which "batteries" of tests were utilized to help "aim" our "armamentarium" in the "conquest" of disease became universally used even when, as in chronic disease or in the care of the terminally ill, it is no longer appropriate. The patient became a battleground on which physicians waged battles with disease; the battlefield, like Verdun 70 years later, was often left devastated. In struggling for the patient's bodily health, the patient as a human being was all too often forgotten.

A superficial examination of history would tend to support the thesis that our concern with moral issues in medicine originated in response to the possibilities raised by the proliferation of science and technology. On the other hand, some have argued that moral issues did not arise out of technology but rather that technology developed "in response to a deeper and a prior moral concern."[29] Man's fear of unknown forces, of death, and of illness, man's search, in other words, for the good life, prompted the exploration of the unknown and the development of technology to deal with it effectively. A closer examination of this relationship would indicate that it is reciprocal: questions of morality and the development of technology are mutually reinforcing. A dialectic between moral concerns and technological options produces a synthesis facilitating the development of both. The old paternalistic model of previous ages was incorporated in the scientific model. The patient's "good" usually continued to be defined on the physician's terms. With more and more attention given to disease, the patient tended to be neglected: the "good" was more often than not seen in terms of "conquering" a particular disease or aberration.

One cannot separate medicine and its values from the culture that nourishes it and in which it functions. Medicine's moral views can differ in emphasis and detail, but they cannot differ substantially. American society, predicated on competition and personal gain, should not be surprised if its practitioners evolve into businessmen vying for a share of the "health-care dollar."[30,31] The quality of the "product" sold to the customer (the patient) must assure customer satisfaction so that the "business" rather than the patient may prosper. The emphasis on customer satisfaction—rather than on patient service or patient "good"—constitutes a change in moral view. An ethic of outward performance is given full reign in the entrepreneurial model of today's emerging medical practice.

Medicine, although it is rooted in the soil of the culture that sustains it, nevertheless has its own separate identity. It cannot be entirely distinct from that culture and shares with its culture a host of values and viewpoints, but it nevertheless has its own distinctive history and, therefore, its own distinctive set of values and precepts. Medicine need not become entirely enmeshed in the entrepreneurial model; rather, medicine can use its historical viewpoints and its traditions to support its own distinctive ethos. Although such an ethos perforce needs to function within specific communities and accommodate its function to them, it nevertheless does not have to have values and viewpoints that are identical when it comes to its own professional function. Furthermore, medicine in discharging its social function may be able to do much to ameliorate what it may see as a point of view inimical to the interest of patients in a wider sense: social conditions have much to do with illness and health, and medicine may well see itself as obliged to try and bring about social (and, therefore, inevitably philosophical) changes in the way the community sees itself (see also Chapter 6 on the physician as citizen).

REFERENCES

1. Clouser, K.D., What is medical ethics? Ann. Intern. Med. 80:657–660, 1974.
2. Churchill, L.R., Bioethical reductionism and our sense of the human, Man Med. 5(4):229–249, 1980.
3. Churchill, L.R., Principles and the search for moral certainty, Soc. Sci. Med. 23(5):461–469, 1986.

4. Loewy, E.H., Clergy and physicians confront medical ethics, *Humane Med.* 3(1):48–51, 1986.
5. Loewy, E.H., Introduction, in: *Ethical Dilemmas in Modern Medicine: A Physician's Viewpoint* (E.H. Loewy, ed.), Edwin Mellen Press, Lewiston, NY, 1986, pp. 1–15.
6. Amundsen, D., History of medical ethics: Ancient near east, in: *Encyclopedia of Bioethics* (W.T. Reich, ed.), The Free Press, New York, 1978, pp. 880–884.
7. Garrison, F.H., *An Introduction to the History of Medicine*, W. B. Saunders, Philadelphia, 1929.
8. Aristotle, Politics III, 15, in: *The Basic Works of Aristotle* (R. McKeon, ed.), Random House, New York, pp. 1127–1324.
9. Carrick, P., *Medical Ethics in Antiquity*, D. Reidel, Boston, 1985.
10. Edelstein, L., The professional ethics of the Greek physician, *Bull. Hist. Med.* 30(5):391–419, 1956.
11. Edelstein, L., The Hippocratic Oath, in: *Ancient Medicine: Selected Papers of Ludwig Edelstein* (O. Temkin and C.L. Temkin, eds.), The Johns Hopkins Press, Baltimore, 1967, pp. 3–63.
12. Deichgräber, K., Professio medici: Zum Vorwort des Scribonius Largus, *Abh. Akad. Mainz.* 9:856–862, 1950.
13. Hamilton, J.S., Scribonius Largus on the medical profession, *Bull. Hist. Med.* 60:209–216, 1986.
14. Ramsey, P., *The Patient as Person*, Yale University Press, New Haven, 1970.
15. *The Bible, New Testament*, Matthew 6:26–28.
16. Amundsen, D.W., History of medieval medical ethics, in: *Encyclopedia of Bioethics* (W.T. Reich, ed.), The Free Press, New York, 1978, pp. 938–951.
17. Marks, G., *The Medieval Plague*, Doubleday, New York, 1979.
18. Hartung, E.F., Medical regulations of Frederick the Second of Hohenstaufen, *Medical Life* 41:587–601, 1934.
19. Gottfried, R.S., *The Black Death*, The Free Press, New York, 1983.
20. Loewy, E.H., Duties, fears and physicians. *Soc. Sci. Med.* 22(12):1363–1366, 1986.
21. Welborn, M.C., The long tradition: A study in 14th century medical deontology, in: *Medieval and Historiographical Essays in Honor of James Westfall Thompson* (J.L. Cates, ed.), University of Chicago Press, Chicago, 1938, pp. 344–357.
22. Rath, G., Ärztliche Ethik in Pestzeiten, *Münch. Med. Wochenschr.* 99(5):158–162, 1957.
23. Schullian, D.M., A manuscript of Dominici in the Army Medical Library, *J. Hist. Med.* 3:395–399, 1948.
24. Amundsen, D.W., Medical deontology and the pestilential disease in the later Middle Ages, *J. Hist. Med.* 32:403–421, 1977.
25. Jonsen, A.R., Medical ethics: Western Europe in the seventeenth century, in: *Encyclopedia of Bioethics* (W.T. Reich, ed.), The Free Press, New York, 1978, pp. 954–957.
26. Amundsen, D.W., The physician's obligation to prolong life: A medical duty without classical roots, *Hastings Cent.* 8(4):23–31, 1978.
27. Lakoff, G., and Johnson, M., *Metaphors We Live By*, University of Chicago Press, Chicago, 1980.
28. Childress, J.F., Ensuring care, respect and fairness for the elderly, *Hastings Cent.* 14(5):27–31, 1984.
29. Carse, J.P., The social effect of changing attitudes towards death, *Ann. N.Y. Acad. Sci.* 315:322–328, 1978.

30. Relman, A.S., The new medical-industrial complex, *N. Engl. J. Med.* 303(17):963–970, 1980.
31. Engelhardt, H.T., Morality for the medical-industrial complex: A code of ethics for the mass marketing of health care, *N. Engl. J. Med.* 319(16):1086–1089, 1988.

CHAPTER 2

Theoretical Considerations

This chapter briefly examines some of the ethical theories that have been useful in dealing with problems in medical ethics. The chapter looks at the way some of these theories have been used and offers a biological way of looking at ethics grounded in suffering. Primary, secondary, and symbolic worth are suggested as a way of analyzing some of the problems of medical ethics. The chapter ends with a brief introduction to macro-allocation issues.

INTRODUCTION

Ethics derives from the Greek *ethos* as morals derives from the Latin *mores*. Both derive from the word for "custom," "manners," or the "disposition peculiar to a given people." In our framework, "ethics," although it still contains that root meaning, transcends it. When it comes to delineating "ethical" from other problems, however, we find it hard to do so. Intuitively we know that prescribing penicillin to a patient with pneumococcal pneumonia is largely a "technical" matter, whereas not supplying nourishment to a terminally ill patient is largely an "ethical" one. But we are stumped when we try to explicate the difference. As with pornography, we may be unable to define it precisely. "Morals" often is used with a rather different shade of meaning. The term tends to be laden with the baggage of a suprarational belief system, with religious and often with sexual overtones. Despite the fact that these terms are often used to connote different things, they are frequently used interchangeably.

Ethics searches for a way of life (secular ethics, Christian ethics), seeks rules of conduct (applied ethics), and inquires about ways of life and conduct (metaethics).[1] Thus, as in ancient times, it is concerned

15

with seeking the "good" life and, more broadly, in defining the "good." Ethics, for our purposes in this book, is held to be other-directed. An act to be considered "ethical" must in some way, however remotely, affect another.[2,3] There are those who, pointing to pure duties to oneself, would deny this. Duties to oneself are a peculiar concept. In general, when duties to self are invoked, they are justified by appealing to the harm that failure to discharge these duties would, in fact, bring to others: relatives, friends, the community, or, ultimately, God. In true duties to self, rights and duties are simultaneous rights and duties: they are owed to and by the same person. Therefore, it would seem that they are disposable by the same person. Duties owed oneself lack a referent except for that self, and thus the arguments cannot escape a certain circularity. Individuals can waive their rights and can, for instance, decide that they do not want to collect a sum owed to them and thereby absolve their debtors of a duty to pay. For purposes of this book, problems of ethical content are limited to those involving another.

DEFINING THE GOOD

In searching for the "good life," the "good" has largely remained elusive and undefinable. Goods may be intrinsic goods ("good in themselves") or instrumental goods (goods that serve as the means for achieving another, and usually higher, good). It is the intrinsic good which has escaped definition. The quest for the *summum bonum*, the ultimate good, that which is good in itself, is sometimes seen as the greatest good in a hierarchy of goods (rationality, for Aristotle), sometimes as the common denominator of all other goods (pleasure, for the hedonist), and, at times, as an almost mystical, religious good (God, for the religious). Our use of the word is more pedestrian, and our referent is the common experience of what men universally call good and what they call bad (joy as a universal good, pain as a universal evil). Other goods, for the purpose of this book, are defined largely in terms of the rational being experiencing and enunciating that good.

ETHICAL THEORY

Some understanding of ethical theory[4] is most helpful if we are to analyze and understand moral problems, just as the principles of pharmacology are necessary if we are to prescribe properly. What follows is a necessarily oversimplified and in many ways, therefore, a somewhat falsified account of ethical theory. At least that degree of acquaintance with theory, however, is most helpful in understanding and working with the practical problems encountered on the ward.

There are, of course, a variety of ethical theories as well as many variations. The principles that each of these theories underwrite seem, at first glance, irreconcilably different. But such principles are fashioned by men to live by and to pursue their goals. They are instruments that lead to the "good life," not narrow exercises here to constrain and oppress man.[5] Our principles vary with innate personality and conditioning, but in spite of this, our decisions are often similar.[6] They reflect the mutual ethos of society, and that ethos has been shaped by the ethical theories which it, in turn, produced.

CONSEQUENCES AND INTENTIONS

There are two traditional ways of looking at the "rightness" or "wrongness" of an act: (1) We can look at the consequences of the act, judging the outcome we value to be good and the outcome we find evil to be bad. If we adopt this consequentialist view, we are apt to search for the "good" in any act as one that "brings about the greatest amount of good for the greatest number," Or (2) we can ignore the consequences of the act, judging that, in any event, the outcome is far from completely under our control, and we can then seek the good in the intention of the actor rather than in the consequences that are brought about. If we adopt this view, we rely on the agent's adherence to duty to judge the merits of his actions. (Of course, consequences are not entirely ignored: rather, consequences here are the intended and not the actualized consequences. As in the previous example, a standard by which to judge what is "good" is missing.) Broadly speaking, the first of these two views has been called "utilitarian." It relies on the works of Jeremy Bentham (1748–1832) and on those of his student John Stuart Mill (1806–1873).[7] The second view is called deontological or, at times, Kantian notwithstanding that Immanuel Kant[2] (1724–1804), its most eloquent proponent, is not the only one.

Kant puts primacy on the autonomous selection of our moral principles. In essence he claims that man is free, or, what he holds to be the same thing, must act as though he were free. Therefore, in order to be deserving of the respect that all rational beings deserve, he must be "self-legislating": i.e., he must set his own (autonomous) moral law. Heteronomous law, in contra-distinction to autonomous law, is not worthy of the respect that a self-legislating moral agent deserves. Heteronomous law is that law extrinsic to the agent; i.e., it is accepted unthinkingly, and therefore adherence to it, for no reason other than that it is the law, is not praiseworthy. Adhering to heteronomous law (law that comes from outside the moral agent and is not selected by him- or herself) may be morally neutral (as when we obey the law not to park in a certain place), morally blameworthy (as when we obey a law forcing us to discriminate against certain races), or praiseworthy, if our adhering to such law is motivated by more than blind obedience.

Kant bases his rule-oriented ("deontological") moral philosophy strictly on those rules which a rational agent legislates for him- or herself (autonomously derived law) and such rules, to be moral, must be universalizable: i.e., a moral agent setting these laws for him- or herself should be able to will that such laws would apply likewise to all other rational beings. We must, Kant says, be willing for the rules we set for ourselves to become a "law of nature"; i.e., we must be willing to have such rules apply universally. The Categorical Imperative, or "universalizability" principle as it may also be called, is one of the fundamental struts of Kantian ethics. Kant holds that one cannot derive rules from things the way they are: the status quo is not right (or wrong) merely because "that's the way things are." Rules, rather, must accord to reason and logic and, therefore, be universalizable. In refusing to grant the status of "ought" to "is," Kant furthermore holds out hope for future changes. He is a true child of the time of the French revolution, albeit that he abhorred its methods.

Utilitarianism, or consequentialist ethics, can be either act or rule utilitarianism. In both, "rightness" or "wrongness" is determined by the actual consequences achieved: in act utilitarianism the rightness of the act, and in rule utilitarianism the rightness of the rule, is judged by the consequences the act or the rule brings about. The trouble with either form of utilitarianism, of course, is that it makes any action which either produces maximal "good" in itself (act utilitarianism) or any action that conforms to a rule seen to maximize the "good" (rule utilitarianism), good only because of the consequences. Consequences to be "good" must achieve the greatest "good" for the greatest number. One of the largest drawbacks, of course, is that the notion of the "good" remains ambiguous.

Both utilitarian and deontological ethics have problems peculiar to themselves. Neither defines the "good" except in the most general terms. By relying purely on consequences in judging an act and its actor, utilitarianism, like all consequentialist theories, ignores fallibility and the unpredictability of events in assessing praise or blame.

An action that turns out badly, no matter what the unforeseeable cause, is bad.

Utilitarianism has lost much of its appeal. When applied to the realm of private relationships, it is rightly deemed to be dangerous: in its name, dangerous experiments on helpless people which could, however, benefit a large number would not be precluded, and a few innocent could readily be sacrificed for a great benefit to the many. In stressing outcome, it ignores motive and fails to account for human fallibility. In a sense, it is an ethic of outward performance rather than one of inner intention. We shall see in later chapters, however, that when we are faced with issues of resource allocation in which we deal not with individuals but with groups, we must inevitably take consequences and the greatest good for the greatest number into account.

Deontological theories, on the other hand, are often accused of being inflexible and of being deficient in their ability to guide our daily decisions. An action considered to be wrong—lying, for example—is wrong under all and every circumstance. The resulting conflict is inevitable in daily life and highlighted in medical practice. (Kant, I believe, may be misunderstood here: see Chapter 3 on Blameworthiness.) Further, Kant's ethic is one of pure form and lacking in content; the Categorical Imperative ("act so that you can will the maxim of the action to be a universal law") is impeccably true but provides little guidance in concrete situations. Moreover, by narrowly twisting language to accommodate a given contingency, almost any maxim could be construed to be a universal.[4] The charge that Kant's ethical philosophy is empty of content is often heard and is not without its justification. In defense, however, it must be said that Kant clearly did not set out to give specific answers in concrete situations. Rather, and quite explicitly, he set out to provide a framework within which decisions affecting concrete situations could be made. And, all criticism since notwithstanding, that framework retains much of its validity.

In dealing with patients within our vision of the patient-physician relationship, inner intention rather than merely outward performance becomes crucial. Kant's philosophy, in stressing motive and duty, does just that. Kant did not intend to produce a cookbook of ethics but a firm foundation on which rational men could build the good life. Perfect duties (those that universalize and are binding on all rational beings at all times: the duty not to murder, for example), contrast with the imperfect duties (those, beneficence for example, that are not binding at all times but cannot be done without). These imperfect duties, among other things, give content and direction[2] (see below under "Virtue Ethics").

JOHN DEWEY

Other ethical theories try to utilize, expand, modify, explicate, and conciliate these two main themes. A pragmatist, John Dewey, for example, looks at inquiry, including the inquiry into moral problems, as consisting of making an "indeterminate situation" more "determinate."[8,9] He seeks to incorporate the concepts of growth, change, and context into our moral reasoning. Dewey is determined to preserve the importance of experience and empirical evidence in the formulation of our ethical choices rather than to base choice on predetermined ethical "principles." He rejects the notion of an "intrinsic right" (or "good") outside the context of experience and feels that judgments about ethical matters are judgments made about the appropriateness of specific actions to achieve specific goals. The goals (or "ends") themselves are determined by a given social context and are not immutable or valid at all times. In doing this, he has profoundly influenced much of contemporary work, especially as it relates to the importance of context and character, in ethics. His work is important not only from a very practical point of view in medical ethics in which context and specifics assume such great importance but likewise in the formulation of what has come to be known as "virtue ethics." The way specific problems as well as problems of moral worth, blameworthiness, and community are examined owes a heavy debt to John Dewey.

VIRTUE ETHICS

Rules we choose to follow, principles we select, and theories we elect to guide us are a reflection of our character. Virtue ethics, as old as the Homeric tradition and as young as contemporary thinkers, tries to base itself on an appreciation not as much of the rightness or wrongness of given acts depending on duties and obligations as it does on the goodness of the persons who select such obligations and rules.[10–15] It inquires into what attributes are characteristic of persons we consider "virtuous" rather than selecting rules and then deciding that persons who follow such rules are, by virtue of rule following, virtuous.

"Virtue" is used here in the sense of competence in the pursuit of moral excellence. In common usage it carries an unfortunate baggage of moralism and comes across almost as mealymouthed. That is not the way it is used here, nor is it what people mean when they speak of "virtue ethics." To Plato, virtue was synonymous with excellence in living a good life, and such excellence could be attained by practice.

Vice, Plato believed, was not so much caused by moral turpitude as it was the result of ignorance: one either lacked knowledge or lacked the ability to reason properly. To Aristotle and later Aquinas, virtue was a disposition to act in the right way. Aristotle strove for balance. Whereas Plato saw virtue as an intellectual trait, Aristotle saw that in practical terms virtue was the result of a balance among intellect, feeling, and action. "Virtue" was a state of character and the result of practice. In turn, practice resulted in habit so that the "virtuous" man could be counted on to act justly. Thinkers from then on have explicitly or implicitly considered virtue and the virtuous man (the man practiced and adept at finding moral goodness in real situations) to be an intrinsic part of ethical behavior. MacIntyre saw that more than internal qualities were involved: goodness is shaped by a social vision of the good.

Even Kant, the example par excellence of a deontologist, distinguished between duties of justice (which he called the "perfect" or "strict" duties) and those of virtue (which he called the "imperfect" or "meritorious" duties). Duties of justice (the "perfect" duties) derived their standing from their logical necessity: no one could logically will them to be otherwise. Duties of virtue (the "imperfect" duties), on the other hand, derived their standing from an incapacity of the will to will otherwise. To demonstrate: truth-telling is a duty of justice because to do other than tell the truth conflicts with reason (truth-telling underwrites the ability to communicate); beneficence is a duty of virtue because never to act charitably would be a contradiction of the will (inevitably, one will depend on the benevolence of others, and although one could logically imagine a world in which benevolence did not exist, one would have trouble willing such a world). Duties of virtue (or the "imperfect" duties) were those that were optional: not always to be foregone but certainly not always dischargeable. Duties of justice were those that were binding at all times: not killing, not lying, etc. Duties of justice depend on behavior (refraining from killing, for instance), whereas duties of virtue depend more on inner disposition.

The problem with virtue ethics, of course, as a single ethic to adhere to is that "goodness" and "virtuousness" are defined on each other's terms: the virtuous man does good things, and good things are those acts a virtuous man does. Nevertheless, other ethical theories, in just as circular a fashion, must link the good with their theory of ethics. Legalistic ethical systems of ethics tend to define right action purely in terms of rules. When used by themselves and with nothing else to guide them, they are very likely to become strait jackets rather than guideposts of the moral life. Ultimately, and if carried to their logical conclusion, they may interfere with decisions that, on human terms, are humane and good. Virtue ethics alone, on the other hand, suffers from an imprecision and "fuzzyness" which, in defining the good in terms of the "virtuous person" runs the danger of ending up in paternalist acts. Both, it seems, can complement and enhance each other. If being virtuous, as Aristotle viewed it, entails striving for balance, virtue ethics may entail the balanced application of principles, and rules in a thoughtful and humane fashion. Problems of ethics cannot be separated from the moral sensibilities that shaped them or isolated from the moral actors which make up their context.[16] Virtue and rules shape each other and permit moral growth and learning. In that sense and in many others, the insights of John Dewey are critical to virtue ethics.

SITUATION ETHICS

A more recent attempt to enunciate a system of ethics was made by Professor Fletcher. Situation ethics, as he calls this type of approach, would judge each situation purely on its own merits, aiming for the most "loving" result that could be brought about.[17,18] Initially Fletcher speaks of this as "Christian love"; in his later works he speaks of it purely as "love." Situationism (or, as it has sometimes been called, "agapism" from the Greek term for "love," which encompasses more than its mere translation denotes) is, of course, a form of act utilitarianism in which each act is judged by its outcome.[19]

A prior insight, of course, as to what constitutes the most loving result is needed. "Love" as a concept on which to ground morality seems at least as ill-defined as are notions of the "good." Situationism, Fletcher agrees, must take place in a framework of general rules: "rules of thumb," as he calls them. But such "rules of thumb" must conform to some prior insight of the "good" or of "love." Such prior insight, in turn, is either the product of rigidly conceived "truth" or will be seen to vary from society to society in its definition.

Appealing, at least superficially, as such act-utilitarianism or "agapism" may be, it breaks down when one considers that what is "right" is not merely determined by the "goodness" (or by the lovingness) of the outcome. Other factors seem to matter: bringing about a "good" circumstance by reprehensible means or performing an accidentally "good" deed (in terms of its outcome) with evil intentions cannot be considered an untarnished "good."

LOOKING AT ETHICAL THEORIES

The variety of ethical theories with their advantages and drawbacks again raises the initial troubling question: What is morality? We can adopt a variety of viewpoints of morality. On the one hand, we can affirm that morality is absolute and that absolute standards of "right" and "wrong" exist. Beyond this, and not quite the same, we may assert that in the human condition such standards are knowable. We can reach such a viewpoint from a number of avenues of approach but inevitably will find that our conclusion is based on the presumption that truth exists and that it is, in principle as well as in fact, knowable. Truth, in this view, depends on neither situation nor context. Beyond this, of course, there are those who claim that truth is, in fact, known and that only the stubborn recalcitrance of the uninitiated prevents it from being generally accepted. This point of view claims that morality exists as a discoverable truth, an absolute which is not fashioned by men but is unchangeable and immutable. "Rights" and "wrongs" are "rights" and "wrongs" quite apart from the stage on which their application is played out. Situations may differ, but at most such differences force us to reinterpret old and forever-valid principles in a new light.

On the other hand, there are those who claim that what is and what is not morally acceptable, vary with the culture in which we live. This claim rests on the assertion that there are many ways of looking at truths and that such truths are fashioned by men within their own framework of understanding. Depending on our vantage point, there are many visions of reality,[20] a fact which the defenders of this doctrine hold to be valid in dealing with the concrete scientific reality of chemistry and physics.[21] Such a claim, it would seem, is even more forceful when dealing with morals. As Engelhardt put it so well: "our construals of reality exist within the embrace of cultural expectations."[22] And our "construals of reality" clearly include our visions of the moral life.

The claim, however, that since our "construals of reality" occur purely within the "embrace of cultural expectations," all visions of reality are necessarily of equal worth and that there are no useful standards that we can employ in judging either what we conceive to be physical or ethical reality, does not necessarily follow. One can, for example, make the claim that some visions of reality are clearly and demonstrably "wrong," supporting such a claim by empirical observation or by showing that certain visions of reality simply do not work. This is the stronger claim. In rejoinder, it will be said that empirical observation and what works are both framed in the very same "embrace." Or one can make the somewhat weaker claim that certain visions, in the context of a given society and historical epoch, seem less valid than others because they confound careful observation or because they simply fail to work when applied to real situations occurring in real societies. Such a move does not deny that our "visions of reality occur within the embrace of cultural expectations." But while such a move affirms that there are many co-existing realities of similar worth, it also suggests that within the specific context of such "cultural expectations," some realities have little and others much validity. Such a view neither throws up its hands and grants automatic equal worth nor rigidly enforces one view: it looks upon the problem as one of learning and growth in which realities (both empirical and ethical) are neither rigidly fixed nor entirely subject to *ad hoc* interpretation.

Consider the Babylonian peasant reared in a small community, a community whose integrity is believed to be safeguarded by the annual sacrifice of a selected firstborn to Moloch. Should such a peasant, when his firstborn is selected for sacrifice, be held blameworthy for sacrificing his child? Or, on the contrary, could a refusal to yield his son be held to be an immoral act endangering the whole village for the sake of his own selfish interests? By what standards are we to judge? By ours, by those of his society, or by an absolute to whose knowledge we pretend?

But hold on! Judging our peasant blameworthy or not is not quite the same thing as judging the act to be or not to be wrong. The peasant may, in his special context, not be to blame (his intentions were good, and he acted according to his own conscience), but the act of infant sacrifice may, on the whole, still be considered wrong. If so, this judgment must accord to some universal principle that all could subscribe to.

When we seek the "good" or, to phrase it another way, seek for an insight as to what "love" is, we tend to go in one of two diametrically opposite directions: either we affirm some absolute vision of the "good" or "love" to which we appeal or we claim that no vision of the truth can be appealed to and that, therefore, standards do not exist. Neither the first nor the second claim has much intuitive appeal: an absolutist vision is not readily shared by others (especially by others from different cultures), and a purely situational claim leaves us with no points of reference to act as guideposts on the road to decision making. A common biological denominator of such good may offer a firmer grounding.

Utilitarianism (and I shall consider situationism to be a form of act utilitarianism) and deontology may, in effect, necessarily presuppose each other. When Kant speaks of intentionality, it is the intention to bring about a consequence that he is speaking about. One cannot, it seems, have an intention without this: To intend something is to wish to bring about a consequence. On the other hand, when utilitarians or agapists set out to maximize the "good" (or to bring about a "loving" outcome), their vision of what it is to do good, or to be loving, is unavoidably rooted in a prior vision of the good. This prior vision of the good conforms to a logically universalizable principle (the particular vision of "good" or "love" must be "universalizable") as well as to a preexisting social vision (the particular notions of good or love current in a particular society). The nature of such a universalizable principle, among sentient beings, must in turn conform to the limits imposed by biology.

A BIOLOGICALLY GROUNDED ETHIC OF SUFFERING

Biology as a basis for morality will, inevitably, be challenged by those who would separate the reasoning process from its biological underpinnings and instead appeal to "pure rationality." The viewpoint that rationality can be separated from its biological underpinnings has, and has had, many adherents. It is a claim which is inherently dualistic in that it would separate "body" and "soul," "brain" and "reason," etc. In suggesting biology as a proper ground of morality we are not claiming that the two ("brain" and "reason") are identical; merely that one is the necessary, even if hardly sufficient, condition of the other. Reason or rationality without brain (and, for that matter, specifically without neocortex) is, in the realm of our experience, unthinkable. Data abound to underline that fact. Claiming that somewhere a creature may exist whose substrate for the reasoning process is other than what we call brain does not defeat our thesis; rather, it points out that such a being would then have some other substrate without which its reasoning could, again, not take place. Reasoning without a substrate that reasons, it seems, is unthinkable.

Morality, of course, is not grounded in biology in a reductionist way; i.e., morality cannot be reduced to biology. What is implied by saying that morality can be biologically grounded is that we, as sentient creatures, can neither escape the framework of our biology (all our functions including the function of thinking and of making judgments can occur only within the framework of our biological possibilities) nor, in that sense, transcend it. That is not to say that we cannot resist biological drives or urges but merely that our ability to resist and, at times, to go counter to such drives is itself expressed in the embrace of biological possibility. Biology is the source of our common experience, moral and otherwise.

In that sense, a biologically grounded ethic can be rationally carved out and can be cautiously employed as a basis for further exploration. Such an ethic is predicated on a "common structure of the mind"[23] which enables all sentient creatures (be they parakeets, chimpanzees, or humans) to appreciate benefit and harm, and, at the least, to suffer. This "common structure of the mind" differs from Kant in that it does not ground itself on rationality but rather finds firmer and broader footing in the capacity of all sentient creatures to suffer. If, as we have consistently claimed, ethics is other-directed, then the capacity now or again in the future to be capable of perceiving benefit or harm, at the very least to suffer, can be seen as central. Not to bring harm (or suffering) to entities capable of experiencing harm may be a meager but a sound basis. Of course, what is harm (or suffering) has to be defined on the terms of the entity itself. The capacity to suffer (with suffering defined by the sufferer), then, is central to such an ethic.

Suffering is not quite the same as perceiving a noxious stimulus or having pain. We may say of someone that he or she is experiencing pain but would be amused to have such pain termed "suffering." A teen-ager having her ear-lobes pierced is an example. On the other hand, we may suffer without having distinct pain: mental suffering aside, for that is perhaps a form of pain, patients with terminal cancer and with their worst pain obtunded may still be suffering intensely.

The capacity to suffer, then, implies more than the mere ability to perceive or to react to pain. Suffering implies a more sustained perception and one which perforce is integrated into memory and linked to thought. I suffer because I may know that my pain is interminable, because my fate is hopeless, because I am powerless, because I see the pain of a loved one, or for many other reasons. Suffering is a composite concept. At the very least, to suffer I must have the capacity to remember what has gone before (remember, for example, that my pain was here a little while ago and is here still) and, in the most primitive sense, anticipate the future. To suffer, then, at whatever level implies a rudimentary ability to sense, to integrate such sensation into however rudimentary a memory and, beyond this, to have a sense of future at however primitive a level. We would then say that organisms that have, however primitive, a neocortex can, and that those who lack a neocortex cannot, suffer. Making the neocortex the necessary condition of the capacity to suffer is not the same as reducing suffering to the neocortex. It is merely to affirm that in biological systems as we know them (not as we might envision them), suffering is inextricably linked to such a substrate.

Grounding an ethic on the capacity to suffer, then, grounds it in a universalizable quality common to all sentient beings. Grounding an ethic on the capacity to experience mere pain forces one into a morass of considerations dealing with the ability to judge such things. When entities experience and when they do not experience pain is difficult to judge: does an amoeba withdrawing from a sharp object or do worms experience pain? Certainly there is evidence that they react to noxious stimuli, that they withdraw or avoid them. But that is not quite the same as "experiencing" pain and a far cry from suffering.

To experience, or to suffer, organisms must at the very least have the ability at however primitive a level to think. Memory may be definable as the ability to re-call however primitively (Kant speaks of this as re-cognizing: "knowing again") past events. To experience anything, rather than merely to react reflexly to sudden and at once forgotten stimuli, at the very least requires such an ability. Thought, on the other hand, inevitably linked to memory, may be defined as the ability to integrate external and internal sense experience into memory. Memory and thought—inextricably dependent upon each other—are the necessary conditions for the capacity to suffer. In biological organisms as we know them, memory and thought are necessarily grounded in a neocortex.

PERSONHOOD AND MORAL WORTH

In going about their daily tasks, physicians are concerned with the hard questions of moral worth. What endows entities or objects with moral worth and why? This is a fundamental question: it seeks to find adequate reasons for differentiating between, say, automobiles and college students as objects of moral worth.

Having moral worth does not endow objects with absolute rights; it merely says that considerations against arbitrary treatment stand in the way. Concepts of moral worth are fundamental to such diverse issues as cadaver organ donation, abortion, and dementia, to name but a few. For the purpose of these pages, we are concerned with three types of moral worth: primary, secondary, and a subset of secondary, symbolic. Any of these confer *prima facie* (not absolute) rights against violating the object in question. To have such worth forms the necessary condition to be an object of moral consideration. Necessary because unless another is somehow actually or potentially benefited or harmed the question of morality cannot come up (see also Chapters 4, 10, and 11 dealing with the patient-physician relationship and with issues at the end and at the beginning of life).

The language of personhood, traditionally used throughout the ethics literature, has never been well defined.[24,25] It basically finds its motivation in Kant's statement that all persons must be objects of respect and in defining objects of respect as those entities capable of moral self-legislation (viz., autonomy). But this definition has been less than entirely helpful in illuminating our ethical gropings when confronted with hard decisions. Is personhood to be granted to the human form (the res extensa, as Descartes would have it), or does it inhere in the res cognitans (the "knowing thing")? Does personhood require continuity (is, for instance, the anesthetized or unconscious patient a person?), and does it need to be actualized (is, for example, the developing fetus a person?). What is the standing of the severely mentally defective, the psychotic, the senile, the vegetative or of the brain dead on the ventilator? Personhood without an agreed-on definition of all that personhood does or does not imply, has proven to be inadequate. And such a definition has never been agreed on. When personhood is used in ethical discourse, we tend to forget the problem at hand in quest of a definition. Personhood today unfortunately carries a heavy load of historical definitions and arguments, and its use has become problematic. The question of what endows objects with moral worth and therefore what must, prima facie, make us hesitate to deal with them merely to our own satisfaction remains.

TYPES OF MORAL WORTH

The question of what endows objects with moral worth is one of the fundamental questions of ethics. How and why do we differentiate among stones, flags, amoebas, dogs, and children? What are the features which permit us to deal with one entity almost at will and with another only under certain circumstances? Moral worth is the ethical feature of entities which we use to discuss this. For our purpose, "moral worth" is discussed in three categories: primary moral worth, secondary moral worth, and symbolic moral worth or the moral worth which attaches to objects because they stand for something else.

Our ethical concerns are prompted by the benefit or harm that can, directly or indirectly, result from our actions to another. Primary moral worth attaches to an object which in itself is capable of being self-knowingly benefited or harmed, which, at the very least, has the capacity to suffer. The capacity to suffer, the necessary condition of primary moral worth, may be actual or potential. Once this stipulation is met, a *prima facie* state mitigating against harming such entities exists. Such a *prima facie* condition is not necessarily absolute. At the least, however, a *prima facie* condition against being harmed raises serious ethical concerns. A lack of the capacity for self-knowing benefit or harm is what, *inter alia*, differentiates inanimate from animate objects and what divides the sentient from the insentient. Self-knowing presupposes a capacity for awareness and for social interaction.[26–29]

To have secondary moral worth, an object must be of material value to another. It would be silly to believe that a model airplane or an automobile could, in itself, be benefited or harmed. But if the model airplane is dear to an 8-year-old, or the automobile belongs to another person, destroying the airplane or the car has obvious moral overtones. Moral worth, in such cases, is conferred by proxy. It is moral worth because the object in question has material value to another who him- or herself is of primary worth. Damaging the object, harms another who him- or herself has the capacity to suffer and is, therefore, of primary moral worth.

Symbolic worth, an aspect of secondary moral worth, endows an entity with value not because it has value to or in itself nor because it has material value to another. Rather, such objects have worth because in the eyes of some they represent important values. Flags, religious symbols and many other objects have symbolic worth. Symbolic value is a frequent concern in medical ethics: it enters into issues of organ donation, brain death, and ways of thinking about disease, to name but a few. What is symbolic at a given time or to a given individual may be meaningless at other times or to other persons. The types of symbols we use are an expression of the "education and discipline of the feelings."[30]

Entities may simultaneously be endowed with primary, secondary, and symbolic worth. A sick animal may be of primary moral worth since it can be benefited or harmed, may have secondary worth in having a "market" value and may also have symbolic value in that it, in some minds, stands for a previous owner who loved it. Kant, in a similar vein, speaks of objects as having "dignity" (primary worth), a "market value" (secondary worth), or an "affective" (an aesthetic or, perhaps, symbolic worth).[2]

Having primary moral worth gives objects a *prima facie* hedge against being capriciously harmed. In the clinical situation this may be helpful. When a patient is anencephalic, brain dead, or permanently comatose or vegetative, primary worth is lost. Such patients are now of symbolic worth to their loved ones and, as representatives of human ity, to the community, and they may be of secondary (material) worth in that they may have the capacity to serve as organ donors.

When an entity loses primary worth, professional obligations change. Consider the patient who is now brain dead or who has lapsed into irreversible coma. Prior to such a time, the physician's obligation was clear: the wishes of the patient were controlling, and those of relatives and context were peripheral to the eventual decision. A conflict between competent patient and next of kin inevitably (or at least inevitably in terms of the ethics of the patient-physician relationship as we currently understand it) was finally resolved in the patient's favor. When, however, patients become permanently brain dead or lapse into irreversible coma, things change: barring a prior agreement, such patients who now can no longer be knowingly harmed in themselves (who have, in other words, permanently lost the ability to suffer) move from center stage. The wishes of family as well as the desires, feelings, and needs of their context (the needs of the ICU or the hospital, for example) now legitimately may move to center stage.

The presumption against capriciously harming entities of primary worth, however, does not go very far. If parakeets, baboons, the mentally retarded and college students all share in this, how can one use such a concept in arriving at concrete decisions in specific cases? Inevitably, in trying to establish hierarchies of value, external standards have to be applied. Arguments that ground themselves on the superior worth of one or another entity by appealing to biological sophistication ("animals are of lesser worth"), intellect, or any other aspect necessarily appeal to an externally determined standard. Quality-of-life judgments are an example.

Accepting a nonexternal standard—a standard determined by subjects for themselves—serves only negatively. It may serve when dealing with a life no longer valued by its possessor: say, a man riddled with metastatic cancer who pleads for death. But a nonexternal standard, a standard that lets each entity determine its own value, cannot serve when it comes to practical problems. Most, if not all, organisms value their life above all others. External standards, when it comes to difficult choices, are inevitable. Many of our judgments in medical ethics perforce will have to grope with this troubling question (see an explication in later chapters).

MACRO-ALLOCATION AND PROBLEMS OF JUSTICE

Medical ethics deals with issues at both the "macro" and the "micro" level (for a more thorough discussion of justice as well as macro-allocation, see Chapter 12). At the "micro" level, physicians determine the use of specific resources for specific patients. Micro-decisions deal with problems of abortion, feeding the vegetative, or using ventilators in the brain dead; they are informed by interpersonal ethics and by our social vision of the patient-physician relationship. Macro-allocation issues, on the other hand, deal with the just distribution of resources not on an individual but on a communal level. They are concerned with broader issues of justice and fairness.

Macro-allocation issues, dealing with resource allocations to institutions or to definable groups of people, must be separated into three levels. First, societies allocate their resources in various broad categories: how much for education, how much for welfare, how much for healthcare, etc. Second, distribution of funds into the constituent enterprises of education, welfare, or healthcare takes place: those responsible now distribute funds to hospitals, nursing homes, public health, and so forth. Third, individual institutions distribute available resources according to their peculiar needs: decisions of how much to give for birthing units, how much for ICUs, and how much for the library of an individual institution are made. Macro-allocation differs from micro-allocation in a critical sense: macro-allocation decisions are made for all the individuals within a given group irrespective of the individuals comprising that group. Physicians faced with micro-allocation decisions are faced with judgments made about individual patients and with the ground rules of their function.[31]

In dealing with ethics, especially ethics on the "macro" level, notions of justice are essential. Whether or not the idea of justice is applicable to the bedside, is problematic,[32] but the moral problems that the physician encounters hardly occur in isolation. Notions of justice have been matters of debate since classical times. Ranging from Plato's notion that justice consisted essentially in attending to one's own business,[33] to Aristotle's view that justice consisted in giving to each his due,[34] the evolution of thoughts about justice has undergone changes intimately tied to social systems. The questions, of course, of what is one's business or what is one's due remain.

John Rawls in his A Theory of Justice[35] has developed the notion of justice as (1) assuring maximal freedom to every member of the community, (2) assuring those with similar skills and abilities equal access to offices and positions, and (3) assuring a distribution to benefit maximally the worst off. He posits a hypothetical "veil of ignorance" behind which all prospective members of a community choose the broad allocation of resources. Members choosing from behind this veil of ignorance do so ignorant of what their own age, sex, or station in life is to be. They are, therefore, unlikely to disadvantage a group to which they may well belong. A community's vision of justice, according to Rawls, is likely to emerge from such a choice.

THE NATURAL LOTTERY

Views of what has been called the "natural lottery"[35,36] intertwine with our notions of justice and our views of community. By the "natural lottery" is meant "chance" or "luck," which distributes poverty, wealth, beauty, and other endowments as well as health or disease. Emphasis is on the "luck of the draw," which determines our individual fates. The natural lottery determines our being struck by lightning or slipping on a banana peel. All those things not directly attributable to the individual's own doing or clearly caused by another are viewed in this way.[37] There are three basic ways of looking at the lottery: (1) The results of the natural lottery are no one's direct doing, no one's responsibility, and, therefore, do not confer any obligation on anyone. Plainly speaking, they are simply regrettable but certainly not unjust. (2) Although no one may be responsible for the results of the natural lottery, the loser has done nothing to deserve being singled out. In that sense, the results are "unjust." Based on beneficence, such a viewpoint may entail an assumption of obligation.[38,39] (3) Lastly, one can view the "natural lottery" as far from that simple. Being struck by lightning or slipping on a banana peel do not adequately describe the situation which exists when we are born to wealth or have a heart attack. Looking at being struck by lightning or being born into grinding poverty as both being mere chance, somehow fails to ring true. The conditions that create, aim, and hurl lightning are as yet out of human control; the conditions that create, perpetuate, and ignore poverty are not.[40,41] It has been shown over and over again that health and disease are intimately linked with poverty and other social conditions.[42–45] At the very least, this makes one's state of health substantially different from being struck by lightning. Most happenings result from a combination of factors in which random selection plays a greater or lesser role. In a complex world, health and disease are conditioned by, if not predominantly due to, a social construct. Our viewpoint of obligation, therefore, may change.

VIEWPOINTS OF COMMUNITY

The way in which we view community largely determines our concept of justice, our sense of mutual obligation, and, ultimately, our laws and procedures.[46] There are two basic and contrasting ways of looking at community.

On the one hand, we can view community as consisting of members united only by duties of refraining from harm one to another. In such communities, freedom becomes the necessary condition of morality (a "side constraint" as Nozick would have it) rather than a fundamental value.[47] Freedom is an absolute and cannot be negotiated. Individual freedom can be restricted only to the extent that it directly interferes with another's freedom. The sole, legitimate power of the community is to enforce and defend individual freedom. Beyond duties of refraining from harming one another, persons have the freedom, although not the duty, of helping each other. Except when such help is freely and explicitly agreed upon by mutual contract, they have no obligation to respond to their neighbor's weal and woe.[12]

On the other hand, community can be seen to have a different structure. Unless they are united by certain ways of behaving one to another, associations of individuals living together cannot long endure. Refraining from doing harm to each other makes coexistence possible. But that, in this other point of view, is insufficient and not the way we ordinarily think of community. In ordinary parlance, a community demands a commons in which its members work towards their own as well as towards their neighbors' good. Freedom, in such a community, may be a fundamental value but it remains a value of the community and not one of its absolute and necessary conditions. As such, it is subject to negotiation. In such a community, a "minimalist ethic"[48] is viewed as insufficient; the Kantian perfect duties (in essence the logically necessary duties of refraining from harm to one another) must be leavened by Kant's more optional imperfect duties (duties because willing their opposite would represent a contradiction of the will).[2]

These two views of community, as do the different views of the natural lottery, entail starkly different consequences. If one views freedom as the absolute condition of morality and, therefore, the community as bound only by duties of noninterference, one will be unable to tax the affluent for the benefit of the poor, unwilling to demand licensure or to control the safety of drugs, and one would be allowed to sell oneself freely into slavery. Freedom would no longer be a bargaining chip. Instead of being a fundamental communal value, one promulgated, secured, and safeguarded by the community, freedom becomes an untouchable absolute. As such it too easily leads to the domination of the weak by the strong, the poor by the rich.[49] Beneficence, in such communities, has no moral standing; it may be "nice" but rather than being a moral obligation, being beneficent is supererogatory, and, essentially, non-moral. Communities based on such a premise have no latitude, and cannot raise funds, for necessary beneficence to their members. Medicine, in communities of this sort, becomes another technical service at the command of the consumer. Its competence, determined by an ethic of outward performance, is bereft of moral content. Health professionals become mere "bureaucrats of health"[22] who hang their moral agency on a rack together with their coats when they go to work.

Considerations and theories of this sort are crucial to our moral function not only as private physicians encountering private patients or as specialized members of a community whose advice is legitimately sought in health matters, but also as members of that very community. Moral theories and the moral principles which emerge from them are most useful if they are used as guideposts along the way of moral reasoning. On the other hand, moral theories and the principles which emerge from them can interfere with moral reasoning providing, instead of guideposts, straitjackets. If moral theories are used in such a way, unnecessarily irresolvable conflicts may result.[6,50] Ethics reduced to principles and applied to problems in a cookie-cutter fashion without being filtered through our moral sensibilities makes a mockery of ethics: instead of being a quest, a search, a sometimes agonizing and always stimulating exploration through which learning and growth can occur, ethics is reduced to another technical occupation. Under such conditions, ethics loses its soul.

REFERENCES

1. Abelson, R., and Nielsen, K., History of ethics, in: The Encyclopedia of Philosophy. Vol. III (P. Edwards, ed.), Macmillan Publishing Company, New York, 1978, pp. 81–117.
2. Kant, I., Foundations of the Metaphysics of Morals, Bobbs-Merrill, Indianapolis, 1980.
3. Kant, I., Duties to oneself, in: Lectures on Ethics (L. Infield, tran.), Peter Smith, Gloucester, MA, 1978, pp. 116–125.
4. Rachels, J., The Elements of Moral Philosophy, Random House, New York, 1986.
5. Cassel, E.J., Life as a work of art, Hastings Center 14(5):35–37, 1984.
6. Toulmin, S., The tyranny of principles, Hastings Center 11(6):31–39, 1981.
7. Mill, J.S., Utilitarianism, Bobbs-Merrill, Indianapolis, 1979.
8. Dewey, J., Logic: The Theory of Inquiry, Henry Holt & Co., New York, 1938.
9. Dewey, J., Ethics, Vol. 5, The Middle Works of John Dewey, (J.A. Boydston, ed.), Southern Illinois University Press, Carbondale, IL, 1983.
10. MacIntyre, A., A Short History of Ethics, Macmillan, New York, 1966.

11. MacIntyre, A., *After Virtue*, University of Notre Dame Press, Notre Dame, IN, 1983.
12. Frankena, W.F., Beneficence in an ethics of virtue, in: *Beneficence and Health Care*, (E.E. Shelp, ed.), D. Reidel, Dordrecht, The Netherlands, 1982, pp. 63–82.
13. Pellegrino, E.D., and Thomasma, D.C., *For the Patient's Good: The Restoration of Beneficence to Health Care*, Oxford University Press, New York, 1988.
14. Von Wright, G.H., *The Varieties of Goodness*, Humanities Press, New York, 1965.
15. Reeder, J.P., Jr., Beneficence, supererogation and role duty, in: *Beneficence and Health Care*, (E.E. Shelp, ed.), D. Reidel, Dordrecht, The Netherlands, 1982, pp. 83–108.
16. Churchill, L.R., Bioethical reductionism and our sense of the human, *Man Med.* 5(4):229–249, 1980.
17. Fletcher, J., *Situation Ethics*, Westminster Press, Philadelphia, 1966.
18. Fletcher, J., Situation ethics revisited, *Rel. Humanism* 16:9–13, 1982.
19. Frankena, W.J., *Ethics*, Prentice-Hall, Englewood Cliffs, NJ, 1973.
20. Fleck, L., *Genesis and Development of a Scientific Fact* (D.J. Trenn and R.K. Merton, eds., F. Bradley and D.J. Trenn, trans.), University of Chicago Press, Chicago, 1979.
21. Kuhn, T., *The Structure of Scientific Revolutions*, University of Chicago Press, Chicago, 1970.
22. Engelhardt, H.T., *The Foundations of Bioethics*, Oxford University Press, New York, 1986.
23. Kant, I., *Critique of Pure Reason* (N.K. Smith, trans.), St. Martin's Press, New York, 1965.
24. Fletcher, J., Indicators of humanhood: A tentative profile of man, *Hastings Center Rep.* 2(5):1–4, 1972.
25. Fletcher, J., Four indicators of humanhood—the inquiry matures, *Hastings Center Rep.* 4(2):4–7, 1974.
26. President's Commission for the Study of Ethical Problems in Medicine and Biomedical and Behavioral Research: *Deciding to Forego Life-Sustaining Treatment*, U.S. Government Printing Office, Washington, 1982.
27. McCormick, R.A., To save or let die: The dilemma of modern medicine, *J.A.M.A.* 229:172–176, 1974.
28. Veatch, R., *Death, Dying and the Biological Revolution*, Yale University Press, New Haven, 1976.
29. Veatch, R., The definition of death: Ethical, philosophical and policy confusion, *Ann. N.Y. Acad. Sci.* 315:307–321, 1978.
30. Tanner, M., Sentimentality, *Proc. Aristotelian Soc.* 77:127–147, 1977.
31. Loewy, E.H., Drunks, livers and values: Should social value judgments enter into transplant decisions? *J. Clin. Gastroenterol.* 9(4):436–441, 1987.
32. Cassel, E.J., Do justice, love mercy: The inappropriateness of the concept of justice applied to bedside decisions, in: *Justice and Health Care* (E.E. Shelp, ed.), D. Reidel, The Netherlands, 1981, pp. 75–82.
33. Plato, *The Republic* (P. Shorey, trans.), in: *Plato: The Collected Dialogues*. (E. Hamilton and H. Cairns, eds.), Princeton University Press, Princeton, 1961.
34. Aristotle, *Nichomachean Ethics*, Bobbs-Merrill, Indianapolis, 1962.
35. Rawls, J., *A Theory of Justice*, Harvard University Press, Cambridge, MA, 1971.
36. Engelhardt, H.T., Health care allocations: Responses to the unjust, the unfortunate and the undesirable, in: *Justice and Health Care* (E.E. Shelp, ed.), D. Reidel, Dordrecht, The Netherlands, 1981, pp. 121–138.

37. Loewy, E.H., Risk and obligation: Health professionals and the risk of AIDS, in: *AIDS: Principles, Practice and Politics* (I. Corless and M. Pittman-Lindeman, eds.), C.V. Mosby, St. Louis, 1988.
38. Outka, G., Social justice and equal access to health care, *J. Relig. Ethics* 2(1):11–32, 1974.
39. Outka, G., Letter to the Editor, *Perspect. Biol. Med.* 19(3):449–452, 1976.
40. Loewy, E.H., Communities, obligations and health care, *Soc. Sci. Med.* 25(7):783–791, 1987.
41. Loewy, E.H., Communities, self-causation and the natural lottery, *Soc. Sci. Med.* 26(11):1133–1139, 1988.
42. Kosa, J., and Zola, I.K., *Poverty and Health: A Sociological Analysis*, Harvard University Press, Cambridge, MA, 1975.
43. Subcommittee on Oversight and Investment, *Infant Mortality Rates: Failure to Close the Black-White Gap*, U.S. Government Printing Office, Washington, 1984.
44. Fuchs, V.R., *Economic Aspects of Health*, University of Chicago Press, Chicago, 1982.
45. U.S. Department of Health and Human Services, *Health Characteristics According to Family and Personal Income*, U.S. Government Printing Office, Washington, 1985.
46. Loewy, E.H., Waste not, want not: Communities and presumed consent, in: *Medical Ethics: A Guide for Health-Professionals* (J.F. Monagle and D.C. Thomasma, eds.), Aspen Publishers, Rockville, MD, 1988, pp. 249–260.
47. Nozick, R., *Anarchy, State and Utopia*, Basic Books, New York, 1974.
48. Callahan, D., Minimalist ethics, *Hastings Center* 11(5):19–25, 1981.
49. Niebuhr, R., Rationing and democracy, in: *Love and Justice* (D.R. Robertson, ed.), Westminster Press, Philadelphia, 1957, pp. 61–63.
50. Churchill, L.R., and Simàn, J.J., Principles and the search for moral certainty. *Soc. Sci. Med.* 23(5):461–468, 1986.

Decision Making, Fallibility, and the Problem of Blameworthiness in Medicine

This chapter examines one of the critical problems in medical practice: that of error in technical medicine as well as in ethical decisionmaking. It deals with the notion of being to blame and, in ethics, of almost inevitably being confronted with one of two or more options, all of which frequently are more or less bad. Accepting blameworthiness in medicine can be a stimulus to learning, growth, and moral development.

In the course of their daily practice, physicians, just like other people in all walks of life, are confronted with choices. Physicians, like all other men and women, must accept the fallibility of these choices. The diagnosis made, the treatment determined, the conclusions drawn, all may be wrong. In the human condition, error is the risk we take. When shoemakers err and, despite prudency and care, spoil a pair of shoes, they must, if possible, remedy their error or at least learn from it. Regrettably, their error may be irretrievable, and a pair of shoes may be lost. When doctors err and, despite prudency and care, misdiagnose, mistreat, or misjudge, they too must try to remedy the error and learn from it. And such errors, even more regrettably tragic, may also be irretrievable: the patient may die. This fallibility, inherent in medicine as it is in any other activity, is the price of action in any field.[1] It is only that in medicine the stakes are so high. But no matter how high the stakes, no matter how dreadful the consequences, mortal man is bound to err.

Medicine, it has been said, should not be like other fields: decisions, actions, and consequences are too critical. Physicians, it is often implied, should not be like other men. Their material is life, and life is too precious to permit error. But workers, no matter how well trained, no matter how alert, no matter how careful, are fallible. They may spoil the material with which they deal, and the nature of the material does not change this basic fact.

Physicians have come to accept the often heavy burden of their potential fallibility and to deal with its regrettable exemplars in their own way. The honest, intelligent, and strong admit, learn, and regretfully put the error behind (except, at times, in their dreams); the honest and less strong often cannot and are sometimes crushed by it; the less honest try to manipulate the facts and structure the evidence until the error of yesterday is seen as no error at all and failure becomes success. Manipulating facts to make what is not appear as what is, is, of course, done in every field. Sometimes it is done unconsciously, an act of repression, as it were. Initially the attempt often is a deliberate one which starts consciously and in which eventually we ourselves come to believe. Instead of using our energies in learning from the mistake we acknowledge, we consume our energies in a senseless quest for the blamelessness we seek.

On the whole, physicians have learned to be, if not comfortable, at least accepting of their technical errors. Often they will acknowledge these only to their inner selves, fearful that honest disclosure will lead to censure or, worse yet, legal suit. This fear, while often unjustified, is frequently potent enough to prevent more public disclosure and, thereby, tends to hamper others from learning from the mistake. There is, however, more than a fear of censure or suit. Physicians, at least as much as other men and women, fear a loss of prestige and the associated loss of an aura of omnipotence. They, at least as much as other men, partake in a process of delusion which starts with an attempt to delude others and ends by deluding one's self. When, however, physicians fail to acknowledge error even to themselves, self-delusion blocks even self-learning, and errors are prone to be repeated.

Knowing that probability is not certainty, and that certainty, at best, is only reasonable certainty,[2] physicians accept uncertainty and error in technical matters as a reasonable price for action.[3] But when it comes to the moral realm, uncertainty is less easily accepted. None of us expects to be right at all times, but at the very least we want to be perceived as scrupulously virtuous. The fear of blame causes us to seek certainty in the very realm least likely to provide it.[3]

Even worse: in making choices about moral matters, we rarely have problems in choosing between the "good" and the "bad." All other things being equal, only psychopaths or fools deliberately or knowingly choose a "bad action" in preference to a "good" one. Our choices are more constricted: we must, in general, sort out one "bad choice" from another more or less "bad" one and then act upon that choice. Such choices rarely leave us with a "good" alternative for action. No matter how hard we try, we are left with a course of action which, when considered by itself, is bad. Blameworthiness, it seems, is difficult to evade.

Actions, objects, or judgments in moral as well as in nonmoral matters may be desirable, undesirable or indifferent to us. We have little trouble choosing between the desirable, on the one, and the indifferent or undesirable, on the other, hand. In choosing, we have no trouble with choosing between having a tooth pulled or seeing *Hamlet*: most people enjoy seeing *Hamlet* and hate having their teeth pulled. It would take a very odd man, indeed, to will pulling a tooth instead of seeing a play (no matter how bad!). Our problem in choosing is in choosing one from among several attractive objects or courses of action or, on the other hand, one object or course of action from among several unattractive ones. In the old legend, the donkey sitting smack in the middle between two equally attractive parcels of food starved to death. His was a true dilemma.

Generally we do not have severe problems choosing among attractive objects or actions. Deciding whether to go to the theater or to the opera leaves us with a choice in and of itself attractive and not to be, in and of itself, regretted. However we choose, we may be sorry not to have picked the other, but we will still be glad to have picked the one. And a normal person is. It would be odd if we let our pleasure at hearing *Don Giovanni* be entirely spoiled by the thought that we missed *Hamlet*. We may say to ourselves or to others: "I am sorry to have missed *Hamlet*," but we do not, therefore, say that seeing *Don Giovanni* was an unpleasant experience. Even if we regret the choice, we regret not having had, as we now see it, a greater pleasure; but we do not therefore conclude that our pleasure, even if less, was pain.

Choosing among unpleasant experiences, say the choice between having a tooth pulled or having a filling put in, leaves us in much the same way. We may conclude that, on the balance, we prefer having a filling, and we go have it done. And we may be glad that we did not choose what we perceive to have been the more painful route. When we come home from the dentist, we may take pleasure in the pain we evaded; we may say that, in comparison, we are glad to have had the smaller rather than the greater pain. But few would now say that having a tooth filled was a pleasure and, on the whole, a nice experience. When we choose between two unpleasant experiences, then, we do not try to pretend that one of them, because we chose the other, is now pleasant or pleasurable. The same holds when we choose one from among several possible pleasant choices: we do not or cannot reasonably claim that what we did not choose was unpleasant but merely, for a variety of reasons, that it was or seemed less pleasant.

But why choose? Why not simply do nothing or toss a coin? Few are willing to abrogate their right to choose; few are willing to say that they are unable to make an intelligent choice. Rarely are the coins so evenly stacked that, simply speaking, there is no relevant difference. When we fail to choose, or when we leave the choice up to chance, we deny our freedom to make a choice, refuse to think deeply and critically about relevant differences or simply are confronted with a situation about which we do not much care and in which thinking deeply or critically is not worth the bother. Whether we go to *Hamlet* or *Don Giovanni* may, basically, be irrelevant to us. We may not wish to expend the time or effort needed to make the choice. And so we toss a coin, or leave it up to our wife, glad not to be directly involved. But, however we allow the choice to be ultimately made, refusing to partake is an expression of not caring very much about what happens. It is a form of "copping out."

There is a difference between the choice made and the process of choosing. Refusing to choose leaves us with a choice made for us by external forces. Choosing between *Hamlet* and *Don Giovanni* or between having a tooth pulled and having it filled is a process internal to us. Like every internal process, it reveals more about us then it does about the problem itself.[4] It speaks to our fears, hopes, and values more then it does to the intrinsic merits of the actual choice. The thing chosen, the choice, is extrinsic to us; it has a life of its own almost, but not quite, regardless of our choosing.

Ethical choices in medicine confront us with similar considerations. Inevitably perplexing situations fail to have "good" answers, and we are left with alternative courses of action any one of which is bad in and of itself. Not treating pneumonia in a vegetative patient may be the most reasonable and, on balance, the "best" alternative, but that fails to make the nontreatment of pneumonia and, thereby, the hastening of death a "good" and "praiseworthy" thing to do. It cannot and should not cause us to go home feeling self-satisfied; it can, and perhaps should, leave us saddened but relieved that, among the terrible alternatives, we have chosen the best available. It does not make us praiseworthy for the act (an act intrinsically and in itself blameworthy), although it might make us praiseworthy for the agony of choosing. The process of choosing and the choice itself are not the same thing.

Not making choices, evading decisions, and hiding behind immediate technical concerns is tempting and is what is, in fact, frequently done. After all, physicians are trained to watch scientific changes and to intervene in the biological process so as to support homeostatic mechanisms tending to promote life and health. Such work is difficult, demands a great deal of skill and is often perplexing. It is easy to hide behind technical factors, pretending to oneself not to have time for other matters. And that pretension is often close to the truth. And yet, if physicians allow themselves to attend only to the task of balancing electrolytes, adjusting blood gases, and choosing antimicrobials, they will not only evade their prior human responsibility as moral agents, but will eventually force others to make such choices for them. Problems in medicine are too critical and too close to the weal and woe of real people to permit the evading of choices. Refusing to make moral choices does not evade blameworthiness. Rather, it transfers such blameworthiness: physicians now are responsible not for the choice not made but for making the choice not to choose and thus for abrogating and denying their moral agency.

In the human condition, and in the human condition confronted by the physician, moral choices often leave us with the necessity of choosing between acts any one of which, to a greater or lesser extent, is blameworthy in and of itself. This notion, if one is theologically inclined, harkens back to notions of original sin in which humans, by their very condition, inevitably must sin (and, according to Luther, should at least sin "boldly," i.e., forthrightly and without dissimulation). In modern clothes, this Augustinian concept is found in many of our choices in medical ethics. When we evade our blameworthiness by rationalizing or manipulating the facts and circumstances of our action until a claim of praiseworthiness emerges, we run the danger of moral callousness. Doing certain things—killing, for instance—must never be looked at as "good" or praiseworthy; when things which are clearly "bad" or blameworthy in themselves are manipulated and glossed over so that they are now presented or seen as "good" or praiseworthy, moral callousness may easily result. Doing such things now suddenly is presented as, and easily becomes, an intrinsically good and praiseworthy act and makes the next such action, even if in different circumstances, all the easier.

On the surface, this realization seems bleak and dark. If, indeed, all humans when confronted with many moral dilemmas are destined to make an inevitably "bad" choice, why choose a field in which the consequences of such choices so often lead to disaster and in which blameworthiness is blameworthiness for such terrible consequences? Why not do something else where decisions, actions, and consequences are not as stark? Why beat yourself to death?

There is a difference between the action or thing chosen and the process of choosing. The action or thing chosen is external to us: it has, as it were, a life of its own. Killing, ripped out of the context of the situation and divorced from the moral actors involved in the actual example, becomes an action subject to dispassionate interrogation or examination. But looking at problems in this fashion and making issues or categories out of real problems change the real problem and make it an artificial and, therefore, a different one.[4] Abstracting the practical problem and making out of it a category to be studied has practical value only if, after examining this now isolated phenomenon for the sake of greater clarity, we rejoin the issue or category to the actual context and its moral actors and now reexamine the actual problem in that light. The "answers" to the problem, examined out of its context and away from the moral actors which ultimately must act, are part of the material of our ultimate choice. Our actual choosing, however, involves more than this part of the material alone. Our choosing and our ultimate choice involve the context and the moral actors no less than they do the category of our problem.

When we examine a given problem in isolation, away from its context and divorced from the moral actors whose agony of choice must, eventually, be translated into agony of action, we may be blameworthy for a course of action chosen. But we may have no other better choice than this unquestionably blameworthy one. In the human condition, choosing inevitably will confront us with this fact: our choice, removed from its context and divorced from its moral actors may inevitably be blameworthy in itself; but in choosing among an array of choices all in themselves blameworthy to a variable degree, we may deserve praise for the agony of that choice rather than choosing not to choose or choosing capriciously or carelessly.

Physicians, in going about their daily tasks, must learn to assume and be accepting of their fallibility in technical as well as in moral matters. Mistakes will be made, errors committed, and undesired outcomes achieved. Doubts, often nagging doubts, will remain. These not only are the price for action but, used properly, can serve as vehicles for learning and for moral growth. Physicians must learn to take not only their technical but their moral fallibility in their stride, to learn from it, and to put it into the perspective of a full and rewarding life. Beating oneself to death or dwelling on errors as opposed to learning from them and then going on is a destructive way of dealing with the realization of one's own mortality. Accepting blameworthiness (rather than immaturely rationalizing that which is worthy of blame to be worthy of praise) and making moral choices in the full realization of fallibility and blameworthiness, serves to enhance the personal growth of compassionate, thinking persons and, therefore, helps make better doctors.

To be blameworthy for initiating or participating in a bad act does not, although we often think of it that way, make us "bad" or evil human beings. We are judged—by ourselves or by others, if they or we choose to be fair—by the totality and inevitability of our actions and choices, not by actions divorced from their context. A good person is not described by a tabulation of single actions and choices bereft of context but rather, as the Greeks already saw it, by their "self-making" or the ability to learn from situations and, in consequence, to change.[5] Our choices say more about us as persons than they do about the problem itself.[4] Whether technical or moral, and the difference is certainly not always clear-cut, our choices are reflective of us as persons and are springboards to moral and intellectual growth. The business of ethics, which cannot be divorced from the business of living or of practicing medicine, is concerned not merely with single problems, with their categorization or with their solution, but also, and with at least as much force, in promoting personal growth and, in a classical sense, the "virtues"[6] (see also the section on "virtue ethics" in Chapter 2).

REFERENCES

1. Gorovitz, S., and MacIntyre, A., Towards a theory of medical fallibility, J. Med. Phil. 1(1):51–71, 1976.
2. Doherty, D.J., Ethically permissible, Arch. Intern. Med. 147(8):1381–1384, 1987.
3. Loewy, E.H., The uncertainty of certainty in clinical ethics, J. Med. Humanities Bioeth. 8(1):26–33, 1987.
4. Churchill, L.R., Bioethical reductionism and our sense of the human, Man Med. 5(4):229–247, 1980.
5. Becker, L.C., The neglect of virtue, Ethics 85:110–122, 1975.
6. Pincoffs, E., Quandary ethics, Mind 80:552–571, 1971.

CHAPTER 4

Doctors and Their Patients, Patients and Their Doctors

The patient-physician relationship is considered in its historical perspectives and the roots of the relationship are briefly sketched. Several suggested models are examined. The good of the patient, basic to any consideration of the patient-physician relationship, is examined. Some of the problems such as confidentiality, conflict of interest, consent, and experimentation are briefly considered in the light of the previous discussion.

INTRODUCTION

The basis of traditional ethics involves two issues: the relationship of individuals with one another and the relationship of individuals with their community. In the parlance of medical ethics, the former involves issues of micro-distribution and the latter problems in macro-allocation (see Chapter 2).

In former days, patients related to their physicians on a direct one-to-one basis in the context of their home and relatives. Few other caregivers or institutions were involved. In medieval times, the clergy began to intrude into the relationship and, as we have seen, to make demands apart from the direct problem of illness. The church often assumed a controlling role. As more modern hospitals emerged, illness began to be institutionalized, and the relationship between patient and physician now took place in a different, and more impersonal, setting. Further, other caregivers began to assume critical roles and to demand recognition of their own expertise and moral agency.

Hospitals play a critical role in communities and, even if privately owned, serve public functions. Therefore, they not only establish internal rules but in turn are governed by a set of external rules with which the community tries to control the integrity of any of its institutions' functions. Additionally, third-party payers (a mish-mash of insurance carriers, industry, various levels of government, HMOs, etc.) have started to play a critical role in American medicine: these third-party payers not only control the hospitals ("he who pays the piper calls the tune") but are beginning to assume a significant role in controlling the function of private physicians in their own offices.

Many patients, furthermore, are not ill: they see physicians to have their health evaluated or certified, to be examined for employment, or to meet a number of other requirements not directly associated with illness. In the last 50 years, the patient-physician relationship has become complicated beyond imagination. And yet, there remains that unavoidably deeply private relationship. Still reflecting a slowly evolving traditional vision, the patient-physician relationship remains inevitably based on trust, fear, and hope.

Our vision of the patient-physician relationship, is central to the way in which we perceive the physician's obligation vis-à-vis individual patients. It has developed slowly over the ages, changing and adapting with its social context. Except in its crudest outlines, the relationship is not one codified in law. It has been affirmed by social contract and has been largely accepted as the ground of the physician's function. A social contract, as used here, implies a tacit understanding among the members of a community which permits societal function. Without this tacit understanding—reinforced here and there by law—disruption would occur. Enforcement of social contract is generally through social mechanisms involving praise, censure, and, at times, even stigmatization.[1]

ROOTS

The physician-patient relationship has at least three roots: (1) a root of social contract relying upon a mutual perception of profession; (2) a root developing out of the historical tradition of society and profession; and (3) a personal root which gains its strength from the specific personality of both physician and patient and from that unique relationship.[2] These three roots nourish a relationship which has found expression in three basic models first described by Szasz and Hollender.[3] These essentially behavioral models (activity-passivity; guidance-cooperations; and mutual participation) coexist with and flesh out the more attitudinal paternalistic, scientific, entrepreneurial, and, lately, interactive models.

The root of social contract is expressed, on the one hand, in the immense privileges and power given to physicians and, on the other hand, in the high expectations for physicians held by communities. Physicians enjoy high status, special prerogatives, unusual rights, and ample material reward. Physicians strip strangers, administer poisons, inflict wounds, and hold legal power over life and death. The community has vested this trust in physicians because of the tacit promise held out by their profession.

Communal expectations are expressed in the community's view of professionals in general and the medical professional in particular. To be a professional means many things.[4] More than the ability to perform certain tasks and the promise of requisite skill to allow a technically successful conclusion is implied. The willingness to perform these tasks, and the personal integrity which prevents the perversion of these skills to an injurious end, are also implicit.[5]

Skills, whether technical or intellectual, are merely the instruments and not the essence of a profession. To be a professional implies a willingness to use requisite skills in a manner consonant with the moral ends implied in the contract. It is to declare oneself freely willing to assume an obligation—in medicine the obligation to "perform a good act of healing in the face of the fact of illness."[4] Technical competence is the necessary condition without which the act is fraudulent: but it is insufficient to describe the professionalism implicit in the social contract which binds doctors to communities and, through this, to their patients. The act of healing implies moral choice and moral sensitivity.[6] Beyond a willingness to perform the technical act is the willingness to participate in and to guide the choice. A social contract, then, binds physicians to technical competence as well as to moral discretion, and it enjoins them to use both.

Social contracts evolve through the ages. In our vision of the physician-patient relationship today, physicians are expected to attend to banal as well as hopeless illness; that same contract in ancient as well as medieval times enjoined no such expectation.[7] The physician-patient relationship, cemented by specific contract (the contract as understood to exist between doctors and patients) as well as by a larger social contract (the communal contract, which promises fidelity to such contracts) evolves with communal notions. It endures and evolves through time.

Within the larger society as well as within the profession, the patient-physician relationship has rested on historical tradition. A patient seeking out a healer has done so with the fundamental assumption that physicians will, above all else, be dedicated to their patients' "good" no matter what. Disagreements about the nature of the "good," about who legitimately defines it, and about the means necessary for its attainment may exist. But as long as the patient-physician relationship has endured, the central fact was never in doubt: physicians, if they are to fulfill the social contract, must be dedicated to their patients' good. Trust validates this assumption. Although from time to time physicians have unscrupulously broken the implicit contract, have sought their own good, or have become the willing tools of the state[6,8,9] (by executing, participating in involuntary experiments or practicing "acute remunerative medicine"), the immediate or at least eventual negative communal response and the physician's evident personally felt need for justification and defense speak for themselves. Many aspects of medical care have changed; many definitions and ways of defining the "good" have come and gone, but the central fact has remained: physicians must seek their patient's good (however defined within a given personal contract and within the community) and never their patient's harm. The patient remains central; the family, the institution, and the state all are peripheral.

Intertwining with the others is a root formed out of the specific personality of physician and patient. Each relationship, therefore, is unique and changing over time. At times, relationships may be deep and pervasive (an old-time patient who has become a friend), at other times, almost nonexistent (the unknown patient brought to the hospital in an unconscious state). Deep, pervasive relationships are informed by the enduring worldview of both parties expressed over time: "they have gotten to know each other." Their relationship is underwritten more by personal than by communal understanding. When, however, no such previous relationship exists, the communal contract, and the symbolism inherent in the contract, come to the fore. Physicians doing their duty as they see it are informed in their vision of the contract by the social forces in which they are enmeshed.

MODELS

The behavioral models posited by Szasz and Hollender reflect these views.[3] A model of activity-passivity in which treatment takes place "irrespective of the patient's contribution and regardless of the outcome" is best adapted to the unconscious, critically ill, or irrational patient. Guidance-cooperation, in which the physician is invested with great power by virtue of the patient's internal coercion by fear or pain, is attuned to situations of serious illness. Here the patient's power and consequent autonomy are reduced, and the physician's authority is enhanced. It is the situation in which most hospitalized ill patients find themselves. In the model of mutual participation, the physician and the patient, cooperating for an end satisfying to both, are seen as mutually interdependent and similar in power. It is the situation which pertains in various chronic states of which diabetes, hypertension, or coronary disease may be examples.

Many physicians have felt most at ease when their power was great but when patient participation and therefore "consent" was possible. They have been willing to assume an entirely active role but have, traditionally, felt unequal to the task of equality. To speak of paternalism in the activity-passivity setting does not ring true. It is a paternalism of necessity. Since, by definition, there is no one else to define the "good" or choose the means, physicians, ultimately and hopefully with the aid of the family, must. It is the second setting, that in which illness has distorted and unbalanced power, which lends itself best to paternalism and in which, ultimately, a certain amount of cautious paternalism is appropriate and inevitable. Here the patient seeks firm guidance and often willingly (and not always wisely) surrenders all decisions into the hands of the physician. Equal participation, never really entirely equal, finds the patient most ready to disagree both with the definition of the "good" sought and the means used. Power is never really entirely equal: the physician still controls pad and pen. But power may go the other way: patients control the purse strings and, in a sense, the reputation. A balance exists, and it is here that skillful and humane interaction and negotiation are most useful and necessary.

Cassel has pointed out that sick persons lose the sense of control over themselves and their world.[10] Often they may lose their adulthood and revert to a more childish form of existence. At that time, their attribution of unrealistic power and competence to the physician is maximal. This is characteristically seen in the "guidance-cooperation" model. Consent here is often token consent: power has been yielded to the physician, and autonomy is virtually lost. Restoring this autonomy is one of the noblest functions of medicine.[11]

Physicians bring technical expertise, experience with similar problems, judgment in analogous situations, and integrity to the relationship. Patients bring their needs, their hopes, and their implicit promise of payment: whether that payment is directly from the patient, through an insurance carrier, or by the government. Patients who, for a variety of reasons, do not pay in a material way still bring enrichment to the physician: they provide physicians with an opportunity to pay a small bit of their great debt to society, enable him or her to feel self-esteem, and promote the physician's feeling of humanity. Further, both physicians and patients see the accomplishment of their task as a social responsibility. Beyond licensure, and despite malpractice suits, the law has little practical impact upon most individual situations in which physicians and patients find themselves.

The sick person can be considered to be, as Cassel in condemning the notion put it, merely a well person carrying "the knapsack of disease";[11,12] or sick persons can be seen as emotionally, socially, and personally changed. The former model tends to look at the relationship as one of a power struggle and at the function of the physician as analogous to that of a garage mechanic replacing a customer's carburetor. The latter model sees the personal interaction of physician and patient as crucial and central and technology as the necessary tool. Neither model is entirely true. Rather, as with the three models discussed above, there is a continuum of ongoing relationships and forces appropriate to the situation and context encountered.

There are other ways and other models with and by which the physician-patient relationship can been described. Simplistically, of course, the relationship of healer to patient can be viewed simply as that of the "healer" attending a "sick" patient. Such a concept evades several important factors: it fails to address the concept "healer" as well as that of "sickness," and, above all, it takes the situation in which the healing act occurs outside its inevitable social and communal matrix.

"Healer" is a broad concept which has evolved from a unitary conception in which religious and medical functions were united in the same person.[13] The term "healer" has had various connotations throughout history and, therefore, has evoked different expectations. The shamans of the pre-historic world and the few surviving today, were not unique in uniting the religious and the "medical" function: from the Asclepiads of the Greeks (who coexisted and at times exchanged patients with their Hippocratic colleagues[14]) to medieval times when many if not most physicians were priests, to the faith healer of today, the function of the "healer" has often been combined with more priestly functions. To physicians, the concept of what "healers" are today may be quite firm and obvious, but these concepts by no means invariably match historical precedents or at times even come close to the varying conceptions of healer by today's lay public. Expectations are closely tied to such concepts.

Furthermore, what has been considered a crime, a disease or a sin has varied throughout history with the particular subject in question sometimes fluctuating among all three.[15] Consider only the fact that masturbation in the 19th century was considered a disease, a disease associated with demonstrable pathological findings, and, furthermore, a disease which not only had a surgical cure but also was listed as a cause of death on death certificates.[16,17] The category in which we place such things (whether we hold them to be crime, disease, sin, or irrelevant condition) makes a radical difference in the way we deal with them. The World Health Organization definition of health as a ". . . state of complete physical, mental and social well-being and not merely the absence of disease and infirmity,"[18] while holding out an unattainable goal, serves as a point of reference. It too, however, requires a social definition of disease and infirmity.

The social matrix in which the healing act occurs and in which doctors and other health professionals, as well as patients, function conditions the way we look at such matters as well as how we look at ourselves. If health and disease are, in fact, social constructs, and if what we consider to be a "healer" is conditioned by societal viewpoints of health and disease, then the physician-patient relationship is also very much molded by the society in which it occurs. Concepts do not have a straight linear arrangement with one another. Rather, concepts interact with each other and, ultimately, with their social context.[19]

The "sick role" is defined by one's particular culture and history.[20] It determines how we as patients behave and what, as professionals, our expectation of patients will be. This can, as has been shown, vary widely in differing cultures.[21–23] In consequence, the physician-patient relationship will be different in differing cultures. Models which seem appropriate to one culture and to one historical epoch, cannot simply be transplanted and be expected to flourish.

A slightly different version of the models outlined in the preceding pages can be historically identified. Fundamental to almost all has been the centrality of acting for the patient's benefit, however that benefit may be defined.[10,24] It is the bringing about of a ". . . proper act of healing in the face of the fact of illness" which has been and remains the proper concern of medicine.[4] It is the definition of what is proper, and who decides, which has given rise to many of the problems today.

One can look at four basic models. The historical model that, with considerable variation has lasted until recently has been the paternalist model. In this model, physicians decide both their patient's ends or goals and the means necessary for their attainment. In such a model, physicians simply decide legitimate goals in specific situations: for example, whether the goal of health by giving a transfusion (the means to reach that goal) is to be preferred over the patient's goal of not jeopardizing salvation or, perhaps, whether a DNR order serves the patient's interests (as defined by the doctor) best. Ends and means are chosen by the physician with the unexamined presumption that "father knows best." Not only does "father" choose the means since, obviously, "father" has much more knowledge and experience with such matters; "father" also feels entitled to choose the goals despite the fact that goals of health, salvation, or beauty are highly individual matters.

The scientific model, ushered in by Francis Bacon (late 16th and early 17th centuries), evolved until by the mid-19th century the patient more and more became an object to be scientifically studied and acted upon. Physicians began to see themselves more and more as scientists serving "science" as much as, and often more than, their patients: meticulous attention to technical details, unfortunately at times associated with callous neglect of the human dimension, followed. The relationship between healer and patient sometimes became one in which the centrality of the patient was lost: instead of science being a means to serving the patient's ends, the roles were reversed, and patients became a means of serving science. This, of course, was especially true in experimental settings, but reflections penetrated into the clinical arena.

As the economics of the marketplace changed and as the Western world progressively became more individualistic and less communitarian, an economic or entrepreneurial model developed. Medicine was seen not so much as a profession as a business, and patients became consumers. Notions of the health-care industry, of packaging, and of obtaining as much of the "health-care dollar" as possible emerged. Physicians as entrepreneurs or as workers in an entrepreneurial enterprise were enmeshed in mutual competition. An ever-growing conflict of interests inevitably followed.[24] The entrepreneurial model, inevitably competitive, makes of patients as well as of other physicians not partners but adversaries. A concern for legal protection from each other grew on both sides.

Clearly the paternalist model is not suitable in the modern world. Patients are not, if they ever were, children whose good we must decide; rather, they are sophisticated beings whose capacity to pick and choose is limited only by their lack of specific medical knowledge and experience as well as by the facts of their illness, which to a greater or lesser extent limits autonomy.[25] Restoring the patient's necessarily more or less limited autonomy and affirming as much of the autonomy which remains as possible are acknowledged to be among the central functions of proper medical practice today.[11] But restoring or affirming autonomy is not equivalent to abandoning patients to their autonomy (see also Chapter 5).

Crucial as science is to the practice of medicine, it forms a proper tool and not a proper goal in dealing with patients in the clinical setting. (The experimental setting is, of course, somewhat different, but the principle of first protecting the patient and not allowing deliberate harm is, at least explicitly, much a part of such endeavors also.) Unless physicians are abruptly to break with a tradition which mandates the centrality of the patient, the patient-physician relationship cannot properly be reduced to this model. Patients come to physicians to be healed, and the patient's, not abstract science's, good must first of all be served.

The entrepreneurial model, likewise, would break with this tradition and would reduce the relationship between healer and patient to one of coldly exchanging goods and, therefore, inevitably to competition. Explicit and, at times, well-written contracts and not human relationships form the basis of such a model.

New models, which are now beginning to emerge, are sorely needed. An emerging interactive model promises not only to be more adaptive to the realities of modern life but also to be more respectful of the evolving tradition.[26,27] This model derives the physician's status from his or her (undoubtedly) greater expertise in medical matters and sees the physician's role as one of enhancing the patient's ability to choose. Physicians and patients in such a model are partners in health care with mutual respect and concern. In this model, the commitment of physician to patient is grounded in a prior commitment to the patient's good and to the necessity of having that good enunciated by the patient. Any relationship in such a model takes place in a social matrix and is shaped by it.[27]

One must not be hamstrung by models. Models serve as convenient examples, but they cannot fully describe relationships between people. Physicians are all different from one another as are their patients. Relationships, as has been mentioned, contain a personal root shaped not only by a particular patient and a particular physician; such relationships are not comprehensible unless one understands the history of the relationship. Furthermore, relationships at any one moment are dependent upon circumstances outside the relationship which impinge on each of the actors. My relationship with a particular student (or patient) at a particular time is informed not only by a social understanding of how students and professors (or patients and doctors) are expected to interact in a given community but also by more personal factors. The way our day has gone, for example, inevitably shapes the way in which we interact with others who, in their turn, shape our further relations. These changes are subtle, but they nevertheless constitute the realities of life as well as, inevitably, those of medical practice.

RANKING THE PATIENT'S GOOD

When patients and physicians interact, they inevitably interact underpinned by an often tacit understanding of fundamental assumptions. Here a ranking of "goods" is helpful. Pellegrino and Thomasma have most helpfully proposed that such ranking can proceed at four levels: (1) the patient's ultimate good or "good of last resort"; (2) the good of the patient as a human person; (3) the patient's particular good; and (4) the biomedical good.[18] It is this ranking, within a social framework, which enables physicians and patients to negotiate goals and treatment plans.

The patient's ultimate good (or "good of last resort" as it is aptly labeled) is the highest good that patients autonomously have chosen for themselves. Obviously such choosing is not entirely "autonomous": the array of choices open to the patient is framed by history and by the community. It is within this framework that choices called "autonomous" are made. Such a good of last resort may be a religious vision, a secularly enunciated belief, or any other which is appealed to when "the chips are down." Paternalism, by reason of respect for persons, is inappropriate in the choice of such goods.

The good of the patient as a human person involves the choice made by the patient concerning his or her vision of himself as a human person. This good is the personal freedom to make choices, and it implies that physicians in honoring such a choice must do everything possible to enhance, and not to interfere with, the patient's competence. Insofar as possible, patients must therefore be supplied with complete information as well as a complete set of options. Drugging patients to insure compliance, or deliberately giving them less than complete information concerning their options is, under most circumstances, ethically suspect.

The particular good a patient may choose emerges from these other considerations. Here the patient chooses whether, in view of the previous considerations, a procedure is or is not worthwhile. A patient may, for example, choose to take or not to take a greater or lesser risk (say, a woman who must decide on various options when breast cancer is diagnosed). Here serious conflict between physicians and patients may occur (as when a patient makes a choice morally intolerable to the physician), and compassionate referral to another health-care professional is sometimes the only option. Compassionate negotiation should, as far as that is possible, precede such a last-resort move.

The biomedical good is the *prima facie* good of the physician-patient interaction. After all, when patients come to see physicians, they come primarily with that good in mind. Only when a higher good interferes will the biomedical good be neglected or postponed. Often it is here that negotiation is at its most fruitful. Within the context of the patient-physician relationship, patients cannot be forced to pursue the biomedical good when it violates a higher value; on the other hand, it is here that patients cannot simply be abandoned to their autonomy.

CONFIDENTIALITY

One of the enduring cornerstones of medical practice is the confidentiality of information obtained in the context of medical practice (see also Chapter 6). This stricture—not to reveal information about patients to anyone and under (almost) any circumstances—has endured through recorded time. Patients expecting to be helped must be truthful with their physician (or with their attorney). In turn, this, according to some, necessitates a strict (almost absolute) obligation of confidentiality. It is codified in law and has come to be seen as an (almost) absolute condition of proper practice.[28] There are those who argue that, for a variety of both utilitarian (encourages full disclosure) and deontological (absolute respect for persons) reasons, it is near absolute.[28] Confidentiality, as Rawls says, is an agreement bound by the principle of fairness.[29] But that does not make it absolute.

Problems of confidentiality, even though at first blush we may think of confidentiality as near absolute, are frequent: with whom to share hospital or office records, to whom to reveal diagnoses, how to safeguard information at a time when multiple health professionals are engaged with and must share information about common patients or are members of the same group or HMO, and how to deal with information of possible communal impact (infectious disease, the revelation of crime, dangerous forms of insanity, etc.). Confidentiality, according to some, has become a "decrepit concept," one that because of the necessity of multiple persons having access to patient's records is nondischargeable in the context of proper medical practice.[30] That does not mean that abuses of confidentiality by inadvertence or idle prattle (which Siegler, probably quite correctly, argues are those breaches the patient fears most) can be condoned. It does mean that, rather than being declared "absolute," the concept needs thoughtful and compassionate attention in the light of current medical realities. Patients must be made aware of the complexity and changing nature of this concept; physicians must exercise caution and prudence when making chart entries. Claiming to be adhering to what, in many instances, is a non-dischargeable obligation adds hypocrisy to the violation.

Saying that confidentiality is an absolute and must never be breached is untrue, impractical, and at times may cause disaster (as when a man kills his wife after telling his psychiatrist that he might do so). Laws, almost universally accepted as legitimate, which safeguard the community and enable public health insist that we report infectious disease; others force us to assign a cause of death on the death certificate. Surely confidentiality can be neither absolute nor untempered by common sense. Sharing information with colleagues is a necessary condition of medical practice; without it, cure often cannot be effected. Most patients assume this as an implicit norm. Providing information to insurance carriers is also usually done with the patient's explicit or implicit consent. Problems may, however, arise when the physician is privy to potentially embarrassing information or to information with legal implications for the patient. Under such conditions, the physician's first obligation is to safeguard the patient's trust, but that obligation is neither absolute nor universal.[31]

The obligation to keep confidentiality can be argued on utilitarian and deontological grounds. There are, however, times at which obligations clash. Such clashes involve a conflict between confidentiality and the rights of the community (public health issues), threatened third parties (as when patients threaten to do harm to others or in cases in which their condition threatens others), and at times conflicts between preserving confidentiality with the patient and not allowing that patient to come to harm (as, for example, when patients threaten suicide).[32]

The rights of the community and the physician's communal obligations may clash with the patient's wishes (see also Chapter 6). The reporting of communicable diseases is an example. Physicians here have a clear legal obligation and sometimes an ethical quandary. Patients, when they seek a physician's help in the context of our community, are generally aware that certain conditions must be reported. This requirement transcends any legal obligation: it forms part of the social contract in which the patient and physician, both as citizens, are enmeshed. Reporting such diseases, then, may be against a patient's expressed will, but has, nevertheless, been tacitly agreed upon by the community. Patients themselves have benefited, and expect to benefit, from such laws. They are part of the community in which such tacit agreements occur. Physicians, however, have an obligation beyond the mere reporting: physicians have the duty to see to it, as best they can, that rules of confidentiality effectively extend beyond their offices so that information still does not become easily accessible or a matter of public record.

Threatened third parties are another, and a troublesome, issue. There is at least a difference of degree between the person who does not wish the nature of his or her illness revealed to their mate (even though the illness may be venereal or, perhaps, fatal), the patient refusing to make a will, and the person who seriously threatens to murder another. Among other considerations, the question of sanity—and, therefore, ultimately of true autonomy—looms larger when a patient seriously threatens physical harm to another. Contracts, agreements, or covenants entered into with the questionably sane and, therefore, questionably autonomous cannot have the same force as contracts, agreements, and covenants under better circumstances. Here clinical judgment (judgment which determines the seriousness of the threat and the mental state of the patient) and discretion are the essence. Ultimately, physicians must make an agonizing choice in the full realization that a violation of covenant (be it with the patient or with the community) is inevitable. A given choice in a particular circumstance, while in itself blameworthy, may be the lesser evil.

When patients refuse to reveal the nature of their illness to others who have a clear need to know (either because those others stand to be infected or, because these others need to know since planning their life is critically dependent upon this knowledge), the physician may, likewise, be placed in a quandary. Often such problems can be solved by speaking with such a patient and convincing him or her to share this information; on rare occasions patients may remain adamant and insist that their mate remain uninformed about venereal disease or, perhaps, about a rapidly fatal condition. The physician's course of action here is unclear. Safeguarding confidentiality at the risk of seriously jeopardizing innocent bystanders is no more appealing than violating a patient's trust. Decisions depend upon the context of individual cases and on a careful analysis of the risks and benefits inherent in each course of action. Negotiation and an offer by the physician to serve as intermediary may have their place here.

The question of confidentiality when patients threaten harm to themselves is a more troubling issue. A man with operable cancer of the colon who refuses surgery and insists that his family not be told, or a woman determined to commit suicide would serve as an example. When physicians intervene in such circumstances, intervention is strictly paternalistic (see Chapter 5). Physicians and patients see the "good" differently, and if physicians break confidence, they are now imposing their vision of the "good" on the patient. Provided the patient is sane, not depressed, and meets the criteria of autonomy (and that, after all, is a largely clinical judgment), a breach of confidence would be hard to defend within the context of our current vision of the physician-patient relationship.

Individual cases will be adjudicated in the light of the obligation envisioned and the context in which the obligation occurs. Physicians have a *prima facie* obligation to preserve confidentiality,[33] but such *prima facie* duties can be overridden for weighty reasons.[34] When confidentiality is breached, no matter what the weight of the argument, physicians are blameworthy (see Chapter 3). Breaching a confidence and violating a trust is not now, nor can ever be, a "good" thing. But it can, on the grounds of harm and benefit to others, be a better alternative than allowing great harm to occur.

CONFLICTS OF INTEREST

Physicians are confronted with a variety of problems unique to the setting of their practice. Practice in a private solo practice, HMOs of various types, practice as the employee of various organizations (hospital, insurance company, industry), or practice within an organ of the state (the armed forces, prisons, etc.) all influence and distort the classical tradition. To remain an honorable physician seeking the patient's good within the context of these various constraints is often difficult. All these contexts offer the carrot of greater pay or advancement in the organization for "proper" behavior, proper, of course, as defined by the organization. Furthermore, rewards and punishments are rarely blatant, and usually they are given a veneer of probity. Such slick hypocrisy is an especially dangerous feature. It remains for physicians to examine themselves and their function in the light of social contract and to reach conclusions with honesty and integrity.

Blatant infringements of the patient-physician relationship occur and have occurred in the service of the state. The yearly reports of Amnesty International do not leave physicians free of blame. As far back as the first century, Scribonius Largus spoke of the duty towards all patients—regardless of war or peace—which united physicians.[14,35] Our current vision of the physician-patient relationship would seem not to endorse practices in which physicians become the allies of others bent on their patient's harm or destruction. Such gross examples as uninformed and unconsented to experimentation,[8,9,36,37] torture, or interrogation (or assisting, aiding, or abetting torture or interrogation),[38,39] or participation in capital punishment with the tools of medicine[6,40,41] are so flagrantly wrong as not to require extensive condemnation. Nevertheless, and despite pronouncements, guidelines, and rules,[42,43] these outrages continue throughout most of the world, regrettably also within our own borders.[38]

Because torture, experimentation on unconsenting subjects, and other outrages are so evidently wrong, they are often less of a problem than the role of physicians in the day-to-day working of jails, prisons, or, at times, within the armed forces. It is here that utmost vigilance is called for. Further, the problems of an entrepreneurial system which rewards physicians for not performing tests, not hospitalizing patients, etc.—in other words, a system which rewards saving and the practice of a minimalist medicine while touting good patient care as its goal—presents similar dangers couched in different terms. Institutional pressures on physicians, pressures which again favor minimalism at almost all costs are likewise considerable.

Physicians frequently experience ever-growing conflicts of interests today.[44] Since physicians in many respects control their own incomes and often generate their own work—by ordering tests which they perform or from which they profit, by having financial interests in diagnostic or surgical centers, and sometimes by financial inducements given by companies whose products they use—the conflict of interests is formidable. In a fee-for-service system this has always, but to a much lesser extent, been the case. The medical care of the patient, which ethically must be the physician's first priority, here conflicts with the physician's desire to maximize his own income. Whether by ordering fewer tests or procedures than needed (so as to satisfy, say, an HMO) or ordering more such tests, procedures, or return visits than needed, or by ordering marginally needed tests, physicians fail in their obligation.

It is difficult to come to terms with these problems. No pat solutions are available. The danger is not so much in the deliberate choice to do more or less than needed (although that danger too is real); the danger is that subconscious self-interest will influence decisions and enter into what should be decisions made on the basis of another's (and not one's own) good. Sensitivity, honesty, and a careful understanding of the roles and obligations of physicians in society can go far toward helping to find reasonable solutions.

Consent

The way we understand and use the notion of consent in dealing with patients is intimately connected to our understanding of the patient-physician relationship. We are often told that "consent" is a new idea, one not thought of in former times, and that undoubtedly is true of formal "consent." Yet, when patients came to Hippocratic or Asclepiad physicians, they came expecting a certain approach, and they were enmeshed in a relationship which they understood in certain ways. They came first of all to be helped and second with a social concept of a physician-patient relationship. Furthermore, surgeons could not "cut for stone" or physicians administer potions unless the patient submitted him- or herself to this. Consent, therefore, although not formal and far from as informed as we require today, nevertheless was a consent of sorts. Then as now, consent is not merely an explicit agreement between two or more individuals but has to be understood as enmeshed in a communal matrix.

Today as never before, we take the necessity of obtaining consent for granted. Often this is merely to protect ourselves from legal repercussions; properly (if by "properly" one means being mindful of the richness of the physician-patient relationship and its consequent obligations) it is in order to make our patient a willing partner in the joint enterprise. Consent to do a thing to another is necessary if we are to respect one another. The act of profession requires us to pursue our patient's "good"; respect for others requires that we define that "good" on that other's terms. A respect for autonomy presupposes a sense of beneficence. Since my "good," under ordinary circumstances, properly is a "good" defined by myself, acting beneficently is to have a regard for and to respect that good. Caring enough for another's welfare to respect their autonomy, ultimately, is a beneficent thing to do.

Consent, as Ramsey has so eloquently stated, can be understood as a "statement of fidelity between the man (or woman) who performs medical procedures and the man (or woman) upon whom they are performed." At its best, consent is grounded in a "canon of loyalty" which requires more than merely sterile assent.[45] Consent implies a fiduciary relationship which assumes that the patient's good is to be done and assumes that patients consent because they fully (or as fully as possible) understand not only what it is that is to be done (the means) but also the ultimate goal (or end) of doing it. The procedure (the means) and the ultimate goal (the end) are necessarily interrelated and interactive; choosing one in a sense determines the other. When fully informed patients consent to a procedure or treatment, they agree both with the goal and with the means towards its achievement. When such patients refuse, they refuse because they disagree with the goal to be achieved, find the means (the suggested therapy) either inappropriate or intolerable, or, at times, have failed to understand the issue.

Rather than merely going through motions, physicians in accepting either consent or refusal as valid must be reasonably certain that patients have, as fully as possible, understood the implications of either course of action.

When patients consent to what we want them to do, we do not question such consent unduly. Persons who agree with our course of action are obviously eminently well informed, sane, and intelligent! When, however, patients disagree with us, we are prone to question the extent of their information, their sanity, or their intelligence. Patients who agree with our recommendations share our goals and are willing to conform to our means, and most do. And yet consent too glibly given should be subject to at least some questioning. Patients may not have understood fully (or, at least, as fully as in their particular circumstances they really can), be frightened into assent (just as others may be frightened into dissenting), or be unaware that they are, in fact, committing themselves to a course of action. Therefore, it behooves physicians to maintain a degree of skepticism for consent too readily given. Physicians should reexamine their patients' depth of understanding either when patients dissent or when consent comes too readily.

When we become ill, our autonomy is, of necessity, diminished.[10,11,25] This is true even when—much as we may not want to admit this—physicians and other health professionals inevitably also become patients. Lay-persons, in addition, have a variable but inevitable lack of cognitive knowledge and a lack of experience with similar cases, which, among other things, distorts their emotive understanding of problems. Further, as if this were not enough, patients—health professionals and others alike—are at least concerned if not in fact frightened, and their ability to think clearly and dispassionately is therefore hampered by the very disease which has made them patients in the first place.

In the clinical situation, power is inevitably unevenly divided. Besides the cognitive, experiential, and biological factors we spoke about, physicians have the entire power of the medical setting at their side. In addition, and not to be underestimated, healers are invariably seen by those they heal (or pretend to heal) as endowed with more than actual power. Therefore, physicians and others who concern themselves with obtaining consent must try, as best they can, to promote as much understanding and offer as much true choice as is possible. The relative weakness of patients does not make them "more deserving," but it introduces a special obligation. Discharging such an obligation requires a great deal of compassion, tact, patience, and understanding.

Decisions must be understood within the patient's peculiar social milieu and its background beliefs. A disagreement about goals or about the relative value of competing goals cannot usually be solved by dispute: the Jehovah's Witness who refuses blood is not apt to be persuaded by lectures on the safety of transfusion or about the threat that such refusal has for life. A misunderstanding about means (as long as these means are not precluded because they are seen as distorting the goals as in the blood transfusion example) is more apt to yield to negotiation and persuasion: persons who fear that a given treatment or procedure would have a dreadful cost in terms of pain or suffering or who, on the other hand, unreasonably fear some outlandish misadventure may be persuaded by reasoning or by supplying additional facts.

EXPERIMENTATION

Experimentation in medicine offers a troublesome dimension. Little formal attention was paid to this until after World War II, when the outrages committed by Nazi doctors revolted the civilized world.[8,46,48] And yet, such outrages were hardly limited to Nazi Germany. From 1932 to 1972 (covering the period preceding the Nazi experiments and extending well beyond their condemnation by the civilized world including the United States), the United States conducted a systematic study in which over 400 black Alabama sharecroppers were studied to determine the effects of untreated syphilis in a day when syphilis was highly treatable (and when, incidentally, the effects of untreated syphilis were well known).[9,48] The Tuskegee Study, funded by the United States Public Health Service, has assumed its rightful place among man's medical atrocities alongside the Nazi and other experiences. And it is hardly an isolated instance.[36,37] Racism aside (and it is difficult in either the Nazi or the Tuskegee experience to put it aside[48]), the dedication of researchers to science has often resulted in experimentation and innovation involving unconsenting human subjects.

It is, of course, not altogether easy to say what does and what does not constitute experimentation, let alone innovation. Physicians and surgeons in trying out a slightly different technique or by prescribing a drug under slightly other than stereotyped circumstances may be accused of experimentation or at least innovation. Some such maneuvers are part and parcel of everyday practice and these are not what we have in mind.

Experimentation, as ordinarily conceived, involves an adventure into what is at least partially unknown. Those who join in the adventure should, at the very least, be fully aware of what is known about the journey and what is not known. As far as possible, risks need to be spelled out. Consent of patients should be freely given. (This raises obvious problems with the use of prisoners, medical students, and others who may be prone to more than usual coercive pressures.) Furthermore, experiments done on sick patients with the hope of curing or somehow beneficially affecting their disease are quite a different matter than experiments engaged in purely to extend our knowledge.

In general, experimentation has come to operate under a set of guidelines constructed to safeguard subjects and meant to assure that research follows ethical standards. Research, whenever possible, should first be done on inanimate models (tissue cultures, computer models, or plants) before being done in animals and should be done on lower before it is done on higher animals. When treating disease in humans, acceptable research should not deny a group of patients suffering from a dangerous illness treatment of their disease in order to establish "no treatment" controls: new treatment for a disease would have to compare current to new rather than current to no treatment. When a treatment for an untreatable disease shows a clear and statistically significant benefit when contrasted to no treatment, the experiment must be stopped, and the new treatment must be offered to all suffering from the disease (for example, when AZT was tested against AIDS and its benefits became clear, the experiment was stopped, and AZT therapy was offered). Guidelines for conducting research on prisoners, children, and the mentally infirm have been evolved.[49–51]

Research, to be acceptable, must be approved by an Institutional Review Board. All institutions conducting human research are expected to have and to utilize such IRBs. This is a laudable, but hardly foolproof, step forward. IRBs are composed of people. At their best people are not entirely impervious to political pressures or unmindful of the fact that their colleague whose research they must approve or not approve today will tomorrow approve or not approve their own. Furthermore, passage by an IRB does little to solve the quandary in which researchers find themselves when they must both look out for a particular patient's welfare and for the welfare of their experiment. Inevitably, at times, they are caught between two mutually exclusive, or at least mutually somewhat contrary, goals.

Inevitably, the physician-patient relationship is distorted or, at the very least, strained by research protocols. And yet, if medicine is to advance, research is vitally necessary. Sometimes it is possible to diffuse the problem (for example, by having two different persons responsible for the treatment, one mainly concerned with the patient's welfare and the other conducting the experiment, with the former having veto power over the latter). Often the best that can be done is to be vigilant, to be aware as much as possible of one's own motivation, to be mindful of the problem, and to be honest in one's dealings with the subjects of the research.

REFERENCES

1. Loewy, E.H., Duties, fears and physicians, *Soc. Sci. Med.* 22(12): 1363–1366, 1986.
2. Loewy, E.H., Moral considerations in dealing with dementia, in: *Ethical Dilemmas in Modern Medicine: A Physician's Viewpoint* (E.H. Loewy, ed.), Edwin Mellen Press, Lewiston, NY, 1986, pp. 237–262.
3. Szasz, T.S., and Hollender, M.H., The basic models of the doctor-patient relationship, *Arch. Intern. Med.* 97:585–592, 1956.
4. Pellegrino, E.D., Toward a reconstruction of medical morality: The primacy of the act of profession and the fact of illness, *J. Med. Phil.* 4(1): 32–55, 1979.
5. Loewy, E.H., Healing or killing: Health professionals and execution, in: *Ethical Dilemmas in Modern Medicine: A Physician's Viewpoint* (E.H. Loewy, ed.), Edwin Mellen Press, Lewiston, NY, 1986, pp. 107–132.
6. Pellegrino, E.D., and Thomasma, D.C., *A Philosophical Basis of Medical Practice*, Oxford University Press, New York, 1981.
7. Amundsen, D.W., The physicians obligation to prolong life: A medical duty without classical roots, *Hastings Center* 8(4):23–31, 1978.
8. Lifton, R., *The Nazi Doctors*, Basic Books, New York, 1986.
9. Jones, J.J., *Bad Blood*, The Free Press, New York, 1981.
10. Cassell, E., *The Healer's Art: A New Approach to the Patient-Physician Relationship*, J.B. Lippincott, Philadelphia, 1976.
11. Cassell, E., The function of medicine, *Hastings Center* 7(6):16–19, 1977.
12. Parsons, T., and Fox, R., Therapy and the modern urban family, *J. Soc. Iss.* 8(4):31–44, 1952.
13. Loewy, E.H., Clergy and physicians encounter medical ethics, *Humane Med.* 3(1):48–51, 1987.
14. Edelstein, L., The professional ethics of the Greek physician, *Bull. Hist. Med.* 30(5):391–419, 1956.
15. Loewy, E.H., Communities, obligations and health-care, *Soc. Sci. Med.* 25(7):783–791, 1987.
16. Engelhardt, H.T., *The Foundations of Bioethics*, Oxford University Press, New York, 1986.
17. Engelhardt, H.T., The disease of masturbation: Values and the concept of disease, *Bull. Hist. Med.* 48:234–248, 1974.
18. World Health Organization, Constitution of the World Health Organization, 22 July 1946, *Public Health Rep.* 61:1268–1271, 1946.
19. Dewey, J., *Logic, the Theory of Inquiry*, Henry Holt, New York, 1938.
20. Parsons, T., Definitions of health and illness in light of American values and social structure, in: *Concepts of Health and Disease* (A. Caplan, H.T. Engelhardt, and J.J. McCartney, eds.), Addison-Wesley, Reading, MA, 1981, pp. 57–82.
21. Glazer, G., The "good" patient, *Nurs. Health Care* 11(3):144–164, 1981.

22. Bhanumathi, P.P., Nurses conception of the "sick-role" and "good-patient behaviour": A cross-cultural comparison, *Int. Nurs. Rev.* 24(1):20–24, 1977.
23. Payer, L., *Medicine and Culture*, Henry Holt, New York, 1988.
24. Lain-Etralgo, P., *Doctor and Patient* (P. Partridge, trans.), McGraw-Hill, New York, 1969.
25. Morison, R.S., The biological limits of autonomy, *Hastings Center Rep.* 14(5):43–49, 1984.
26. Ozar, D., Patient's autonomy: Three models of professional-lay relationships in medicine, *Theor. Med.* 5:61–68, 1984.
27. Pellegrino, E.D., and Thomasma, D.C., *For the Patient's Good: The Restoration of Beneficence in Health Care*, Oxford University Press, New York, 1988.
28. Kottow, M.H., Medical confidentiality: An intransigent and absolute obligation, *J. Med. Ethics* 12:117–122, 1986.
29. Rawls, J., *A Theory of Justice*, Belknap Press, Cambridge, MA, 1971.
30. Siegler, M., Confidentiality in medicine: A decrepit concept, *N. Engl. J. Med.* 307(24):1518–1521, 1982.
31. Thompson, I.E., The nature of confidentiality, *J. Med. Ethics* 8:12–18, 1982.
32. Walters, L., Ethical aspects of medical confidentiality, *J. Clin. Comput.* 4(1):9–20, 1974.
33. Ross, W.D., *The Right and the Good*, Clarendon Press, Oxford, 1930.
34. Frankena, W., *Ethics*, Prentice Hall, Englewood Cliffs, NJ, 1973.
35. Hamilton, J.S., Scribonius Largus on the medical profession, *Bull. Hist. Med.* 60(4):209–216, 1986.
36. Capron, A.M., Medical research in prisons: Should a moratorium be called? *Hastings Center Rep.* 3(2):3–5, 1973.
37. Ward, R., Krugman, S., Giles J.P., et al., Infectious hepatitis: Studies of its natural history and prevention, *N. Engl. J. Med.* 258(9):407–416, 1958.
38. Jonsen, A.R., and Sagan, L., Torture and the ethics of medicine, *Man Med.* 3:33–49, 1978.
39. Whymant, R., The butchers of Harbin, *Conn Med.* 47(3):163–165, 1983.
40. Curran, W,J., and Cascells, W., The ethics of medical participation in capital punishment by intravenous drug injection, *N. Engl. J. Med.* 302(4):226–230, 1980.
41. Cascells, W., and Curran, W.J., Doctors, the death penalty and lethal injection, *N. Engl. J. Med.* 307:1532–1533, 1982.
42. World Medical Association, Declaration of Tokyo, *Bull. Am. Coll. Physicians* 17(6):15, 1976.
43. United Nations General Assembly Resolution Adopted by the General Assembly, *Principles of Medical Ethics*, CIOMS, Geneva, 1983.
44. Relman, A.S., Dealing with conflicts of interest, *N. Engl. J. Med.* 313(12):749–751, 1985.
45. Ramsey, P., *The Patient as Person*, Yale University Press, New Haven, 1979.
46. Pross, C., and Winau, R., *Das Krankenhaus Moabit*, Hentrich Verlag, Berlin, 1984.
47. Alexander, L., Medical science under a dictatorship, *N. Engl. J. Med.* 241:39–47, 1949.
48. Brandt, A.M., Racism and research: The case of the Tuskeegee study, *Hastings Center Rep.* 8(6):26–29, 1978.
49. National Commission for the Protection of Human Subjects of Biomedical and Behavioral Research, *Report and Recommendations: Research Involving Children*, U.S. Department of Health, Education and Welfare, Washington, 1977.

50. National Commission for the Protection of Human Subjects of Biomedical and Behavioral Research, *Report and Recommendations: Research Involving Prisoners*, U.S. Department of Health, Education and Welfare, Washington, 1976.
51. National Commission for the Protection of Human Subjects of Biomedical and Behavioral Research, *Report and Recommendations: Research Involving Those Institutionalized as Mentally Infirm*, U.S. Department of Health, Education and Welfare, Washington, 1978.

CHAPTER 5

The Ongoing Dialectic between
Autonomy and Responsibility

Autonomy and responsibility form the two limbs of a dialectic which helps form our communal ethos. This tension is studied not only as it pertains to medicine but also as it is reflected in other social issues of caring for members of community. In examining this issue, the chapter scrutinizes autonomy and sets out criteria for determining that a decision is or is not an autonomous one. Truth-telling, as it relates to autonomy, is briefly discussed.

Autonomy, as usually understood, implies the ability to govern oneself. It is an ideal never fully realized or realizable in the human condition. Biological (including genetic) factors impose very real limits on our abilities; environmental factors create conditions to which, whether we like it or not, we must adapt; and matters of cultural background, upbringing, and the social conditions in which we find ourselves severely constrain our willing as well as our acting.[1] Kant, whose name is most closely associated with the concept of autonomy, understood this very well when he stated that only the "divine being" is truly autonomous.[2] But not being entirely autonomous does not mean that man is totally at the mercy of external forces or totally "the slave of the passions."[3] The limits of autonomy are set by forces in a sense external to the will and beyond the control of man (and these may vary from time to time and situation to situation), but man's freedom to operate within those limits is what we commonly mean when we speak, loosely, of free will or of an "autonomous act."[4]

The feeling of responsibility is a response to an externally imposed or perceived condition. Thus, we may be responsible because of our role (or the way in which we and others conceive that role), because of a promise freely given or a contract freely entered, because of something that we have done (broken a cup or given the wrong treatment, for example), or because of the promptings of an internally felt *noblesse oblige* (as when we see a helpless creature in need of help). Our view of community and obligation to one another conditions our sense of responsibility and consequently our actions (see Chapter 2). In the sense of causal responsibility (as in breaking a cup or treating in the wrong way) and, in some respects, in the sense of role responsibility, responsibility is externally determined and judged. In role responsibility, however, the delineation is largely a changing social construct determined over time. Communities determine role responsibility as a composite expression of the internally felt responsibility of their individual members. Internally felt responsibility, while to some extent conditioned by extrinsic factors, is also, to some degree, the product of autonomous, rational choice. It is a function of how we view ourselves in relation to others and in relation to community. In that sense, the choices we make and the responsibilities we assume say more about us as moral actors than they do about the problem.[5]

Responsibility for one another may clash with autonomy. Physicians, feeling responsible for their patients, may choose to treat against the patients' wishes. Or physicians, out of respect for autonomy, may allow patients to pursue a course leading to disaster. Medicine is but a microcosm of this daily struggle: when we allow our homeless to wander the streets and freeze to death (mostly because communities lack even reasonably adequate facilities but sometimes because we accept that some of the homeless allegedly "wish" to do this) without, forcefully if need be, taking responsibility, the same issue is at play. Unthinkingly and unfeelingly abandoning persons to their autonomy is the flip side of paternalism.

Paternalism (or parentalism as it has lately begun to be called) seeks to do one's own good to another instead of facilitating that other's (self-selected) good. It often arises out of a sense of responsibility in which the paternalist's claim to greater knowledge, foresight, wisdom or experience is the ostensible excuse. The fact that such claims are not always without foundation makes paternalism all the more insidious and, therefore, dangerous. If paternalism were simply a crass act of one human being callously superimposing values on another, the problem would be easy. Forcing persons to listen to Mozart (or to rock music) because we happen to like Mozart (or rock music) is clearly indefensible. But forcing panicky patients to undergo emergency treatment to save their life (or forcing a homeless person to seek shelter in a snowstorm) may be another matter.

Furthermore, responsibility in the contemporary world and with the awesome power of technology which may be used for good or evil has changed. We cannot evade the responsibility that comes with this change—the responsibility to use technology wisely, not only for the sake of our patients but for the sake of the future. In a sense, we need to be able to foretell the future, to reenunciate norms and standards as substitutes for the norms and standards left behind by technology. If we fail to do this, the future is bleak.[6]

The modern concept of autonomy, as mentioned above, originated with Kant. The will is not only subject to the moral law; to be autonomous and therefore "worthy of respect," it has to be subject to its own self-legislated, universalizable law. This autonomy comes from within the individual. But autonomy itself does not seem to be enough if one reads Kant clearly. "Nothing in this world . . . can possibly be conceived to be good without qualification, except a good will."[2] And so, autonomy can only be an instrumental good, one which depends for its goodness or badness upon the will and the—unfortunately not entirely clear—"goodness" which guides it.[2,7] Mill, in his entirely different utilitarian concept of the bases of morality, likewise considers autonomy to be a fundamental fact of the moral life.[8,9] Autonomy of action must be one of the fundamental principles in order to maximize the good of society. So long as persons' actions do not directly infringe upon their neighbors', such actions must be permitted.

In a society in which personal liberty, freedom of thought, and eventually of action were severely restricted, the ideal of autonomy served well. Men were downtrodden by a rapacious state that simultaneously inhibited its citizens' freedom and denied responsibility. Where the state was forced to assume responsibility, it did so hesitatingly, grudgingly, and with humiliating condescension. Charity itself became a tainted word, responsibility for one's fellowman an impoverished concept, and autonomy a dangerous thing. Whether interpreted from the philosophical slant of Kant or of Mill, autonomy of will and action underwrote the promise of the American, the French, and later the Russian revolutions.[10]

If we hold freedom to be an absolute condition of the moral life and look at communities as collections of men united merely by duties of not bringing harm one to another, we will place a supreme value upon autonomy and will find the place of responsibility for one another to be, except under contractually stipulated conditions, quaint.[11,12] If, on the other hand, we hold freedom to have a high communal value but not to be an absolute, and if we look at community as being united by more than the minimal duties of refraining from harm one to another, a different kind of responsibility enters the equation.[13] It seems doubtful that many of us, not knowing what station in life we were to occupy or what our fate is to be, would deliberately choose a community in which beneficence were to have no moral standing.[14] Neither a minimalist ethic (built only on duties of refraining and bereft of the duties of charity, benevolence, and kindness)[15] nor an ethic in which men are coerced to follow another's vision of the good presents the sort of society most rational men would envision for themselves.

In society at large and in medical practice, there is an ongoing dialectic between autonomy on the one hand and paternalism (couched in terms of responsibility) on the other. Autonomy, seeking to maximize personal moral agency, and responsibility, as an expression of benevolence, both have their place. Neither can become a moral obsession.[16] Autonomy as a moral obsession leads to neglect: it is often a moral "cop-out," an excuse for pursuing our own interests mindless of the often very obvious needs of others. Benevolence as an obsession, on the other hand, too easily eventuates in personal or communal tyranny: it easily serves as an excuse for repressive acts of the crassest kind. In choosing between alternative courses of action, reason must guide us to choose the least restrictive.[17]

It has been said that there must be a presumption against paternalistic acts and in favor of autonomy.[18] If individual and communal tyranny is to be prevented, both society and medicine share the need for this presumption. Autonomy, never complete, always variable, is an ideal and not a concrete fact. By itself, and not integrated with a sense of community and responsibility to one another, it leads to a callous and uncaring society.

There should, as we have said, be a presumption against paternalistic acts: the burden of proof is (and, if we are to prevent tyranny, should be) on the paternalist. Such an initial presumption, however, must be measured against another: the presumption against allowing others to come to harm.[18] The problem, of course, is the strength of one presumption as against the other and the meaning of what it is to come to harm. There can, at times, be a justification for paternalism just as, at other times, there can be a justification for allowing persons to come to harm in respect of their autonomy.

Allowing respect for autonomy to result in personal harm to our fellow man, or to our patient, requires justification just as does violating their autonomy. When one or the other presumption must prevail, the initial presumption usually will be to safeguard one another. That, if nothing else, will buy time. In critical emergencies (say, when a patient is in imminent danger) a presumption against allowing another to come to harm seems very much in order. When situations are less critical, however, the presumption against paternalistic acts becomes more persuasive. The rational patient bent on suicide may try again; the irrational patient allowed to die is denied that second chance. Once the criteria for autonomous action have been met, the presumption against paternalistic acts should prevail (see also Chapter 7).

To be autonomous, an action must meet certain minimal criteria: it must be amply informed, it must be the product of sufficient deliberation, it must be free of internal or external coercion, and it must be consistent with an enduring worldview.[19] A judgment as to when such criteria are sufficiently met (and what is considered to be sufficient) is often difficult. Keeping these criteria carefully in mind, however, at least distinguishes the clearly autonomous decision (say, when a life-long Jehovah's Witness staunchly refuses permission for blood) from one clearly not so (say, when a hysterical person, confused and in severe pain, refuses a critically needed intervention).

Ample information, in and of itself, may be problematic. Telling patients technical details that are often not understood or entirely out of the range of the patient's experience is not truly "informing." Every attempt to enable patients to truly understand and understand in simple, nontechnical terms not only procedures and diagnoses but options and choices must be made. An autonomous decision is predicated on an understanding of the facts, an internalization of external data. More than the giving of data is therefore involved. Physicians must remember the impact that the emotions of the moment and, often, the lack of experience have and must try to minimize the gap of understanding between themselves and their patients (see also the section on consent in Chapter 4).

Sufficient deliberation implies time and time, as much as possible, away from the acute pressures of critical situations. Time, however, is often just what is not easily at hand. Here physicians can only try to provide as much time as possible: pressuring patients in order to meet the needs of a busy schedule defeats that purpose. Allowing a patient sufficient time to deliberate and make choices consistent with their own values has to be, at times, balanced against the exigencies of a critical situation; but all too often physicians are apt to serve their own convenience by pleading the urgency of a situation to hide the fact that their own convenience is what is being served.

Coercion can come in many guises. Patients may be coerced by external circumstances to act not according to their own will but according to the will of others. Often the physician can sense this in the context of situations in office or hospital. Elderly patients wishing to please their children, husbands wishing to please their wives, and patients wishing to please the medical team not rarely fall into this category. It is the physician's job to understand and to perceive sensitively such problems and to counter them by speaking to the patient with understanding, with compassion, and, when possible, alone. But coercion, as often as not, is internal. Panic, fear, pain, and hope all can be coercive and can help obliterate or, at the very least, impair autonomy.

Familiarity with the patient's worldview is, perhaps, of the greatest help. Choices made under the influence of fear or pain, for example, may nevertheless be considered autonomous if they are consistent with a previous enduring and well-understood worldview. Knowledge of a patient's prior worldview is best obtained in the context of an ongoing and enduring physician-patient relationship. Ideally, sympathy and understanding for each other's worldviews have slowly developed over time. Unfortunately, such relationships are more the exception than the rule today. More often, physicians and patients are virtual strangers, and often physicians must deal with acutely ill patients about whom they know little or nothing. At best, impressions can be gleaned from many inevitably biased sources, which may (or may not) have the patient's "best interest" (defined on the patient's and not on their own terms) in mind. Such impressions must then be distilled by an equally biased physician. Often the final picture resembles more what we would like it to be than what it is.

Deciding whether a patient's action is acceptably autonomous is not an easy task. Individual decisions will depend upon specific circumstances, on prior knowledge, and on consultation with the patient's family, colleagues, and other members of the health care team. At times, psychologically schooled personnel may give invaluable assistance for an understanding of the dynamics informing patients' decisions. But, when all is said and done, the final decision—to accept or not to accept a patient's choice—will have to be made by the physician.

Since we assume ourselves to be competent, we rarely question competence when patients make choices consistent with our own. When, on the other hand, the patient's choice conflicts with our own, questions about the validity of the choice tend to come up. The more blatant the conflict and the more we disagree with the road chosen, the more do we tend to question the patient's ability to choose. And that is natural. Conflicts of this sort may arise from a lack of factual material, a different understanding of such facts, or a profound difference of worldviews (see also Chapter 4). Problems of judging competence or autonomy arise because competence and autonomy are not absolutes. A patient may, for example, be incompetent to handle his own finances but be quite competent to order dinner or determine which theater to go to. Competence to make one's own will and competence to determine one's own course of therapy are not necessarily identical matters. Determining that patients are or are not competent to consent to or to refuse treatment must be adjudicated on a one-to-one basis depending upon individual circumstances. We cannot presume that incompetence is an all-or-nothing phenomenon or that it does not change with time and circumstance. Denying competence to choose a course of treatment may, on the one hand, deny the patient's individual dignity when autonomy to choose such treatment is maintained; on the other hand, affirming that a frightened, ill-informed, or otherwise incapable patient is capable of refusing may deny the beneficent responsibility which lies at the core of medicine. Abandoning patients to their autonomy is all too easily done. Respecting autonomy in the competent person presupposes beneficence: when persons are competent to choose, even when the choice is not one we ourselves would make, respecting their choice is a beneficent act. It allows their will to be done in circumstances directly affecting them. Respecting autonomy in the incompetent, however, is a hollow mockery denoting rather than beneficence a callow noncaring. Allowing an uninformed, coerced, or confused will to be done makes a mockery both of autonomy and of beneficence.

Using the criteria for autonomy cited above may help sort out specific cases. Physicians are obligated to provide patients with all pertinent information concerning their case necessary for informed choice, and they are obligated to provide it in a manner understandable to the patient. Further, physicians should make sure that such information is truly comprehended. Comprehension means more than merely the ability to parrot facts. True understanding, in addition to an essential cognitive part, includes understanding on an emotional as well as where possible an experiential plane. Often physicians assume that their patients understand far more than is actually the case. A little time spent asking some gentle but penetrating questions may be most helpful. In addition, and where possible, time for deliberation must be provided, and "snap" judgments guarded against. Seeing that patients are as free from coercion as possible during this time and gently probing the patient's prior worldview likewise are obligations of the health care team. Forcing patients to make hurried choices with inadequate information sometimes presented in an unnecessarily threatening manner violates basic respect for autonomy and incidentally is destructive to the physician-patient relationship.

At best, problems remain. Patients may make apparently autonomous decisions and then, when the situation is upon them, change their mind. This confronts the health care team with agonizing problems. In general, but by no means always, we tend to honor the more recent rather than the more distant choice. However, such decisions are predicated on the assumption that both decisions were autonomous, that both were competent choices.[20] When patients change their mind in circumstances when reasonable autonomy appears present (when, in other words, information and time for deliberation are reasonable, coercion is held to a minimum and the change is not entirely at variance with a previously enduring worldview) respect for the more recent over the more remote decision will readily be granted. When, however, the choice appears to be the result of ignorance, fear, or panic, matters may stand differently. It is at such times that difficult choices will have to be made.

Truth-telling is intimately linked with problems of autonomy. Persons who hold autonomy to be an absolute principle will, under all circumstances, tell their patients the absolute and unvarnished truth. Paternalists, on the other hand, are apt to judge what is, in their view, to the patient's benefit to know and what not and will act accordingly. The fact that paternalists often misjudge their patient's good,[21] substituting conjectures and personal values instead, has become well known. In practice, a presumption for telling patients the truth can be overcome only by extremely weighty evidence. But truth-telling, like other principles, acts as a guideline to moral behavior and not as an absolute. Blindly following principles (e.g., always telling the truth) can become an end in itself instead of a means to a moral end.[22] Following principles in this way substitutes iron-clad rules for moral deliberation and severely limits moral agency and its necessary choices. Although there is a heavy presumption for truth-telling, ethics reduced to pat principles applied to preconceived problems without being filtered through our moral sensibilities is a technical and not a moral activity.[23]

Not telling the truth (never a praiseworthy and invariably a blameworthy act) may yet be the best choice to make from a range of poor options. Patients at times may not wish to have the truth told to them and may ask to be spared certain knowledge. And while this is rare and while it certainly imposes a heavy burden on the physician, the patient's desire not to know is as autonomous a decision as is the opposite. Rarely there may be other reasons for being less than candid with an occasional patient. The decision to be less than candid must, at all times, be a weighty one, not one made for the sake of expedience, convenience, or cowardice. On some occasions it may, all things being equal, be the only humane option open to the physician. When truth-telling succeeds only in removing all hope from dying patients, discharging an absolute moral duty exacts a heavy price. Ethics not tempered by compassion and understanding becomes like "random chords on a piano"[23] and loses its intrinsic value.

REFERENCES

1. Morison, R.S., The limits of autonomy, Hastings Center 14(6):43–49, 1984.
2. Kant, I., Foundations of the Metaphysics of Morals (L. W. Beck, trans.), Macmillan, New York, 1986.
3. Hume, D., A Treatise of Human Nature, Book II, Part III, Sect. III, Clarendon Press, Oxford, 1968.
4. Dennet, D.C., Elbow Room: The Varieties of Free Will Worth Having, MIT Press, Cambridge, MA, 1985.
5. Churchill, L.R., Bioethical reductionism and our sense of the human, Man Med. 5(4):229–249, 1980.
6. Jonas, H., Technology and responsibility, in: Philosophical Essays (H. Jonas, ed.), Prentice Hall, Englewood Cliffs, NJ, 1974, pp. 3–20.
7. Paton, J., The Categorical Imperative, University of Pennsylvania Press, Philadelphia, 1971.
8. Mill, J.S., Utilitarianism, Bobbs-Merrill, Indianapolis, 1979.
9. Mill, J.S., On Liberty, W.W. Norton, New York, 1975.
10. Loewy, E.H., Paternalism or responsibility: Dirty words or necessary elements of medical practice? in: Ethical Dilemmas in Modern Medicine: A Physician's Viewpoint (E.H. Loewy, ed.), Edwin Mellen Press, Lewiston, NY, 1986, pp. 57–88.
11. Engelhardt, H.T., The Foundations of Bioethics, Oxford University Press, New York, 1986.
12. Nozick, R., Anarchy, State and Utopia, Basic Books, New York 1972.
13. Loewy, E.H., Communities, obligations and health care, Soc. Sci. Med. 25(7):783–791, 1987.
14. Rawls, J., A Theory of Justice, Harvard University Press, Cambridge, MA, 1971.
15. Callahan, D., Minimalist ethics, Hastings Center 11(6):19–25, 1981.
16. Callahan, D., Autonomy: A moral good, not a moral obsession, Hastings Center 14(6):40–41, 1984.
17. Dworkin, G., Paternalism, Monist 56(1):64–84, 1972.
18. Bassford, H.A., The justification of medical paternalism, Soc. Sci. Med. 16:731–739, 1982.
19. Loewy, E.H., Patient, family, physician: Agreement, disagreement and resolution, Family Med. 18(6):375–378, 1986.
20. Loewy, E.H., Changing one's mind: Is Odysseus to be believed? J. Gen. Intern. Med. 3(1):54–58, 1987.
21. Kübler-Ross, E., On Death and Dying, Macmillan, New York, 1975.
22. Churchill, L.R., and Simán, J.J., Principles and the search for moral certainty, Soc. Sci. Med. 23(5):461–468, 1986.
23. Cassel, E.J., Life as a work of art, Hastings Center 14(5):35–37, 1984.

CHAPTER 6

The Physician as Citizen

Physicians are acknowledged to have roles which transcend particular physician-patient relationships. This chapter examines two views: one sees the physician's role as citizen deriving from his or her role as personal physician to patients; the other sees the role of the physician taking form from his or her more public responsibilities. The consequences of these views as they relate to issues of public health, confidentiality, and caring for social ills are discussed.

Men and women partake of various roles in life. Each of these has constraints, duties and obligations peculiar to itself. Nevertheless, and fundamentally, all people are members of a community, "citizens" in the sense of being members bound by social contract with one another and, therefore, sharing in a different but more universal set of constraints, duties, and obligations. The communal set embodies and underwrites the strictures peculiar to the citizen's specific role. While clashes between these are inevitable (the duty as a citizen to report criminals conflicts with the physician's obligation for confidentiality to the patient who is a housebreaker, for example), it is nevertheless essential to remember that role constraints, duties, and obligations developed in a communal setting are sustained by communal values and are therefore informed by communal strictures and expectations. In the last analysis, even the obligation to confidentiality which prompts the physician not to report his patient who is a housebreaker to the police is the product of communal values, strictures, and expectations.

Expectations do not necessarily determine what is and what is not moral.[1] We may expect an acquaintance to lend us money, for example, but his not doing so, although perhaps irksome and even unkind, is not immoral. No moral duties are entailed by one-sided expectations. But in an evolutionary sense, in the sense in which roles in society emerged and were affirmed, expectations for one another are important in determining the morality of an act. When such expectations are, in fact, fulfilled, when, let us say, firemen are expected to enter burning buildings and do so, or physicians are expected to take risks of infection and take such risks, expectations are confirmed by practice, underwritten by values, and, at times, affirmed by legal (or at least social) strictures and sanctions. A functional precedent is set. Communal expectations, legitimized by consistent performance, thus form part of the matrix of considerations which determines the morality of an action.

Our viewpoint of community determines our viewpoint toward obligations (see also Chapter 2). Are communities to be viewed as collections of individuals held together merely by duties of refraining from harm to one another? If, in such communities, freedom is the absolute condition of morality and not a value to be adjusted mindful of other values, communal obligations are limited to securing absolute liberty (short of harming each other) for all. The obligations of physicians are then purely those stipulated by freely entered upon contract.[2,3] If, on the other hand, we consider refraining from doing harm to each other to be the necessary but insufficient condition of community, and if, furthermore, we concede to freedom the standing of "value" to be cautiously traded and bartered for other goods, the duties and obligations of community as well as those of its component institutions (including medicine) emerge in a different light.[4,5]

It is easy to demand that "physicians meet their social responsibilities" in the practice of medicine. No one will seriously doubt that if physicians are to discharge their obligations adequately more than merely medical function is entailed. The World Medical Organization, in its statement on health, defines health as ". . . a state of complete physical, mental and social well-being and not merely the absence of disease and infirmity."[6] This definition, while holding out an unattainable ideal goal, nevertheless serves as a point of reference. If, in the context of this definition, physicians are obliged to care for the health of their patients, social responsibilities cannot be evaded. On the other hand, if we subscribe to the narrower definition of health as being merely the absence of disease, then the physician's obligation, too, is narrower. But even here, we may argue that at the very least the unavoidable public health, occupational, and social aspects of many diseases will, of necessity, involve the physician in social concerns.

The recognition that diseases have, in part, social causes is not new. The manner of life conducive to health which Hippocrates wrote about, includes rules for self-care and diet affordable only by the wealthy leisure class.[7] Detailed instructions for those of other classes tacitly make the point that, even without mentioning the insights into public health, physicians in ancient times already were well aware of the social implications of medicine. The descriptions of the different diseases afflicting various social classes—gladiators, slaves working in mines, sailors, etc.—make the same point.

That different occupational groups suffered from different diseases and that therefore, and at least to that extent, disease is a social construct was systematized by Ramazzini in the 17th century.[8] In the last century, social activists in medicine pointed out the intimate association between health and social conditions and, hence, the physician's necessary function as social architect. Virchow was not alone in his sentiment that the physician should be the "natural attorney for the poor."[9,10] Among Central European physicians, socialism, stemming from social concern for patients, was not rare. To become, as Lowinger asks physicians to, "healers of social as well as individual pathology"[11] is a fine sentiment—but it is also a tall order. Nevertheless, physicians if they are truly to discharge their obligations must, at least to some degree, involve themselves with social issues. This is an analytic statement if one accepts the physician's function as being concerned, at least, with the patient's health and acknowledges that social factors invariably modulate and at times cause disease.

Physicians subserve roles other than primary patient care: they, after all, teach, work as public health officials, for insurance companies and in a host of other settings each of which entails different obligations. The responsibility of most physicians, directly or indirectly, is involved with the cure of disease. Thus, physicians have the primary obligation to show "due care and personal concern for their patients."[12] In the view of Jonsen and Jameton, other concerns are not primary and are not to be met at the expense of direct patient-physician obligations.

One can, as Childress points out, start with the social and political responsibilities of all citizens one to another and to the community, and derive activities of physicians expressive of these; or one can start in the opposite direction and examine those special roles of physicians which give rise to communal or social responsibilities.[13] In the former view, the obligations as citizen are primary and are modified by the special expertise, experience, and role duties of physicians; in the latter view, obligations to specific patients are central, and communal obligations are a spin-off.

If one starts with the social presumption and derives the physician's duty from those of the citizen (specialized and at times modified by technical expertise in the field of medicine), one will conclude that physicians are, *inter alia*, obligated to strive for justice in health care. If, on the other hand, one starts with the physician's charge of maintaining the personal health of the patient, physicians, because of their special knowledge and expertise, will be obliged to attend to public health matters within their purview. Except as citizens, however, they would at first blush seem to have no special obligation to strive for justice in health care. But even here, if one accepts that all members of a just community have the obligation to work for and maintain just institutions, affirms that physicians are part of the greater community, and accepts that physicians are technically expert in matters dealing with health and disease, one will perforce conclude that physicians have an obligation to work for justice in the availability of medical care for all patients. Whichever direction the argument takes, whether we start with the duty of physicians to patients or with the duties of physicians as citizens, physicians, to varying degrees and with varying force, have obligations to be concerned with the social parameters of disease and with social justice.

Furthermore, responsibility in the contemporary world and with the awesome power of technology to be used for good or evil has changed. We cannot evade the responsibility which comes with this change—responsibility to use technology wisely, not only for the sake of our patients but for the sake of the future. In a sense, we need to be able to foretell the future, to re-enunciate norms and standards as substitutes for the norms and standards left behind by technology. If we fail to do this, the future is bleak.[14]

The obligation of physicians to their community, depending upon the way we derive them, entail at least a few obvious duties: duties to discharge their professional obligations with competence and fidelity, duties to serve as advisors in health matters, duties to participate in disaster and other public service to name but a few. Like all such duties of positive action, discretion will have to guide individual performance under specific circumstances, but medicine, as an organized group, is obliged to fulfill these roles. Organized medicine has the broader responsibility of seeing that communal obligations are met and to see to it, if need be by sanctions, that individual practitioners fulfill their individual obligations.

Physicians, if they are to concern themselves with matters which threaten the health of their patients rather than only with alleviating established disease, are obliged to concern themselves, at least in the context of their particular practice, with issues of prevention. In a wider sense, however, they are obligated not only to speak out for such things as sanitary conditions, clean water, safe food, and rational immunization programs but likewise to concern themselves with wider issues. This obligation emerges from the physician's citizenship obligation refined through the peculiar technical expertise and knowledge which physicians, as a result of their training, are expected to possess. Physicians are thus obligated to concern themselves with issues of hunger, inadequate housing, and other social conditions which inevitably threaten health. Physicians, therefore, inevitably and to a greater or lesser extent cannot evade the obligation to be social architects (or, at least, advisors to social architects) and, in Virchow's words, "attorneys for the poor."

Beyond such issues are issues of pollution, war, and peace. Few things in the modern world threaten the health of our patients as much as such issues. The ravages visited upon our environment threaten far more than the economic well-being of parts of this earth. They have been shown to be intimately associated with a large variety of diseases. Even beyond this, the threat of war on today's terms is perhaps the ultimate threat to public health. The consequences of war, not to speak of nuclear war, are consequences which physicians cannot, if they are to meet their obligations, help but work against. Organizations such as the International Physicians for the Prevention of Nuclear War and Physicians for Social Responsibility have made an admirable beginning and the AMA in its *Journal* has likewise spoken out against the insanity which impels nations to dance on the edge of this volcano. Physicians will have to rethink their obligations: when asked to help "prepare" for nuclear or other war, they are put before a difficult ethical choice. On the one hand, physicians may feel impelled to help in such preparations in order to try to ameliorate (if that is possible) the effects of such a holocaust. On the other hand, by helping in such preparations, physicians not only give tacit approval but help to lull the public into the belief that preparing for nuclear war is, in fact, a viable possibility.

The public health role of the physician extends beyond the reporting of disease and compliance with public health laws. Physicians, since ancient times, have been obligated to be teachers (the term "doctor," after all, is derived from teacher). As such their obligation extends beyond the technical application of specific treatment to specific disease. Physicians must teach other health professionals (and in turn be receptive to their teaching) and they must teach their patients how to live healthy lives. To the extent that health is threatened by social conditions, physicians are obliged to speak out. Physicians, while primarily obliged by their occupation to deal with immediate matters of health and disease, cannot in good faith ignore such social conditions as poverty, pollution, dangers in the workplace, accident prevention, and the greatest threat to the lives and well-being of patients, war.

In practical terms and in the context of day-to-day practice, there are specific issues dealing with the tension between public and private duties. Reporting disease, under usual conditions, is commonly expected to be part of the physician's function. This function is well accepted and rarely poses special problems. But in reporting disease to governmental agencies, the physician is obligated to ascertain that all information will, to the maximal degree possible, remain confidential. At times and under special conditions, problems may arise (AIDS is an example). When unreasoning hysteria threatens to undermine the security of confidential information so that severe stigmatization may result, physicians are in a quandary: the public health duties to safeguard communities and their individual members are now opposed to the physician's obligation to the patient. A great deal of technical knowledge (What does a positive HIV antibody titer really mean? How transmissible is the disease?) as well as discretion based on knowledge of individual life-styles and situations is necessary before any decision can be made.

The tension between the duty to safeguard innocent others and to maintain confidentiality is not readily resolved (see also Chapter 4). The physician's role, after all, is socially constructed, and confidentiality, like many other aspects of other roles, may be inconvenient in a given situation. Nevertheless, as long as our current vision of the physician's role persists, there is a *prima facie*, even if not an absolute, duty to maintain confidentiality. Arguing that this is virtually absolute,[15] although an attractive argument, is unreasonable; protecting the innocent (say from a raving maniac intent on killing his family or from a patient with highly contagious disease planning deliberately to infect as many persons as possible) certainly is a duty which also cannot be ignored. Creating absolutes (the absolute of confidentiality, say) rather than deliberating over each individual choice in the light of its particular context surrenders moral agency to preordained dogma (now called "principle"). It reduces moral to technical choice.

Ambiguous relationships not only lead to conflicts of obligation but may also lead to complete fragmentation of loyalties. Physicians share in such dilemmas and, in their everyday practice, must strive to come to terms with them.[16] Obligations are rarely, if indeed ever, absolute. In everyday life and in medical practice we live with a hierarchy of values. Expressed in the language of obligations, this can be translated into the unarguable fact that when obligations collide, one will have to be slighted to fulfill another. Obligations have *prima facie* claims; that is, they must be discharged unless another obligation higher on the hierarchical scale of values obviously must take precedence.[17] Determining the scale of hierarchical values is an amalgam of social forces, expectations, and personal views of morality. It is a forceful reason for teaching ethics and for having persons engage in moral discourse. Beyond this, however, our often ambiguous relationships with one another and with our community may give rise to divisions of loyalty that are "fully and generally irreconcilable."[16] Such quandaries form the moral tragedies of ancient and modern times.

When values, obligations, and loyalties conflict, the specifics are all-important and no ready, pat solutions are at hand. Safeguarding and caring for patients has a *prima facie* claim on the physician's actions and choices. But safeguarding and caring for patients takes place in a context which, furthermore, has played a dominant role in fashioning our conception of what it is to safeguard and care. It can, therefore, not be ignored. Individual problems will demand individual choices and actions made by thoughtful, responsible, and compassionate people.

REFERENCES

1. Murray, T.H., Divided loyalties for physicians: Social context and moral problems, *Soc. Sci. Med.* 23(8):827–832, 1986.
2. Nozick, R., *Anarchy, State and Utopia*, Basic Books, New York 1974.
3. Engelhardt, H.T., *The Foundations of Bioethics*, Oxford University Press, New York, 1986
4. Rawls, J., *A Theory of Justice*, Harvard University Press, Cambridge, MA, 1971.
5. Loewy, E.H., Communities, obligations and health care, *Soc. Sci. Med.* 25(7):783–791, 1987.
6. World Health Organization, Constitution of the World Health Organization, 22 July 1946, *J.A.M.A.* 131(17):1431–1434, 1946.
7. Edelstein, L., Antike Diätetik, *Antike* 7:255–270, 1931.
8. Garrison, F.H., Life as an occupational disease, *Bull. N.Y. Acad. Med.* 10:679–693, 1933.
9. Ackerknecht, E.H., *Rudolf Virchow*, University of Wisconsin Press, Madison, 1953.
10. Terris, M., Concepts of social medicine, *Soc. Servi. Rev.* 31:164–178, 1957.
11. Lowinger, P., The doctor as political activist, *Am. J. Psychother.* 22:616–625, 1968.
12. Jonsen, A.R., and Jameton, A.L., Social and political responsibilities of physicians, *J. Med. Phil.* 2(4):376–400, 1977.
13. Childress, J.F., Citizen and physician: Harmonious or conflicting responsibilities, *J. Med. Phil.* 2(4):401–409, 1977.
14. Jonas, H., Technology and responsibility, in: *Philosophical Essays* (H. Jonas, ed.), Prentice Hall, Englewood Cliffs, NJ, 1974, pp. 3–20.
15. Kottow, M.H., Medical confidentiality: An intransigent and absolute obligation, *J. Med. Ethics* 12:117–122, 1986.
16. Toulmin, S., Divided loyalties and ambiguous relationships, *Soc. Sci. Med.* 23(8):783–787, 1986.
17. Ross, W.D., *The Right and the Good*, Clarendon Press, Oxford, 1938.

CHAPTER 7

Physicians and Patients in a Pluralist World

This chapter examines the problem which physicians inevitably encounter in dealing with patients from sometimes starkly differing belief systems. It examines physicians as moral agents dealing with their patients in a nonpaternalist fashion and contrasts this to physicians functioning as bureaucrats of health.

We live in a pluralist world in which crassly different forms of belief must coexist or extinguish each other. Worldviews differ, often radically, and can at times not be reconciled. Attempting to coerce each other into behaving in certain ways is not only impractical; in a deeper sense it is immoral. Coercing each other seems immoral because it inevitably is a violation by the stronger of the personal freedom and moral agency of the weaker and thus ends by defining "might" as "right" and "is" as "ought." By that type of analysis, one would assume that guidelines and norms do not exist and that ultimately all ethical decision becomes merely a matter of personal whim and caprice. Between these two extreme beliefs, the one a variation of "do as I say (or do) because I say (or do) so" and the other an "anything goes" approach, there is a middle ground which would make some, but very few, rights and wrongs normative except as they are normative in and for a given context (see Chapter 2).

Basically, ethical considerations arise because our actions impinge on others. Were this not so, ethics would make no sense. We think, on balance, that to do right is not to harm another (or to harm another as little as possible under existing circumstances); to do wrong is to bring unnecessary, or needlessly severe, harm to another. As previously discussed (see Chapter 2), objects of primary moral worth are objects of concern since they can be harmed or benefited in themselves; objects of secondary worth (or those of symbolic worth) are of value because our acting as concerns them harms or benefits another and not the object itself. But in all ethical considerations, the harm or benefit done, or potentially done, to another is at stake.

This, then, is a basic norm: not to bring needless harm to another. Such a norm is rooted in the realization that man's common structure of the mind[1] allows us all to share the ability to rejoice and to suffer. Rejoicing or suffering, in differing societies and among different individuals, may be brought about by starkly different things. But the capacity for joy and pain is a universal of sentient beings, a shared quality and value which may serve as a starting point in the quest for peaceful agreement. It is a reference point—a norm—against which to judge our actions as moral or not.

Differing civilizations, and differing enclaves within the same civilization, define the "good" in different ways. It is this lack of uniformity which underlies the often radically different judgments made by patients and their physicians; it is this which causes us "not to understand" the Jehovah's Witness or comprehend divergent attitudes towards abortion. Nevertheless, no matter how described, all sentient beings strive for their good and are, on their own terms, benefited by its realization and harmed by its removal or interdiction.

The universal of harm and benefit, the universal of the capacity to suffer and rejoice, is not a trivial consideration. While self-evident, it is often ignored. We are only too ready to inflict suffering for the sake of doing others our (instead of their) good and to rationalize this by an appeal to a "universal" standard which, when carefully examined, is our own rather than universal. The crusades, the religious wars, the behavior of communist and capitalist alike, all provide ample examples of man's incessant desire to convert—forcefully if necessary—the world to one particular and peculiar belief. On a practical level, the world has become too small and the weapons have become too powerful to permit intolerance of this sort. Medicine, embodied in this world, must likewise examine its own standards, norms, and behaviors if it is effectively to accomplish its mission in such a world.

The pluralist society in which we live, then, is in need of reconciliation and understanding.[2] Not only is this true in comparing, say, Uganda to Sweden; in a fluid world, it is just as true within national entities such as the United States. Many social, economic, cultural, and moral issues must be addressed if this reconciliation, understanding, and ability to live and work together is to be effected. Extravagant social and economic differences (not only between regions of the world but within the very borders of what we tend to consider as national entities, including our own) must be leveled at least to a tolerable degree; cultural exchanges enabling understanding and facilitating cultural diffusion must occur; ethical systems must be reconciled sufficiently to permit mutual toleration and function towards a common goal if "man is to live."[3]

Medicine exists in a community. Prevalent attitudes and prevalent moral senses are shared. A contentious and intolerant society, unwilling to allow others to pursue a different vision of the "good" and bent on enforcing one view of life as "correct," is unlikely to produce professionals otherwise inclined. A society entirely without moral standards, on the other hand, will tolerate amoral physicians who see themselves merely as biomedical facilitators of their patients wishes. In the first instance, crass paternalism running roughshod over other values and views will result, and patients will be left in physicians' hands to "enjoy" (or suffer) the "good" purely as defined by the professional. In such an intolerant society, the patient-physician relationship is seen as intensely personal, dominated by the physician's personality and totally unequal. The enterprise of medicine now has an evangelical flavor. In the second instance, physicians abrogate their moral agency and become their patients' technical agents[4] to be bound merely by strict contract devoid of beneficence or a sense of mutual obligation. Here the relationship is one in which patients bring their complaints and desires to buy a "cure" from the now entirely technically defined physician. In this model, the physician in the role of physician, assumes the character of the civil servant, the bureaucrat who operates under bureaucratic rules and during working hours leaves his notions of right and wrong at home.[4] If one subscribes to such a worldview, moral agency is replaced by bureaucratic rules and professionals become vending machines dispensing their bureaucratically stipulated wares to all comers provided only that payment is made.

If we subscribe to the bureaucratic model, the problem of conflicting moral agency is resolved by being abolished. A conflict between moral agents cannot occur as long as the patient's request for services does not fall outside arbitrarily established and legally stipulated norms. The traditional vision of the patient-physician relationship is replaced by one in which physicians are competent technicians whose technical competency alone is their moral duty. It is a point of view to which this work does not subscribe. In examining the clash of moral agents, the legitimate moral agency of both is presumed.

Problems of medical ethics frequently involve deeply divisive and fundamental issues, highlight moral systems, and are intimately associated with emotive, aesthetic, and religious considerations. For that reason, medical ethics provide suitable paradigms to examine the more basic problem: the coexistence of diverse ethical beliefs.

Moral agents are sentient beings capable of making moral choices. In Kantian terms, the moral agent is capable of making a moral choice, and moral agency is the action taken by a moral agent in the moral sphere.[5] Moral agency will be defined as the assumption of moral responsibility for one's acts. It denotes deliberate choice made in the light of moral belief and, consequently, responsibility and accountability for choice and action. A decision to act, if it can be said to be moral, is not made on technical grounds alone but involves a careful consideration of alternate options and of the moral issues involved. Sentient beings are, by definition, capable of moral choice, and exerting moral agency is their primary ethical duty. When physicians, as professionals and as sentient beings, refuse to partake in the agony of decision making and leave decisions to whim, chance, or to the luck of the draw, they have violated this first of all moral precept without which all others stand moot. Both patients and physicians are moral agents in their own right, with neither, therefore, entitled to run roughshod over the other's beliefs or convictions. If one subscribes to the bureaucratic model, on the other hand, the physician's moral agency, like the physician's overcoat, is hung up and suspended for the duration of his or her professional function.

Human beings in exerting moral agency will conflict, often sharply, in what moral sense to follow. While practical decisions among men of good will are often—but not by any means invariably—similar to one another, the principles to which such decisions are appealed often differ greatly.[6] Physicians deal with patients of kaleidoscopically differing backgrounds and beliefs. It is not surprising that conflicts and misunderstandings occur.

Physicians are faced with a variety of ethical dilemmas in medical practice which must be resolved or adjudicated before deliberate action can take place. These dilemmas are of two kinds. The first is the universal internal human dilemma in which agents confront themselves, their beliefs, and their own clashing contexts with often differing claims. Physicians, like all individuals, are a composite of often conflicting forces which must be internally reconciled; the outcome of this internal dilemma creates our worldview and determines moral attitudes held towards broad categories of problems. The second is the external dilemma in which physicians and patients must reconcile their viewpoints with each other and with the family, the other team members, and with the demands of community and law. Physicians must justify the conclusions and the process internally and externally and must try to produce consensus and understanding. And finally, they must act and must assume responsibility for that action.[7] In adjudicating either the internal or the external dilemma of conflicting beliefs, points of view, and contexts, a search for shared values is essential. Such "shared values" are values that exist prior to any of the conflicting specific beliefs.[8]

Like all human beings, physicians first of all have to come to terms internally with their own, often conflicting, backgrounds and beliefs. This is especially true in our fluid world in which people rarely are born, live, and die in the same or in very similar contexts. During the process of education, many previously tacit beliefs are questioned and examined. Many new points of view may clash with older ones, and many previously cherished and often tacit beliefs are, according to new standards, found wanting. During their education, physicians especially have to confront not only new ideas but new ways of looking at old ideas. This is a process which goes on one's whole life. The microcosm of clashing beliefs to be reconciled within us is a mirror of the larger world. We ourselves may be professionals of some sort, members of a given religious group, live in a certain neighborhood, belong to certain social groups, and have certain political convictions. Every one of these is underwritten by certain tacit conditions and shared beliefs and at times one will clash with another. Each of us as we are today is the product of the reconciliation of many differing attitudes and of many yesterdays. When physicians and patients clash, a similar situation is at hand. The attempt to understand each other's beliefs and, where possible, their reconciliation through deeper shared values can be an instrument to learning and growth.

Disagreements between physicians and patients can be disagreements about the desired ends to be gained, about the means utilized to gain an agreed-upon end, or about the moral issues involved at any point in that process.[3] Conflicts about ends may arise when these ends have not been examined. This usually happens when certain key assumptions are taken for granted: the assumption, for example, that the end to be pursued under all circumstances is the patient's life and health. Disputes about means may be technical (the patient and physician may disagree about the best means of delivering a baby) or moral, and they may involve a hierarchy of values concerning desirable ends: the Jehovah's Witness, for example, may desperately want to live but be unwilling to take blood and, within his or her belief system, jeopardize salvation.

These dilemmas are, in many respects, clashes between autonomy and beneficence (see Chapter 5). Pellegrino and Thomasma, in addressing this problem, have suggested that physicians use a model holding beneficence in trust. By beneficence-in-trust, they mean that physicians and patients both have obligations to each other, albeit that physicians, because of their greater power and because of the patient's illness, bear a heavier responsibility. Beneficence, in their viewpoint, necessitates a decent respect for one another's autonomy.[9]

The patient's good, itself, is a fourfold good with a hierarchy of values: (1) At the top of the hierarchy is the "good of last resort," which is the good that acts as the organizing force of our lives. It is the good which not only is placed above all other "goods" but the "good" we use as the ordering principle when other goods clash. (2) The "good of the patient as a human person" is the "good" that entitles patients to make their own autonomous choices. Competence underwrites this good, and it is this "good" which physicians, because of their respect for persons, are compelled to enhance. In this view, enhancing autonomy by all available means (e.g., by supplying patients sufficient information and by refraining from coercing "compliance" by oversedation) is a physician's obligation.[9,10] (3) The patient's "particular good" is the patient's own appreciation of his or her good in a given situation. It is here that patients—in accordance with their overarching "good of last resort"—make specific treatment choices. (4) The "biomedical good," although it is hierarchically the least, is the "good" usually central to the physician-patient relationship. When other "goods" do not conflict with it—and they usually do not—it is the "biomedical good" which defines the ultimate decision made. When conflicts occur, negotiation and dialogue will help order the "goods."[9] In this dialogue an earnest search for shared values is crucial.

Physicians may disagree with their patients about the need for intervention in either emergency or nonemergency, life-saving or non-life-saving situations. In emergency situations in which the patient's life is at stake (say a patient refusing needed surgery to stanch hemorrhage), the presumption will be to act so as to safeguard life. Allowing the patient to refuse entails the conviction that the patient's refusal is autonomous and not the product of panic or fear. The "reasonable person" doctrine, which holds that in emergency circumstances where consent can either not be obtained or refusal seems confused by the patient's state, the physician should proceed to do that which the "reasonable person" would want under such circumstances, is the doctrine usually applied to handle such cases. This doctrine, of course, can be dangerous, for it presupposes that majority views are reasonable and other views are "unreasonable." Under emergency circumstances, however, physicians must either proceed to save the life of their patient or forego action. Using the "reasonable man" doctrine under such circumstances merely affirms the obvious wisdom in pursuing the more likely rather than the less likely course. If nothing more, it buys the necessary time so that a deliberate autonomous choice, instead of death, may take place.

In nonemergency situations (whether the situation is one with the patient's life ultimately at stake or not), more deliberate effort to ascertain the patient's state of mind and worldview is possible. An example of this might be the patient with a small colon cancer who refuses surgery or a leukemia victim who refuses chemotherapy. When the patient's decision seems to be autonomous (i.e., when it meets the criteria of sufficient information; sufficient time for deliberation; lack of coercion; and consistency with prior worldview), the patient's will is the ultimate deciding factor. Physicians here too have the option of relegating further care to another physician. What individual physicians will do in individual cases depends on their personality, their own worldview, the specific relationship between the physician and the patient, and the context in which the problem occurs. But dealing roughshod with their patients' wishes is not an acceptable moral option.

Patients may desire their physicians to treat them in ways which are morally repugnant to the physician. Examples of this, of course, deal with abortion, birth control, and many more. Here the problem usually involves the morality of the means; in abortion and birth control, the end, not being pregnant, for example, is not in dispute. Physicians subscribing to the bureaucratic model will encounter no problems. Their moral feelings are left entirely at home. When, however, physicians see themselves as persons extended through time with their worldviews, opinions, and idiosyncracies intact, obvious problems come to the fore.

In a free society, physicians are neither compelled to subjugate their personal moral views nor entitled to impose such views on others. Problems of this kind can only be resolved by frank and compassionate discussion which enables patients to make their own choices and to reach their own conclusions. Often resolutions can be found when compassionate and caring persons who have respect for each other and for each others points of view together search for a basis of shared values. When physicians and patients continue to be unable to resolve their differences and continue to differ in these circumstances, physicians should refer their patients to equally competent practitioners more in tune with the patient's moral views. Physicians who do not offer patients undisparaged referral act in a crassly paternalistic fashion. As their patients' medical advisers, they are bound to offer their reasons for their own beliefs, but they are not entitled to prevent patients from following their own moral dictates. Physicians who proselytize or argue with their patients (as distinct from merely offering their reasons for their own views), abuse their implicit power and take unfair advantage of the physician-patient relationship in an attempt to change their patients' minds and convert them to the physician's view. On the other hand, physicians who simply comply with their patients' wishes and perform procedures or do other things which they themselves find morally repugnant, abrogate their moral agency and, by abrogating their moral agency can be argued to be acting immorally.

Emergencies may change the complexion of the problem. When physicians are unexpectedly and unsolicitedly confronted with a dying patient whose life could easily be saved but who refuses the intervention which could save it and whose refusal meets the criteria for autonomous choice (say, an actively hemorrhaging lifelong Jehovah's Witness), a true dilemma is evident. On the one hand, the patient's choice is clearly autonomous; on the other, the physician's worldview and personal belief may be equally strong. Between the option of running roughshod over the patient's autonomous choice and the alternative of acting contrary to one's own autonomously accepted moral law, there is little to choose. A decision here rests on a hierarchy of personal values and is neither "right" nor "wrong" in the usual sense. If physicians attach primacy to the preservation of life and the restoration of health, they act one way; if respect for persons constitutes the ultimate value in their hierarchy, a quite different decision will be made. In either case, the decision can be "moral" in the sense of being consistent with the physician's ethical system and code. But there are other considerations: to watch as vital signs flicker, pupils dilate, and death ensues while having the ability to reverse the process is a devastating, demoralizing, and dehumanizing experience. The considerations here are not merely moral and, as in all decisions, morality may be only one of the factors entering into the composite final choice. The resolution of this problem—on moral, not on legal, grounds—is not possible except on a personal basis predicated on the physician's (neither right nor wrong) hierarchy of values.

We have only considered the clash of moral values and agency between physicians and patients. Although within our current vision of the physician-patient relationship, the relationship of doctor and patient is central, other clashes are not without importance. These include disagreements with rules of the institution or with current laws, differences among the various moral views of other team members (nursing, social work, etc.), problems with family members, etc. Physicians in their role as teachers must strive to explain, adjudicate, and, when possible, convince; they cannot simply override or curtly dismiss other concerned views. But in the final analysis, physicians, as long as nothing contrary to their own moral sense is demanded, remain, ultimately, their patient's agent and must seek and defend the patient's vision of the good.

REFERENCES

1. Kant, I., A Critique of Pure Reason (N. K. Smith, trans.), St. Martin's Press, New York, 1965.
2. Engelhardt, H.T., Bioethics in pluralist society, Perspect. Biol. Med. 26:64–78, 1982.
3. Loewy, E.H., Physicians and patients: Moral agency in a pluralist world, J. Med. Humanit. Bioeth. 7(1):57–68, 1986.
4. Engelhardt, H.T., The Foundations of Bioethics, Oxford University Press, New York, 1986.
5. Kant, I., Foundations of the Metaphysics of Morals (L.W. Beck, trans.), Bobbs-Merrill, Indianapolis, 1978.
6. Toulmin, S., The tyranny of principles, Hastings Center 11(6):31–39, 1981.
7. Loewy, E.H., Patient, family, physician: Agreement, disagreement, and resolution, Fam. Med. 18(6):375–378, 1986.
8. Gorovitz, S., Resolving moral conflict, in: Doctor's Dilemmas: Moral Conflict and Medical Care (S. Gorovitz, ed.), Oxford University Press, 1982.
9. Pellegrino, E.D., and Thomasma, D.C., For the Patient's Good: The Restoration of Beneficence in Health Care, Oxford University Press, New York, 1988.
10. Cassell, E., The function of medicine, Hastings Center 7(6):16–19, 1977.

CHAPTER 8

Risk Taking:
Health Professionals and Risk

Using AIDS as a paradigm, this chapter examines risk taking and the factors which motivate or fail to motivate us in taking such risks. A brief discussion of decision analysis is followed by an examination of professional risk taking from a historical perspective. Social contract is discussed, and the way that health professionals view community is shown to be central to their assumption of risks. Two points of view of obligation in the face of risk are briefly explained and discussed.

A second-year medical student about to enter his third year and begin his clinical activities came to see me. He was very disturbed about going on the ward and feared having to deal with patients infected with AIDS. It was, he felt, more than he had bargained for. The realization of having to deal with problems of this sort had not really "hit" him until now, and he did not know what he should do. Aside from the point that such fears are very much exaggerated and that the first thing to do was to supply him with "facts" (or, at least, what seemed to be the valid and relevant facts at the time), there was the more fundamental point of risk taking to be considered.

Risk is grounded in uncertainty. When we make a decision to do or not to do something (be that something a treatment or a personal choice to undertake a risky course of action), we consciously or unconsciously weigh risks and benefits. What has come to be called "decision analysis" in medicine tries to deal with uncertainty on mathematical terms. Decision analysis (whether informal or formal) tries to apply what is known about the consequences of a given course of action and to factor in the multitude of variables which ultimately determine an outcome. It is an attempt to make the implicit and tacit explicit and to reduce it to numerical terms.[1] In informal decision analysis, physicians implicitly use an informal hypothesis-testing approach to solve problems. They try to factor in a host of tacit considerations among which are their experience, their "hunches," and what they think is "best" for any one patient. How adept physicians are at doing this depends upon their educational level, their experience, and the nature of the case.[2] Formal decision analysis, on the other hand, is an attempt to deal with uncertainty and risks by an overt mathematical calculus.

One of the problems with formal decision analysis when it comes to making decisions involving, as they inevitably do in medical practice, personal values is that personal values are often excluded from the calculus of utilities (the consequence which results when one weighs risks and benefits).[3] When it comes to the ultimate decision in medicine, the risks we are willing to assume to reach a given goal are highly variable from person to person. When patients make choices of treatment, they ideally do so on the basis of "complete" information about the various possible outcomes and of the chances that an outcome will or will not occur. This, of course, includes risks as well as benefits. Individuals, however, vary in the weight that they attach to different risks. Some patients value life more than others, and some may find that being housebound or on dialysis is unacceptable; the variation in personal goals and values is almost infinite. Formal decision analysis, then, can help guide decisions by pointing out the chances of benefit and disbenefit from a given course of action. It does so, of course, within a framework of values which has labeled certain outcomes as "beneficial" and others as "harmful." Formal decision analysis, or the more informal kind, however, cannot make decisions for us: it cannot factor into the choice the widely differing values and goals which inform the ultimate choice individuals may or may not make. When physicians do informal decision analysis and "apply" that decision to a patient rather than use the results of that analysis to help guide and advise the patient, they do so unmindful of the patient's personal or cultural beliefs, aspirations, or preferences. Even though the physician may have the patient's "good" in mind, that "good" is "good" according to the physician's personal or cultural aspirations and preferences: stark paternalism, no matter how well such paternalism is meant, inevitably results. When formal decision analysis is used to make, rather than to help guide, a decision, it is even harder to factor in such personal values, and an even colder paternalism easily eventuates.

Persons choosing their life's work must make choices which are deeply embedded in their own values and personality. In choosing their life's work, they assume certain known risks: firemen may get burned, policemen shot and health professionals infected. Risks, however, are also to some extent at least imponderable and may appear during the course of a life's work: firefighting equipment and the nature of blazes change, criminals adopt new methods and weapons, and the nature of a given infection evolves. Every occupation has its advantages and drawbacks, its risks and benefits. Medicine is no exception.

Physicians and other health professionals are exposed to risks throughout their professional lives. These risks are rarely explicitly spelled out; nor can they be. Members of social structures in first coming together have established communities with far differing notions of what communities are all about (see also Chapters 2 and 12). When members of a social structure first came together to establish communities, they assumed implicit obligations to one another. These implicit obligations underwrite our social structures, the legitimate expectations we have for one another, and ultimately the laws which explicitly govern our particular communities. These obligations are enforced by communal approval and disapproval of certain actions, by social sanctions, and ultimately, here and there, by laws. This social contract, as it has been termed, is defined as the tacit rules binding groups of people together. These rules of behavior are what makes communal life (be it the life of a family, a nation or the community of man) possible.

No matter what our notions of the specifics of this contract may be, its existence cannot be much in doubt. The alternative, no social contract, no understanding or agreement of mutual obligation, however the specifics may be perceived, cannot be called a community. Nor is community merely a collection of individuals held together only by explicit undertakings. Such explicit compacts, such affirmations of mutual responsibility, cannot come about without the tacit undertakings which enabled them in the very beginning.[4]

Theories of social contract vary.[5] The notion of social contract goes back at least to Cicero and finds its reflection in Roman law. The notion was developed further in the Middle Ages and reached full bloom from the time of the Reformation on.[6] Most persons today, in one way or another, will assume social contract as being the basis for the tacit understandings that govern communities and derive their justification and their power from that coming together.

In assuming a social contract, it is said, we assume a situation in which individuals precede and ultimately form communities. According to Hobbes, the "state of nature" prior to the time of such covenants consisted of a collection of individuals not associated in any way and

living in mutual terror of one another.[7] Such an association is predicated on fear and terror. What results are notions of a minimalist ethic
in which men are united merely by duties of refraining from harm to
one another. It is a covenant based on terror and ultimately is an association whose stability is made possible only by absolute obedience to a
sovereign.[7]

There are, however, other ways of thinking about such contracts.
Locke sees social contract as an association of equally free men united
by an evolving trust rather than by terror. Locke's justification is based
on a belief in "natural law," resting ultimately on God's will. It makes
the execution of laws the duty of the individual and not merely the
function of an omnipotent sovereign.[8] Such thoughts, of course, underwrote the later political notions of Jefferson and others. Still, in such a
theory, individuals ontologically precede communities and freedom
remains (almost) an absolute. Rousseau takes this theory further. In his
view, social structures create individual morality.[9] As Rousseau envi-
sions social contract, individuals can only be properly appreciated
within the nexus of their social connections. Just as with Locke, such
associations do far more than prevent harm: they actively promote
"good," which is here seen as a social "good" incomprehensible outside its social nexus. Individuals—most prominently in Hobbes, least
prominently in Rousseau—still are believed to develop prior to community. Individuals came first and it is they who then, and in various
ways, structured community.

One can, however, think of social contract in other ways. Instead of
seeing individuals as "covenanting" with one another only after emerging from a prepolitical state of nature, a presocial state as a necessary
condition of such a contract may not be acknowledged. Men can be
seen as always having huddled together, be it in families or in looser
and more tribal associations. Their contracts, far from having been
underwritten by mutual terror, can rather be seen as having been underwritten by mutual needs, trust, and, inescapably, biosocial interde-
pendence. The very notion of nonharm to one another, in such a view,
must be seen as underwritten by trust if it is to come about in the first
place or if it is to endure in the final analysis.[4] Without trust, men
would be unlikely to emerge from behind their rock or tree to covenant.
Unless there is mutual trust, man cannot even think of entering an
association, of "covenanting" together; unless there is mutual need (of
which the need for protection from harm by possible others in the
group is only a small part), no impulse for entering such associations
exists. Trust, in turn, presupposes that, at the very least, our fellows
care for our welfare and, where possible, are willing to come to our aid.

A feeling of beneficence, therefore, is basic to such a theory, and beneficence assumes moral proportions.

In a view of community which sees beneficence and, in some sense, benevolence and mutual needs as forces shaping community, individuals and their community are seen as interdependent, intertwined, and not separable. Individuals are, to a large extent, seen as the product of their communal upbringing, as conditioned, shaped, and nurtured by their communities and therefore inseparable from them. To ask "which came first: the community or the individual" is, in that view, a "chicken and egg" question of little practical consequence. In a Lockean sense, such communities are seen as based on a continuing understanding and as evolving; the difference is that the ethic of this latter community tends not to be based merely on autonomy but necessarily to encompass moral obligations of beneficence. Since beneficence enabled the coming together of such communities, beneficence now is not a supererogatory but a very real obligation. Rather than a merely minimalist ethic, a beneficence-based ethic results. These considerations form the underpinnings of our thinking when it comes to professional risk taking.

A view of what we owe to one another as individuals, as professionals, and as members of community when faced with a fear of "coming to harm" is inevitably grounded in our view of social contract. If social contract is perceived as motivated by terror, and obligations, therefore, are either merely those of refraining from harming one another or those freely assumed by explicit contract, then professional obligations to those not encompassed by such explicit contracts are meager. The rights of the community in safeguarding itself and the obligation of infected patients to their community are likewise minimal. Communities which subscribe to such a view are not empowered to violate the freedom of their members: they cannot involuntarily test, restrain, or in any way limit the personal freedom of infected patients. On the other hand, such communities have no obligation to help those members of the community who may be in need of help. Professionals, in such communities, are obligated to their patients only within the limits of mutually agreed upon contractual stipulations, and no other professional obligation need be recognized.

If, on the other hand, a more generous notion of social contract informs us, the obligations of professionals, communities, and, ultimately, patients will be perceived quite differently. Communities of this sort will feel empowered to negotiate means of safeguarding themselves perhaps by cautiously limiting the totally free expression of personal desires. Such communities will also feel the moral necessity of coming to their neighbors' aid. Professionals, in communities so conceived, recognize beneficence as a moral obligation and, therefore, will feel compelled to take reasonable risks in treating their patients.

Historically, health professionals, when confronted with infectious disease, have inevitably had to fear contagion. Fear (here defined as a sensation or feeling of anxiety caused by the realization, perception, or expectation of impotency in the face of perceived or expected danger or evil) subsumes qualities of dread and awe and further has other emotive and aesthetic elements.[10] Counterpoised against such fears are the presumed duties of the profession, here defined as obligations assumed by moral agents in recognition of the moral law as distilled through the vision of specific social contract by particular societies. Courage ("the disposition to voluntarily act, perhaps fearfully, in dangerous circumstances," its essence being "the mastery of fear for the preservation of a perceived good against dangers"[11]) gives the edge to doing what one perceives to be the right thing despite one's fears.[10] What, however, health professionals perceive to be "the right thing" derives from their understanding of social contract applied, in this instance, to the way in which the implicit covenant with the community is envisioned. And such a vision is historically grounded.

Health professionals throughout history have assumed obligations to treat patients despite personal risks. Presuming that health professionals were aware of the possibility of contagion (and that, therefore, they were quite mindful that they could contact the disease in epidemics), epidemic disease can serve as a paradigm for such an examination. Although the knowledge of what causes infection was still far in the future, there is sound evidence that man soon realized that some disease could be spread by personal contact. Thucydides, in describing the plague of Athens (fifth century B.C.E.), mentions the disproportionate number of physicians who died there, and Hippocrates carefully instructed physicians in methods of avoiding infection. By the time of the Justinian plague (540–590 C.E.), there is no question that a knowledge of contagion (albeit, hardly of its mechanisms) was firmly entrenched. Lay persons as well as professionals obviously were quite aware of the risks.

Physicians (some notable examples notwithstanding) have largely felt compelled to stay with their patients and to treat infectious disease. This is the case whether we look at the Athenian plague in the fifth century before the common era, the Justinian plague in the sixth century of our era, or the later Medieval plague. In more recent times it is the case as physicians have dealt with typhoid, yellow fever, tuberculosis, influenza, or poliomyelitis. Their reason for taking such risks is, perhaps, best articulated by Guy de Chauliac (surgeon during the Medieval plague) who, speaking about his fears, wrote: ". . . and I, to avoid infamy, dared not absent myself but with continual fear preserved myself as best I could. . . ."[12]

The "infamy" which Guy de Chauliac feared, is a reflection of a perceived social contract in which obligations to one's patients form the tacit underpinning of medical professionalism. Such "infamy" is further reflected in the literature of the era, which looks upon physicians who fled with disapprobation and on those who stayed with approval. It is evident that throughout history societies expected its functionaries to continue their duties in good times and in bad.[13]

Many factors enter into our clinical or personal decisions to take, or not to take, risks. Some of these factors are technical: "What kind of risk am I taking?" "How much risk is there?" to name but two. The answers here are crucial to our ethical deliberations. If undertaking a given course would result in certain death, a different set of considerations pertains than if the risk is small. Even in the first instance, there is a critical difference between the heroism which gives a life to save another and an action which gives a life with no hope of saving another. Giving one's life to save another may be, under most circumstances, a supererogatory act; doing so with no hope of saving a life in turn for one's own may surely be even more problematic. Under most circumstances, neither can be simply viewed as a moral obligation which must be discharged.

For physicians and other health professionals, there is, furthermore, a consideration at least as important as the saving of life. There is a great deal of difference whether, beyond saving a life, significant comfort can be given. The obligation of health professionals clearly does not end with the saving of life. Historically the obligation to give comfort is far more enduring than is the obligation to save life, and this ancient obligation is presumed today.[14] Health professionals must consider both the saving of life and the amelioration of suffering. When a disease is hopeless, ameliorating suffering moves into the foreground of professional obligation. As long as patients have not irretrievably lost consciousness, health professionals are obligated to provide what comforts they can. Such an obligation is grounded in the shared historical vision of the patient-physician relationship (see also Chapter 4).

When people refuse to take risks, fear is one of the main motivating forces. There are many elements which enter into the concept of fear and even more factors which enter our personal and clinical decisions when confronted with fear. Repugnance adds to fear and, with fear, may preclude action. We may fear to be shocked by some apparatus at the bedside but may overcome this fear and, when necessary, use it; yet, when the same instrument is covered with slime, we may choose not to do so. The two sensations—disgust and fear, in this case—are mutually reinforcing and preclude action. Health professionals fearing contagion unassociated with other repulsive qualities may—with fear and trembling, perhaps, but nevertheless—treat; but if, in addition, the disease is associated in their minds with strong negative aesthetic, emotive, or moral considerations, they may fail to act.

Fear, furthermore, may be a force countering itself: there may be fear of contagion as well as fear of censure or disapprobation (by the community or, perhaps even more so, by oneself) if duty is shirked. The fear of contagion here is balanced by another fear, and the ultimate action is a composite of many forces. The more strongly social contract is felt, the more strongly individuals feel connected to their fellows, and the more strongly beneficence is seen as a moral duty (and not merely as an aesthetic "niceness"), the more will the fear of what is seen as just censure influence action.[16]

Health professionals can, at times, abrogate tacit contracts just as can other members of the community. None can do so completely. A physician can abrogate the contract by leaving the profession or narrow it by limiting the field of practice. As long as contracts are discharge-able, as long as both parties have the ability to hold up their end of the bargain, both parties must be involved in changing the contract. Since contract implies mutuality, any limitation or abrogation of contract must, at the very least, be publicly stated and must have been heard. Once understood and accepted by the community, such limitations may, under ordinary circumstances, be valid. But even when such re-fusal or limitation has been announced and understood, circumstances of great communal crisis or need may alter such changed personal obligations.[10]

The meaning of profession includes a tacit willingness to exercise whatever expertise is professed. Without such willingness, expertise cannot be translated into profession. In acknowledging willingness, we imply a realization that negative elements may be encountered. When we made our decision to do a certain thing, benefits and risks were implicitly or explicitly considered. To be willing to do an entirely pleasant thing without even the remotest risk of encountering negative elements does not require discussion. Assuming, at least to some minor degree, some discomfort or risk is an inevitable and implicit element of willingness.

Physicians and other health professionals are not (and ethically cannot be) asked to assume risks of certain death or certain infection.

That is not the issue. Even during times of vast, poorly understood epidemics, many survived. Health professionals were asked to assume reasonable risks—"reasonable" within the context of their community, of the situation within it, and of the prevalent vision of social contract. This vision of social contract and the powerful forces of the social mechanisms of approbation and censure made explicit contract or legal sanction only rarely necessary. What is considered "reasonable" evolves and may be different at certain times and under certain circumstances. But what is "reasonable" is a communal vision, mutually entered into and assured by social contract.

Both physicians and communities have historically profited from their vision of the social contract. Physicians (and to a regrettably far lesser degree other health professionals) gain a tremendous amount from their side of the bargain. Physicians have been blessed with immense privilege, prerogatives and power as well as with considerable material reward; communities have profited from their healer's skill and from the security entailed in the knowledge that the contract will be honored in times of need. Like all contracts, social contract implies mutuality and bilateral agreement.

Why all the "fuss" about treating AIDS? Is AIDS somehow "different"? Health professionals have more and more frequently been strongly tempted to refuse care to patients infected with AIDS, and some have given in to their temptations. AIDS has been seen as different from hepatitis (although it is transmitted in a similar fashion) and has been treated differently than plague, influenza, tuberculosis, or poliomyelitis. AIDS is seen as subtly distinctive. It is seen as absolutely fatal (although we are by no means entirely sure of that fact and even less sure of what happens to patients who merely carry HIV antibodies) as well as seen as carrying the stigma of "sin." After all, it is associated with sex (and frequently with a form of sexual expression seen as "perverse"), addiction, and other "morally questionable" acts. There is the tacit but very real flavor of God's punishment for past doings. AIDS is viewed as "dirty."[17] Health professionals fear that contracting AIDS, even when AIDS is contracted while doing one's duty, will cause a stigma in addition to conferring an illness. Stigmatization is not rare, and hypocrisy tempts many to affirm their own moral virtue by pointing a finger to another.

Further, AIDS, once full-blown, seems to be entirely incurable today. Those infected, if they actually develop the disease, are believed doomed to death. Infected persons may or may not come down with AIDS, but more and more evidence suggests that most if not all will. Other infectious disease rarely carries the risk of almost certain death today, and we, in and outside of medicine, have become spoiled. No longer do we take our own mortality for granted. Individuals within the greater community have lower ethical expectations for themselves and a lower sense of obligation to their fellows than they did only a short time ago (even if they often have inflated expectations of their neighbors and a considerable sense that their neighbors owe them much!). Health professionals being first of all members of this greater community, share this lowering of communally perceived responsibility for one another. Our media and our propaganda extol "rugged individualism," often demean social action, and tend to accept the notion of absolute freedom as an individual's birthright. A minimalist community easily results from such views. Our treatment of AIDS, then, reflects these and many other forces prevalent in society and in medicine today.

If health professionals share the presumptions of the minimalist community and lack explicit contract with the AIDS patient, they will feel entirely entitled to refuse care (and if they accept such a view of community they will also inevitably have to oppose nonvoluntary testing, reporting, etc.). Seeing community in a minimalist way, they regard freedom as a nonnegotiable condition of morality which can be restricted only when the exercise of individual freedom would directly impinge on the freedom of another member. For this reason and traditionally, persons who hold this viewpoint have opposed pure food and drug laws, licensing of health professionals and reporting of communicable disease. For such persons, freedom is not negotiable. If, on the other hand, health professionals are inclined to a more generous view that makes beneficence a moral obligation and is mindful of the ancient tradition of medical ethics, they will have to take reasonable risks in caring for such patients (and, inevitably, will have to see nonvoluntary testing and reporting as a negotiable communal option).[16] Freedom as a value instead of as a condition of the moral life allows a more flexible community which can, perhaps, more easily adapt and grow.

Those who favor a minimalist community do so largely because they fear that doing otherwise would endanger individual rights and give what they feel is uncalled-for power to the community. They fear that a community based on beneficence will easily tend to become paternalistic and define "my" good in its own particular way. On the other hand, those who favor a beneficence-based community and ethic, see a decent regard for autonomy as a necessary condition of beneficence: to act beneficently is to respect another's autonomy. They fear that a minimalist community easily becomes cold and noncaring: a community in which everyone seeks only his or her own self-defined good heedless of the good of others. Such a community, when it finally must limit individual liberty (say, when it finds that AIDS is a sufficient danger so that testing or restricting becomes necessary for survival), has little with which to negotiate. Negotiating values by a political process is not the way such communities usually operate. The likelihood that such communities will end up with a tyranny of the strong over the weak and the rich over the poor (that such communities will bring tyranny by means of the Trojan horse of freedom) is a danger and one which has historical precedent. A mean, seeking a balance between making autonomy an absolute and allowing beneficence to degenerate into crass paternalism, is achieved by a negotiation of communal values.

How much risk, then, should we expect health professionals to take? Are health professionals expected to take substantial risk to themselves in caring for their patients? Consider cardiac surgeons who routinely perform complicated procedures lasting many hours and frequently "stick" themselves with needles or other instruments. They risk daily infection when they perform such complicated procedures on HIV-positive patients. Are such surgeons obligated to operate on HIV-positive patients or does their obligation somehow diminish as the risk grows? Suppose that in the course of a surgeon's career he or she has already managed to infect him/herself with hepatitis but luckily has survived without ill effects. Is it proper to expect such a person to assume the risk of AIDS while others in the profession risk so little?

An excellent argument can be made using an essentially utilitarian calculus which would adjust obligations to the amount of risk taken and the capacity of the professional to take precautions.[18] The limits of the risk, as Ozar sees it, are formed by the extent of the risk and the health professional's ability to control the risk. If the risk is very great and no precautions are available, the obligation would be attenuated; if the risk were great but effective precautions could be taken, professionals would have the duty to take such precautions and to proceed on. When risks are exceptional, caregivers "may be justified in declining care." In fact, Ozar feels that they may even, under circumstances of very grave risk, be obligated (because of duties to other patients, to their families, etc.) to decline care to such patients.

Obligations which diminish as risk increases constitute one way to view such a situation. It is, however, not intuitively or necessarily logically clear why obligations should diminish as risks increase. If I am obligated to pay back ten dollars but find that doing so would make it impossible for me to eat dinner, my obligation would not vanish: it merely would be quite understandable if, all things considered, I ate dinner instead of paying back the money. The obligation, nevertheless, would not be changed. The fact that an obligation is difficult, dangerous or even inadvisable to discharge does not change the fact that it is an obligation.

Health professionals who refuse to take care of AIDS patients when the risk is negligible and those who refuse such care when the risk is great may, nevertheless, both be said to have the obligation to care for such patients. Physicians who fail to care for patients who put them at severe risk may be (and very likely are) blameworthy for not doing so. Yet their blameworthiness is of a different order than is the blameworthiness of physicians who refuse to take a minimal risk or who will not allow themselves to be inconvenienced. The necessity of making difficult choices, often the necessity of choosing to do a blameworthy thing and sometimes the inevitability of doing so, is part and parcel of the human condition (see also Chapter 3).

Ethical quandaries rarely give us "good" vis-à-vis "bad" options. Choices in medical ethics often highlight this human problem: we are forced to make an inevitably bad (even if "better" than the alternatives) choice and to be blameworthy for putting it into action (even when we may be praiseworthy for the agony of choosing). Acknowledging blameworthiness can be a prod to growth and learning and, ultimately, can enable the next choice to be perhaps somewhat better (see also Chapter 3).

What we are putting ourselves at risk for, likewise makes a great deal of difference. Doing desperate forms of complicated cardiac surgery on patients whose life span at the very best is severely limited is not quite the same as giving such patients comfort in their last days. The one is a highly specialized and technical feat, the other a common human as well as professional obligation. One could, perhaps, argue that the obligation to provide comfort has far more human than merely technical roots and is, for that very reason among others, a far more enduring one.

What is considered to be a grave or a trivial risk is largely a decision made by an individual under specific circumstances. It is underwritten and informed by the communal ethos, which guides all such decisions, and ultimately it is determined by the character of the individual who must act. What is a trivial or a grave risk will vary from time to time, from place to place, and from circumstance to circumstance. It is not a determination which can be made outside the context of real situations in which real people find themselves.

REFERENCES

1. Raiffa, H., *Decision Analysis: Introductory Lectures on Choices Under Uncertainty*, Addison-Wesley, Reading, MA, 1968.

2. Elstein, A.S., Shulman, L.S., and Sprafka, S.A., *Medical Problem Solving: An Analysis of Clinical Reasoning*, Harvard University Press, Cambridge, MA, 1978.
3. Pellegrino, E.D., and Thomasma, D.C., *For the Patient's Good: The Restoration of Beneficence in Health Care*, Oxford University Press, New York, 1988.
4. Loewy, E.H., Communities, self-causation and the natural lottery, *Soc. Sci. Med.* 26:1133–1139, 1988.
5. Gough, W., *The Social Contract*, Oxford University Press, New York, 1957.
6. Laslett, P., Social contract, in: *The Encyclopedia of Philosophy*, (P. Edwards, ed.), Macmillan, New York, 1972.
7. Hobbes, T., *Leviathan*, Collier, New York, 1962.
8. Locke, J., *Second Treatise of Government* (C.E. Macpherson, ed.), Hackett Publishing, Indianapolis, 1980.
9. Rousseau, J.J., *The Social Contract* (M. Cranston, trans.), Penguin Books, New York, 1968.
10. Shelp, E.E., Courage: A neglected virtue in the patient-physician relationship, *Soc. Sci. Med.* 18(4):351–360, 1984.
11. Loewy, E.H., Duties, fears and physicians, *Soc. Sci. Med.* 22(12):1363–1366, 1986.
12. Campbell, A.M., *The Black Death and Men of Learning*, AMS Press, New York, 1966.
13. Rath, G., Ärtzliche Ethik in Pestzeiten, *Münch. Med. Wochenschr.* 1957; 99(5):158–162, 1957.
14. Amundsen, D.W., The physician's obligation to prolong life: A medical duty without classical roots, *Hastings Center* 8(4):23–31, 1978.
15. Loewy, E.H., Risk and obligation: Health professionals and the risk of AIDS, in: *AIDS: Principles, Practice and Politics* (I. Corless and M. Pittman-Lindeman, eds.), C.V. Mosby, St. Louis, 1988.
16. Loewy, E.H., AIDS and the human community, *Soc. Sci. Med.* 27(4):297–303, 1988.
17. Churchill, L.R., AIDS and dirt, *Theor. Med.* (in press).
18. Ozar, D., AIDS, risk, and the obligations of health professionals, in: *Biomedical Ethics Reviews: 1988* (J. Humber and R. Almeder, eds.), Humana Press, New York (in press).

CHAPTER 9

Organ Donation

Advances in organ transplantation have made transplantation an option for the treatment of many formerly hopeless conditions. This has raised many ethical problems, and many persist today. In this chapter, the history of transplantation is sketched, the concept of "organs as resources" is discussed and objections to organ donation as well as counterarguments to the objections are considered. Available instruments of donation and the use of related and nonrelated living persons as donors are discussed. The use of social value judgments in making critical decisions in organ allocation are considered.

The possibility of transplanting organs has become a reality. Made possible not only by advances in transplantation technology but especially by new insights into immunology, transplantation has been helped along the way by allowing brain death as the point at which death may, officially, be declared. Nevertheless, serious obstacles remain in the way of utilizing transplantable organs as fully as possible. The problem is examined from the following perspectives: (1) a brief history; (2) organs as resources; (3) objections raised to organ transplantation and counterarguments; (4) possible instruments of donation; (5) live organ donors and using relatives or strangers as donors; and (6) social value judgments in transplanting organs.

A Brief History

The idea of transplanting organs is not new, even though the reality of doing so is.[1] The miraculous transplantation of organs was spoken about in medieval times, and a 16th century picture by Fernando del Rincón, hanging in the Prado, shows a sacristan whose leg had become gangrenous receiving the healthy leg of a black man, presumably a slave (the instrument of consent and the outcome of this venture are, unfortunately, not stated!). A probably apocryphal story speaks of Pope Innocent VIII being transfused in 1492 with the blood of two youngsters conveniently sacrificed for this purpose.[2]

There is no clear-cut evidence that tissue transfer took place prior to the 17th century when Richard Lower of England first transfused blood from one animal to another.[3] Shortly thereafter, Denys in Paris transfused animal blood into man, but a failure of one such procedure and a suit brought by the patient's widow (who, it was later found, had murdered her husband and blamed the physician) soured physicians.[4] No further attempts were made to transfuse blood until Blundell in 1818 at Guy's Hospital first transfused blood from man to man. From then on, transfusions (tissue transplants in their own right) were carried out with variable success. It was not until Landsteiner in 1900 described blood groups (and until he and Wiener further refined our understanding by finding the Rh factor) that at least some of the disasters which sometimes befell recipients were understood and avoided.[3]

Successful skin grafting and early transplantation awaited the late 19th and early 20th centuries. Ullman in Vienna and Alexis Carrel in New York first successfully transplanted the kidney of one animal into another in 1902, and occasionally successful experimental transplantation of other organs from animal to animal soon followed.

Transplantation of kidneys from one identical twin to another were first done in the middle of this century. Successful transplantation in humans from nontwins or at least from nonrelated donors awaited a better understanding of the immune process and, where needed, its relatively safe suppression. Tissue transplants other than those of the cornea (not usually subject to rejection) and blood (transfusible since the development of blood grouping) have become a reality only in very recent times.

Transplanting corneas is one thing, kidneys another, and hearts or heart-lung transplantation a quite different matter. A kidney as well as blood and bone marrow can be taken from a live donor leaving the donor substantially unimpeded. This is not true when it comes to other organs. When one harvests corneas much more time is available to harvest the eye than there is for harvesting of other tissues. Storage for a reasonable time is possible, and rejection is rarely a problem. Kidney transplantation is unique in that dialysis, as an alternative to transplantation and as a stop-gap when rejection occurs, is readily available. On an individual basis this makes the problem less immediate and makes rejection less devastating. With other organs (except perhaps with hearts, and then only experimentally and for a brief time) this is not possible today. Kidneys and livers are best obtained from patients whose homeostasis is maintained up to the time of harvesting, and permissible storage time is brief. Rejection is very much a problem here. Heart and heart-lung transplants likewise must be harvested while the organ is functioning, and time from harvest to transplantation is even more constrained. These technical differences elaborate subtly different ethical questions.

ORGANS AS RESOURCES

Somehow we think of organs as a different kind of resource than, say, ventilators, drugs, or ambulances. Cadaver organs, especially, have overtones which we intuitively feel makes them different from all other resources. There is, rationally, good reason for this. Cadaver organs, among other things, differ from other resources in that they (1) cannot be renewed (although they could most certainly be made more available), (2) are of vital use to persons whose organs they are but, except under most unusual circumstances, are of no use to anyone else (except, perhaps, as articles of food!), and (3) are not, once a person is dead, the property of any specific person except, perhaps, for purposes of burial or organ donation. Besides this, cadaver organs recently were an organic part of a living, breathing, thinking member of community and, as such, are of symbolic value to others and, peripherally, to the community.[5] The newly dead whose organs are suitable for transplantation have symbolic worth to those who knew them as well as to the larger community and they have secondary (or material) worth to those other members of community in need of a transplantable organ. Organs from the newly dead are thus different in being not only unrenewable but also in having been the functioning part of a person connected in fact and in symbol with the community in which such transplantation occurs. A legitimately greater concern for the proper fate of such organs exists than it does for renewable and potentially plentiful objects which were never the part of such persons.[5]

Organs voluntarily donated by the living are somewhat different. Obviously unrenewable, they are still of use to the donor who here voluntarily surrenders their use to another. The donation of organs by the living for the living is thus an example of altruism. Their donation is hedged by other considerations dealing mainly with issues of free consent.

OBJECTIONS TO THE TRANSPLANTATION OF ORGANS AND COUNTERARGUMENTS

The thought of transplanting the organs of the newly dead into the living makes some people uncomfortable. Transplanting organs from the living donor into the needy recipient often meets with other objections. These attitudes are enmeshed in a not unreasonable fear of technocracy and of the philosophy so prevalent today which says that what can be done must and ought, therefore, be done.[6] A sustained religious tradition, which endows the physical remains with mystic qualities beyond the symbolic often also underpins some of these objections.[7,8]

Among others, three main philosophical objections have been raised: (1) the fear of "mutilation" and the fear of disturbing wholeness[8]; (2) the concern that making body parts between individuals interchangeable might serve to make individuals looked upon as organs of the community to be disposed of at will[8]; (3) the misgiving that diluting the respect for natural symbols will weaken a necessary communal respect for symbols.[8] A practical objection has likewise been raised. It is the fear that critically ill but not yet brain-dead persons may have the type of care given influenced by their being potential donors: as a result, it is feared, attention may shift too early to preserving organs rather than to sustaining the ill themselves.[9]

The argument from wholeness essentially takes the following form. (1) Capriciously removing a part of an organism (say, hacking off my ear merely for the sake of doing this) is not only irrational[10] but is "mutilation" and unacceptable. Persons are their body's stewards and compelled not to treat their bodies in injurious ways. (A hidden premise, beyond the rational, often is that this is offensive to God.) (2) Persons are justified in removing a part of their body threatening the integrity of the whole. In the context of stewardship, such "self-mutilation" is not only permissible but, perhaps, since it promotes wholeness, mandatory. (3) Mutilation of the body by removing a part is impermissible for any reason, even that of helping one's neighbor, other than to preserve the integrity of the whole body of which it is a part (this, again, has religious rather than rational roots). (4) The idea of totality to be preserved intact when man dies persists (this, of course, harkens back to issues dealing with resurrection).

Allowing the invasion of one body for the sake of another, according to the second objection, creates a society less mindful of individual rights. It is connected with the argument from wholeness and takes the following form (1) Man's wholeness may be disrupted only for the sake of preserving man's own personal integrity. (2) Communities and their members relate to each other in ways substantially different from the relationship of individuals to their parts. (3) Although one might hope for more, individuals and their communities are bound together merely by duties of refraining from harm to one another and not by any other duties. (4) If one allows men to be invaded for the sake of other men or of the community, one is apt to produce a state of affairs in which the individual becomes merely another organ of the community and is disposable for the needs of the state.

The newly dead serve, among other things, as symbols for the living. A decent respect for symbols is one of the things that unites communities and makes them what they are. Customarily salvaging tissues, it is feared, will lessen communal respect for other symbols and, hence, for the reality which they portray.[7]

Some physicians have expressed the fear that customarily salvaging organs may make the health care team tend to look at the very critically ill patient more as an organ donor whose organs are to be preserved at all costs than as a salvageable patient to be healed. Efforts, therefore, may be bent to doing things calculated to preserve organs (giving large amounts of fluids, for example), rather than doing things to save patients (restricting fluids in cerebral edema, for example). Customarily salvaging organs, so the argument goes, produces a mind-set which would favor salvaging organs from a possibly but not yet certainly moribund patient rather than bending every effort to save the patient. By creating a conflict situation for the attending physician and tending to jeopardize the patient, making organ donations routine is inimical to the traditional vision of the physician-patient relationship.[9]

The counterarguments which have been made to these objections often fail to meet them entirely. The underpinnings on which many of the objections rest frequently are religious: they predicate themselves, for instance, on "wholeness" as a totality to be resurrected, on the body as, ultimately, the property of the Deity. Justifying objections by an appeal to a suprarational system of beliefs excludes these objections from rational argument. That does not, by any means, make these objections trivial. In a pluralist society, respect for other belief systems underpins the possibility of peaceful coexistence. But it does mean that the persuasiveness of such an appeal is limited to a specific moral enclave and, therefore, cannot be rationally translated to the wider community.

Many of the arguments opposing organ donation (especially those from the newly dead) are couched in terms of symbols. Symbols come into being as epiphenomena of a reality which they come to represent.[1] Symbols, wherever found, relate to reality. They may outlast it or be distorted and hard to recognize. Nevertheless, symbols must either represent our perception of reality or, occasionally, be derived from yet another symbol itself ultimately grounded in such reality. Symbols comfort the bereaved and allow the abrupt transition from life to death to be softened, and, in a sense, they slow the moment of loss. They are thus important to our discussion even if we cannot allow them the same standing as we give to the reality they represent. Confounding the symbol with the reality it represents, or holding it to have the same value, ultimately sells out reality. When symbols, rather than the things they stand for, assume primary value, the sentiment of benevolence is replaced by sentimentality.[11]

Not surprisingly, many of the objections to salvage are couched in language which expresses a conclusion while posing a question. Speaking of "mutilation" introduces a repulsive metaphor which inclines one against the act; it carries unwarranted and unnecessary connotational baggage. People facing gall-bladder surgery do not think of it as "mutilation," and even amputation is not generally couched in such terms! "Wholeness," on the other hand, which "mutilation" is said to disrupt, carries a pleasing sense and one which one generally would not wish to disturb. Once again, as in so many other issues, the language in which we frame the problem helps to determine its solution.

The practical objection, which fears that critically ill patients as potential organ donors will be treated more as organ donors than as sick patients, seems unrealistic. Under established protocol, the team treating the patient must be distinct from the team dealing with transplantation. Aside from this, the argument confuses (as it fears we may) the newly dead with the not yet newly dead. Treating the not yet newly dead as though they were newly dead is not only a category error: it is, in fact, malpractice and, therefore, subject to the same controls and sanctions applied in all such cases. Abandoning practice because, occasionally, malpractice may occur does not seem an altogether wise move!

Most faiths today have accepted organ transplantation as a legitimate medical practice. A residue of distaste remains in some and a few differ. In terms of secular ethics, our duty to the newly dead (who, since no longer capable of being harmed or benefited, are no longer of primary worth) is one of respect for what has been and for the value that others place in them. Largely, then, the newly dead are of secondary worth (both materially and symbolically). Our main ethical obligation now is to others: family, loved ones, members of the health care team, and others in the greater community, both those who may stand in critical need of viable organs and those who don't. All of these have legitimate interests for which arguments can be made, and such arguments will need to be adjudicated. However, our duty to the living who may, by proper transplantation, regain health and function cannot be dismissed. In a sense these duties pit respect for what has been against what is, symbol against reality, and feeling against need. Instruments of donation become an essential part of this discussion.

INSTRUMENTS OF DONATION

Communities may decide that the needs of the living properly preempt the rights of the newly dead and of their families.[12] In such communities, instruments of donation will not be thought necessary and routine salvage of all available organs will occur. Salvaging organs routinely, presupposes that (1) a dead person no longer can own anything; (2) while a person can will his possessions to others and while his testators then own this property, organs are a different matter; and (3) a society which freely uses the organs of the dead to benefit the living is a more mature, generous and humane society than one that does not. However, the routine salvage of organs, in our society, is intuitively felt to violate the dignity of the newly dead and of the family with its still poignantly close connection to the deceased. Respect for persons, we often feel, demands that we acquiesce to, facilitate, or at least not hinder autonomously made rational decisions. Treating the newly dead merely as a means to another's end and ignoring the family's expressed wishes offends that respect. Some means of attaining the goal of maximizing the salvage of organs while maintaining a decent respect for others must, we feel, be possible.

The other option available is some sort of voluntarism in which either consent for or refusal of donation is presumed. Currently a distinction is drawn between the voluntarism which establishes refusal as the norm (which is what is generally called "voluntarism") and the voluntarism that makes of consent a norm and is therefore called "presumed consent." It must, however, be borne in mind that both are forms of voluntarism.

In most of the United States today, refusal is the presumed norm.[13] Individuals prior to death or families after the death of the next of kin must specifically give their consent so that the retrieval of organs may proceed. In theory, it is the will of the newly dead which controls even if the family is opposed; in fact, donation does not proceed unless the family also consents. Stimulated or encouraged consent actively promotes the signing of donor cards. Those inclined to find the entire enterprise of organ transplantation more or less distasteful will, in general, support this type of voluntarism since it is, indeed, hedged with the greatest number of safeguards against removing organs without ironclad consent. Further, as Ramsey argues, this type of voluntarism affords an opportunity for expressing human generosity. The impulse for generosity, he feels, would be thwarted by other methods of donation.[8] At the present time, and with current instruments of consent, however, only 10% to 15% of suitable donors ever become actual ones, and even these rarely end up donating fully. Donation is looked at as a supererogatory act.

In some other parts of the world, voluntarism takes a different form.[14] Called "presumed consent," this form of voluntarism presumes that most persons, when the chips are down, will be inclined to donate an organ useless to themselves to another who critically needs the organ.[1,6,15,16] Under such rules, persons, or their surviving relatives, have a right to refuse donation, and they must be explicitly given that chance. In the absence of such refusal, however, organs are taken. In presuming that when given the chance most, in fact, would be willing to donate their useless organs to a neighbor in critical need, presumed consent makes of organ donation a species of beneficence with all the ethical overtones that this implies. Far from thwarting a generous impulse, presumed consent presumes that individuals nurtured by generous communities which take the obligation to help their neighbor as an implicit norm will themselves act generously. Instead of decreasing the impulse to be generous, presumed consent makes generosity the implicit norm and fosters it.

No matter which form of consent is used, problems with staff cooperation persist.[14] Potential donors are often victims of sudden illness or accident and only rarely succumb to a chronic process where death is expected. Such sudden events often occur in outlying hospitals in which transplants are not performed and in which the staff lacks the stimulation of an ongoing program. They do not see the survivors of transplantation leading happy and productive lives; they merely see the newly dead and the bereaved. Others, whose sight or life may depend on sustained action, are unseen and unknown; they are strangers. Not having personal experience with the benefits of transplantation makes it even more difficult to approach the family engulfed in grief, a grief, furthermore, in which the staff shares. Therefore, organ donation often goes by the boards.

Recent legislation in many states has made requesting organ donation mandatory. Health professionals, when patients who might be suitable donors die, are required to ask the relatives for their consent. Objections to this quite similar to the objections raised against presumed consent have again been raised, especially the objection that this would convert possibly viable patients into premature organ donors.[9] Objections of this sort are, as Caplan has pointed out, largely wrong.[17] "In enacting required request legislation, our society has indicated its collective desire that people routinely be given the option of organ and tissue donation. . . ." Required request laws thus are, as Caplan points out, an alternative to presumed consent statutes and "reflect a sensitivity to the key values of voluntarism, altruism and informed choice."[17]

When all is said and done, we are still confronted with wasting as little tissue from the newly dead as possible while meaningfully showing respect for the symbolism so dear to members of our community. Wasting tissues and thereby wasting lives or function which might otherwise easily be saved in itself is a troubling ethical question. Designing instruments of consent which strike a proper balance between the needs of the community and the peculiar interests of the individual is, therefore, a pressing concern. Such decisions are made by thoughtful communities aware of their priorities, values, and history. They are, like most things, not issues which can, once and for all, be settled.

LIVE ORGAN DONORS AND STRANGERS AS DONORS

According to transplant policy today, live donors are acceptable only if (1) their consent is freely given and the implications of their act are, as fully as possible, understood by them; (2) the donor's state of health allows donation; (3) there is a good chance for a successful outcome; and (4) donor and recipient are related by blood or are, at least, husband and wife.

The first requirement, informed consent (the cornerstone of presupposing autonomous action), is necessary if we are to speak of "donation" rather than of piracy. The second reason, demanding that the general health of the donor permit safe donation, is similarly clear. Only if we are to think of freedom as an absolute would a community allow donors to severely jeopardize themselves by donation. Arguments to the contrary, it is difficult to conceive of a situation in which one could properly allow donors to severely jeopardize their own health, and one would find no physician within the current vision of our patient-physician relationship who would consent to take such a kidney. The third reason—a successful outcome—is more problematic. Surely no one would quibble with not transplanting a kidney from a healthy donor into one whose chance of success was almost nil. The problem of "where to draw the line," the problem of what constitutes a "good" chance, remains. What if a parent wishes to donate to a child whose possibility of success is only, perhaps, 50%?

The fourth requirement—that donors must be blood relatives or spouses of recipients—is far more problematic. The dogma of transplantation in America today holds that people who would donate an organ to a stranger (or even to a friend) are psychologically at best peculiar. This opinion, for it is merely that, is predicated on a deeply felt view of responsibility and kinship which almost seems to have tribal roots. Persons donating a kidney to a sibling whom they have always detested, who has, perhaps, done them serious harm, and from whom they may be almost totally estranged are acceptable as donors; persons donating to their best friend are not. Instead, such persons are held to be emotionally unstable. Facts speak otherwise. Not only are donors willing to come to their neighbor's help not found to be "peculiar" or "disturbed," they are found to be rational people for whom the act of donation has deep inner meaning and worth.[18–21] The rather unclear argument supporting the present policy of not accepting other than related donors (or spouses) runs as follows: (1) only psychiatrically stable persons can be permitted to donate; (2) wishing to donate organs to nonrelatives (or nonspouses) is a measure of psychiatric instability; (3) therefore, donations from non-family-members (or nonspouses) cannot be accepted since such persons are psychiatrically unstable.

This peculiarly circular argument assumes risk taking for the sake of strangers to be psychiatrically suspect, and society must restrain, or at least not facilitate, such a notion. An analogy might serve: Mr. Jones, a fair but not an excellent swimmer, is walking by a stream swollen by spring rain. He hears a drowning stranger's cry for help. Taking off his clothes, Mr. Jones dives into the stream and rescues the stranger. This is a risky act, and Mr. Jones might well have drowned in the attempt. The victim is unknown to Mr. Jones, and Jones is not the world's best swimmer. Should he be restrained? Should one refuse to help in the rescue by holding Jones's clothes? Is Mr. Jones doing his duty, acting irresponsibly, or is he irrational? What if the stranger were his best friend, his wife, his brother? Mr. Jones's failure to jump into the swollen stream would certainly be understandable. But is his effecting the rescue of a stranger a sign of a deranged mind?

Giving an organ to a stranger is, in our view of community, at least a supererogatory act not required by our vision of fairness or justice. It is an act of generosity and not one which one can demand of another. All evidence to the contrary, however, some would hold such an attempt to be a sign of mental instability.

Social Value Judgments in Organ Transplantation

The question of social value judgments entering into the distribution of scarce resources has been debated for many years. (Please see Chapter 12 for a discussion of the broader issues.) When patients are selected on medical or "technical" criteria, too large a number of potential recipients remains. Technical judgments, furthermore, are problematic in themselves: not only do they change with further data and leave yesterday's decisions as "wrong"; they are themselves informed by an often tacit web of assumptions and values (for example, the decision not to transplant hearts into patients beyond a certain age is not made on technical grounds alone). The attempt to hide criteria of social worth and call them prognostic, psychological, or environmental is an ever-present danger.[22]

To decide that some people are less socially desirable than others and, therefore, to allocate life-saving resources on the basis of "social worth" has justifiably been in disrepute. Not only do such judgments disrespect all notions of primary worth, they easily open the door to arbitrary value judgments in which national origin, race, religion, or social class become determining factors.[23] This "slippery slope" argument is, of course, impeccable. If we allow social worth criteria to protrude into our medical judgments when it comes to the allocation of scarce resources, we are indeed violating the respect for sentient beings that forms one of the cornerstones of contemporary ethics.

In order to allocate scarce resources when there are not enough to go around, several methods are possible. We can, for example, use a market approach in which resources are available to the highest bidder, use a lottery in which blind luck determines who will and who will not live, or use a first-come first-served approach (see also Chapter 12 for a brief discussion of these options).

In allocating organs (as distinct, for example, from allocating kidney machines), the uniqueness of organs must be borne in mind.

Not only are they irreplaceable (which, given sufficient funding, kidney machines or any other man-made devices are not), they were the organs of a member of the same community enunciating their values. In that way they could, perhaps, be seen to be different.[5] Criteria in organ donation must, first of all, be criteria of medical acceptability. These, inevitably laden with value judgments, must be kept as free of at least the coarser elements of such judgments as possible. Once these changeable and difficult criteria with all their problems of arbitrary cut-off lines are satisfied, groups using other criteria must be enunciated. Only when all other attempts at solving problems are exhausted may considerations of social worth enter. Such criteria may be just or unjust, but their justice or injustice is at least determinable by and appealable to the community of which the recipients are members and whose values they know and, at least to some significant extent, share.[5]

In making allocation decisions, physicians will, within the current vision of the physician-patient relationship, do the best that they can for each individual patient regardless of a particular patient's social qualifications. When, however, communities make allocation decisions social value judgments may have to intrude into macro-allocation decisions which offer to practicing physicians the array of possible options they can use (see a discussion of this in Chapter 12).

REFERENCES

1. Loewy, E.H., Waste not, want not: Communities and presumed consent, in: *Medical Ethics: A Guide for Health Professionals*, (D.C. Thomasma and J.F. Monagle, eds.), Aspen Publishers, Rockville, MD, 1987.
2. Joughin, J.L., Blood Transfusion in 1492, *J.A.M.A.* 62:553–554, 1914.
3. Garrison, F.H., *An Introduction to the History of Medicine*, W.B. Saunders, Philadelphia, 1929.
4. Singer, C., and Underwood, E.A., *A Short History of Medicine*, Oxford University Press, New York, 1962.
5. Loewy, E.H., Drunks, livers and values: Should social value judgments enter into transplant decisions? *J. Clin. Gastroenterol.* 9(4):436–441, 1987.
6. Loewy, E.H., Presumed consent in organ donation: Values and means in the distribution of a scarce resource, in: *Ethical Dilemmas in Modern Medicine: A Physician's Viewpoint* (E.H. Loewy, ed.), Edwin Mellen Press, Lewiston, NY, 1986, pp. 133–154.
7. May, W., Attitudes towards the newly dead, *Hastings Center* 3(1):3–13, 1973.
8. Ramsey, P., *The Patient as Person*, Yale University Press, New Haven, 1970.
9. Martyn, S., Wright, R., and Clark, L., Required request for organ donation: Moral, clinical and legal problems, *Hastings Center* 18(2):27–34, 1988.
10. Gert, B., *The Moral Rules*, Harper Torch, New York, 1973.
11. Feinberg, J., The mistreatment of dead bodies, *Hastings Center* 15(1):31–37, 1985.
12. Perry, C., The right of public access to cadaver organs, *Soc. Sci. Med.* 15(F):163–166, 1981.

13. Sadler, A.M., Sadler, B.L., and Stason, E.B., The uniform anatomical gift act, *J.A.M.A.* 206:2501–2506, 1968.
14. Stuart, F.P., Veith, F.J., and Cranford, R.E., Brain death laws and patterns of consent to remove organs for transplantation from cadavers in the United States and 28 other countries, *Transplant* 31(4):238–244, 1981.
15. Dukeminier, J., and Sanders, D., Organ transplantation: A proposal for routine salvaging of cadaver organs, *N. Engl. J. Med.* 279(8):413–419, 1968.
16. Muyskens, J.L., An alternative policy for obtaining cadaver organs for transplantation, *Phil. Public. Affairs* 8(1):88–99, 1978.
17. Caplan, A.L., Professional arrogance and public misunderstanding, *Hastings Center* 18(2):34–37, 1988.
18. Fellner, C.H., Organ donation: For whose sake? *Ann. Intern. Med.* 79(4):589–592, 1973.
19. Fellner, C.H., and Schwartz, S.H., Altruism in disrepute, *N. Engl. J. Med.* 284(11):582–585, 1971.
20. Sadler, H.H., Davison, L., Carroll, C., et al., The living genetically unrelated donor, *Semin. Psychol.* 3:86–101, 1971.
21. Steinbrook, R., Unrelated volunteers as bone marrow donors, *Hastings Center* 10(1):11–20, 1980.
22. Perkoff, G., Slatopolsky, E., Morris, A., et al., Long term dialysis programs: New selection criteria, new problems, *Hastings Center* 6(3):8–13, 1976.
23. Annas, G.J., The prostitute, the playboy and the poet: Rationing schemes for organ transplantation, *Am. J. Public Health* 75(2):187–189, 1985.
24. Atterbury, C.E., The alcoholic in the lifeboat: Should drinkers be candidates for liver transplants? *J. Clin. Gastroenterol.* 8(1):1–4, 1986.

CHAPTER 10

Problems in the Care of the
Terminally Ill

*Among the most frequent and the most spoken about problems in medical
ethics are those involving the termination of life support. This chapter dis-
cusses the way that our society views death and from this goes on to examine
attitudes toward the maintenance of life. The vitalist and nonvitalist positions
are contrasted. These considerations are used to examine a variety of issues,
including no code (or "DNR") decisions, decisions not to leave home, the
acognitive state (brain death, permanent coma, and the vegetative state), the
locked-in syndrome, dementia and limiting of treatment, fluids and/or nutrition in the terminally ill, suicide, and euthanasia. The chapter ends with a
short section dealing with talking with patients and with economic issues.*

INTRODUCTION

Caring for the terminally ill frequently requires a reorientation of current medical values. Concerns for prolonging life often will yield to
concerns for bringing comfort or, at the very least, for ameliorating
suffering. In ordinary practice physicians, while they try to avoid causing pain, do not see the avoidance or the amelioration of pain and
suffering as their prime concern. The primary function is to heal patients and to return them to useful and enjoyable life. When, in terminally ill patients, all reasonable hope for a return to acceptable function
has vanished, healing patients is no longer possible. In such circumstances, physicians and other health professionals will often be heard
to say that "nothing more" can be done. But that is not true: much relief
and comfort, by medical as well as by simply human means, can still be

given. Physicians and other members of the health care team must be aware of some of the issues if they truly are to be prepared to help patients who are terminally ill.

Issues at the end of life bear a resemblance to issues at the beginning of life in that they must deal with what we think life is and what its purposes are. Why, for example, is killing or purposely letting people die wrong? This is a simple question and one that we are apt to wave aside as silly. The answer to the question seems obvious: it is wrong to kill people or to unnecessarily let them die because by so doing such persons end up dead, and few of us want to be dead. Such an answer, however, is facile and insufficient, for some of us do, in fact, want to be dead, and others, we may feel, are best served by being dead. There must, then, be more to this answer than meets the eye.

As Rachels has so aptly pointed out, killing people (or letting them die unnecessarily) is seen as wrong not because it ends life itself but because it writes *"finis"* to a "biographical life" with its capacity for hopes, aspirations and social interconnections.[1] It is the difference between "being alive" and "having a life," the former a necessary condition for the latter but not, by itself, sufficient. We will, later on, have occasion to examine this more closely.

When physicians and other health care professionals deal with critically ill or dying patients, their own philosophy of life and death tacitly informs many of their actions. When patients deal with their own death, similar concerns inform the patient's hopes, fears, and, ultimately, actions. Often the worldviews of physicians and patients differ, and such differences form the basis of many, often poorly understood, conflicts. It is helpful to examine the ways in which death is generally viewed when dealing with death and dying issues: issues dealing with any aspect of death but especially those dealing with suicide, euthanasia, allowing death to occur, or even questions of how we talk about the fact that death may be imminent or that a prognosis is dismal. In examining these ways of looking at death, we are emphasizing Western and largely omitting Eastern points of view, not out of disrespect for Eastern viewpoints but because of a lack of emotive and experiential understanding of Eastern culture.

The problem of dying can be addressed from a number of vantage points. We can inquire what the criteria for death are, we can examine the dying process, or we can concern ourselves with how we envision the state of death to be. Criteria for death are a largely technical issue in which tests to a state previously philosophically defined are applied ("criteria for" a thing are not that thing). Likewise, the dying process deals with a number of technical issues (pain, psychological changes, etc.), and although these are crucially important and help formulate our final attitudes, there is a prior concern when we consider attitudes towards death. That prior concern is the way in which we envision the state of death: how we think that being dead is. This often tacit prior concern is critical when we deal with dying patients, especially patients whose life we may shorten by adequately treating pain or patients who request the means for ending their own life from us. Although, as Freud has pointed out, none of us are capable of imagining ourselves as dead, we, nevertheless, and deep in our bones, know that death occurs and that, ultimately and relentlessly, we too must die.

There are, as Carrick has pointed out, four ways of looking at the state of being dead.[2] (1) The Homeric tradition, also approximated in Egypt, sees death as terrible and unconquerable. The dead are shadows, morosely wandering through the underworld. The chthonic (from under the earth) religions see immortal persons (not only their souls) as spiritless, pale, and eternal wanderers: "Oh shining Odysseus, never try to console me for dying. I would rather follow the plow as a thrall to another man—one with no land allotted to him and not much to live on—than be a king over the perished dead."[3] (2) The Orphic-Pythagorean and later Christian (albeit quite different and varied among Christians) concept is that of immortality of the soul as conceived by Plato and Socrates. (3) The genetic survival ("species survival" as Carrick would have it) concept of Aristotle in which we live on through our offspring and fellow-creatures. (4) The personal extinction of the Stoics and Epicureans accepts death as a true end of all existence.[2]

Except for the chthonic view, which has largely lost currency, these basic points of view of what it is like to be dead continue to influence us. Understanding the function of these concepts in our everyday lives, and the linguistic and conceptual symbolism of these ideas, is critical if we are to understand not only our own but our patients' attitudes towards the very practical problems of life support, euthanasia, and suicide. Inevitably, as we deal with dying patients, our notions of what it is like to be dead produce feelings ranging from extremes of fear and revulsion to envy.

The Pythagorean and ancient Greek model sees in the continuation of the soul an uninterrupted continuum. The soul, freed of the body, continues on in another existence. Socrates, certain of this in his own mind, drank the hemlock and calmly waited for his own soul to be freed.[4] Christians—at least the early Christians and many today—see the immortality of the soul differently. At death, the body and soul die, the soul to be resurrected.[5] *Not exactly*

Depending on the specific sect or church, Christianity today has varied (and, at times, no set) views of immortality. Some conceive of the immortality of the soul as a continuous and uninterrupted process; others affirm that resurrection is a function of God's grace, which may or, in some views, may not be mediated through our actions on earth. Hebrew thought, by no means clear or uniform on this issue, differs in viewing the relationship of man with God as one of covenant in which each must do his or her part. Life, in the traditional Jewish viewpoint, is to be valued above all else and, therefore, to be preserved at all costs. Western physicians are profoundly affected by this melange of cultural assumptions. Religious or not, the ideology of our culture plays a dominant role in tacitly forming and shaping our individual beliefs.

Genetic or "species survival" (as Carrick calls it) is the scientific answer to immortality. Our gene pool, our DNA, survives and is passed on as long as there is life. One may extend this and subscribe to a chemical survival in which our building blocks survive as building blocks for other and, perhaps, even different forms of existence or life: a mechanistic, material adaptation of a belief in reincarnation.

Personal extinction—the "when I am dead, I am dead" philosophy—rooted in Epicurean and Stoic belief is ostensibly shared by many today. Many of those who enunciate such beliefs will still find it difficult to believe that their own ability to feel and know will be no more. We can, and only with difficulty, imagine a world in which we have not existed, but we find it difficult to conceive of a continuing world in which those we know and love act without our participation. Indeed, we may find it difficult to believe that those we love (or hate) are distinct from that love (or hate) and not, somehow, contingent upon it. Our deep-seated Cartesian dualism—which allows our body as the res extensa to perish—does not allow us to conceive that our knowing self, our res cogitans, will vanish.

Both the "species survival" and the "when I am dead, I am dead" view are bereft of personal satisfaction except in the negative sense: if no personal "I" persists, then when that "I" can no longer know or feel, no further evil can befall it. What matters, the Epicureans, Stoics, and those who share their belief today agree, is to live honorably and well. Life, then, is viewed as the necessary condition of experience rather than as a free-standing value. When the possibility for positive experience is no more and the future holds only negative experience, ending life no longer seems an impossible or immoral choice to make.[6]

Such views profoundly influence the way that physicians and nurses deal with their critically ill or dying patients. Our own unexamined philosophy of such things can become a stumbling block when it runs across the patient's equally unexamined and often quite different philosophy. Misunderstandings are then bound to occur.

Attitudes toward Maintaining Life

To the vitalist, life is a good regardless of anything else. To the vitalist all life (or, at least, all human life) is sacred. The vitalist, therefore, is committed to supporting at least human life at all costs. When it comes to saving or prolonging life, vitalists do not concern themselves with whether life is or is not worthwhile. If life is held to be a primary good (one that is good in itself and not good only as a means to an end), the question of it being or not being worthwhile is incoherent. Being alive, rather than having a life, is what concerns vitalists.

The vitalist stance is sometimes blindly appealed to by those who speak of the sanctity of life. Few persons even among the "right to life" group, however, truly adhere to such a position. If one holds all life (or at least all human life) to be sacred, than a tissue culture of any imaginable human tissue one may choose shares in that sanctity. After all, such tissue has the right number of chromosomes and has those biological attributes which we require to call anything life. If one is to be consistent, tissue cultures could not be destroyed.

Many, but by no means all, physicians and nurses today have abandoned the vitalist position. Nevertheless, this position is often unthinkingly invoked and is, at times, at the root of attitudes which tacitly guide the actions of the health care team as it continues to treat in hopeless situations. At other times the team gets so involved in the complicated business of correcting chemical imbalance, correcting acidosis, or maintaining sinus rhythm that the goal of treatment is forgotten. This in no way is meant to fault the necessary attention to the patient's biomedical needs or to underestimate the primary importance of technical competence; it is, once again, to point to the inescapable fact that biomedical competence serves a purpose beyond itself. Biomedical competence is the necessary, but insufficient, condition of responsible medical practice.

The nonvitalist position, on the other hand, denies that human life itself, just because it is human life, is necessarily "sacred." Instead, it holds that life, far from being a good in itself, is merely an instrumental good: a means toward an end beyond itself. This position sees life either as a condition for experience and life's being or not being worthwhile as dependent upon the nature of the experience, or it sees life as a bridge to eternity. Attitudes differ from very rigorously supporting life as long as the slightest possibility of again experiencing "good" (or working for salvation) remains to being more ready to abandon support where that possibility seems slim. But life, in the nonvitalist's conception, is a means and not an end in itself.

An attitude among health care professionals which refuses to examine either the vitalist or the nonvitalist position is, perhaps, more frequent than is the pure vitalist stance. Refusal to examine the position does so on the premise that the health care team is a skilled team dedicated to the skillful application of all applicable and available technology. "Ours not to reason why, ours but to do or die" is the motto of those who would make of technology an end in itself. The use of the ventilator, for example, is justified by a living patient's lack of respiratory drive and the availability of the technology in question. Technology becomes a sufficient reason for its own existence and use. The underlying philosophy, that what can be done ought to be done, informs many of the actions we see in hospitals today. Such unthinking attitudes make of health care professionals technicians whose purposes inevitably must be controlled by another. Health care professionals, if they think this way, make of themselves automatons whose only choices deal with a selection of means appropriate to an end which is selected entirely by others.

Those who presume that life is a condition for experience and not an end in itself, will, of course, have difficulty in determining when, and when not, that experience is, or is not, worthwhile. Concerns with determining whether the nature of the experience is worthwhile, often called "quality of life" issues, are of extreme importance. However, the threat that the quality of one's life will be determined for us by another is the hidden danger in such situations. Here, as in most other areas where such judgments must be made, every attempt to make such judgments on the patient's and not on the health professional's terms are in order if crass paternalism is to be avoided and a decent respect for persons is to be maintained. Only when patients are clearly incompetent to make such judgments and when their will is unknown and unknowable are substitute judgments acceptable.

Although at times inevitable, quality-of-life decisions are fraught with danger. All too often we are prone to judge another's quality of life on our own terms. Whenever possible "quality of life" is judged by him or her whose life it is. Even then there are problems: temporary events may influence decisions profoundly, and depression or fear may, likewise, skew judgments. The many persons who attempt suicide and later are happy and content to have been saved attest to this. Physicians must take great care in accepting quality-of-life judgments which are not the product of sufficient information or of adequate deliberation. Judgments, furthermore and especially in the medical situation, may be coerced by internal or external forces: pain, fear, a surge of adrenalin or anoxia, are all powerful forces coercing judgments, and economic and social forces should not be underestimated. In general, finally, judgments which are inconsistent with what is known about the patient's prior world view must be held to be suspect. Judgments which fly in the face of a long-held worldview may well be judgments made under the influence of panic or fear (see also Chapters 4 and 5).

Quality-of-life judgments not made by the person about him- or herself under acceptable conditions are problematic. Inevitably my judgment of another's quality of life is filtered through my own values. It has been shown that when physicians judge their patients' quality of life they are very likely to be wrong.[7] Judgments of this sort made for another are, as Pellegrino and Thomasma have convincingly argued, possible when "life no longer has any possibility of satisfaction to the patient," as in the terminally ill patient in pain. Continuing treatment under such circumstances represents "a kind of therapeutic belligerency."[8] But under circumstances not quite as bad as this, judgments of this sort need to be carefully hedged.

Quality-of-life decisions at times must be made for patients who are incompetent. Inevitably such judgments are made by setting external standards; that is, standards which are external to the person choosing. Setting external standards is one of the fundamental problems in ethics. In respecting autonomy, sentient creatures should set standards for themselves or, when unable to enunciate them, have such standards set by persons who can reasonably be believed to have not only the patient's best interest in mind but also to be persons willing and able to define that best interest on the patient's own terms. Such judgments, called surrogate judgments are made under the presumption that those closest to the patient would have his or her best interest at heart and would define that best interest on the patient's terms. The health care team, in accepting surrogate judgments, takes on a heavy responsibility: it cannot assume that surrogates, merely because they happen to be the legal next of kin, truly have the patient's best interest at heart or that they are defining that interest on the patient's terms. At times relatives have their own agenda, which may differ radically from that of the patient, and may, in fact, be pursuing their own instead of the patient's best interests. In accepting surrogate judgments, physicians and other health care professionals must, as far as that is possible, understand the prior relationship and its nuances. Accepting such judgments is often made easier when decisions are made in an ongoing dialogue among the members of the health care team and those most closely associated with the patient. Such conferences can go far in clarifying interests and sorting out options.

When no surrogates are available, substitute judgments are the last resort. Here the health care team must make determinations in situations in which the patient is incapable of speaking effectively in his or her own behalf and in which surrogates are either unavailable or unreliable. Inevitably such decisions invoke the values of the health care team. Physicians are well advised to counsel informally or formally with others concerned in the patient's care and, where severe doubts persist, to obtain consultation or refer the case to an ethics committee. Ultimately, however, physicians must act in their patient's behalf. Obtaining consultation helps delineate and clarify options; counseling with others enables the treating community to approach a problem with a unified focus. When, however, a decision is finally made, it must be a decision acceptable to the physician and to the other members of the health care team involved in carrying it out (see also the section on consent in Chapter 4).

No Code Decisions

When physicians decide to treat, they do so under two presuppositions: (1) a technical judgment that treatment has a reasonable chance of being technically successful (i.e., that a given intervention is likely to ameliorate the condition for which it is instituted) and (2) an ethical judgment that treatment has a reasonable chance of bringing about a desirable or at least tolerable (on the patient's terms) state.

Cessation of treatment is done under the converse presupposition: (1) a technical judgment that treatment does not have a reasonable chance of technical success (e.g., that restarting the heart is useless because it cannot continue beating) or (2) an ethical judgment, that even if there is technical success, the patient's ability to profit from this life is nonexistent or perhaps that prolonging life would lead only to suffering (e.g., that restoring the heartbeat might be successful for a given length of time but that the patient is hopelessly ill and that restoring the heartbeat would either result in intolerable suffering or would be irrelevant to a permanently insentient patient).

In the first instance, when treatment is technically almost certain to be futile, treatment is not only unnecessary but is, in fact, a logical contradiction. Treating the untreatable makes no sense. In such instances, writing a DNR order does not necessarily involve obtaining consent. Physicians are not obligated (and are, in fact, ill-advised) to offer useless treatment options to their patients. Not unreasonably, patients expect that an option brought up for discussion has some possible merit. Getting consent for not resuscitating a patient who cannot be resuscitated is, in many ways, analogous to getting consent for not treating patients suffering from viral hepatitis with penicillin: both are not technically useful options, and offering them to patients is merely confusing. Saying to the patient and family that, unfortunately, no treatment is possible and that, therefore and regretfully, none will be given is all that can be done.[9] Writing a DNR order under such circumstances is a judgment made on technical grounds that such treatment is useless. It is not a moral choice that such treatment, while technically possible, is inadvisable in a given patient. What follows concerns itself with the more frequent ethical quandary of not resuscitating in situations in which resuscitation is technically feasible.

Writing "Do Not Resuscitate" orders has become a daily reality in our hospitals. In former days, men died in the midst of their families, friends, and loved ones, or they died alone. Dying, as it were, was a private process. Today, however, deciding to withhold treatment is no longer a matter which concerns merely the patient, the family, and the physician. Dying has become institutionalized and therefore public and necessarily hedged with a multitude of restrictions. Deciding to allow a patient to die peacefully and to withhold treatment or support is far less easy. Under ordinary circumstances, hospitals are properly seen as institutions here to preserve life by all available means, and the burden of proof is, properly, on the person who would refrain from using all possible means to sustain life.

Most orders written in a hospital setting are positive orders directing other members of the health care team to do something. Only when "doing something" is the norm is an order not to do that thing necessary. After it was shown that in certain instances resuscitation could be effective and could restore some patients to a meaningful life, resuscitating those who died suddenly became routine. It became routine for quite a proper reason: when patients arrest there is no time to deliberate. If resuscitation is to be successful, literally every second counts. Therefore, a specific order not to resuscitate is needed if the properly conditioned reflex of the hospital team is to be forestalled.

The primary goal of medicine as conceived today is the restoration of health, at least to the degree possible, and the saving of life. Leaving aside the fact that this was not always the case (see Chapter 1), abandoning what has come to be considered the traditional goal of medicine requires justification and the delineation of new goals. When we write a DNR order, we acknowledge either that resuscitation is not technically feasible or that the circumstances of the case would make the prolongation of life unwise.

The duty to relieve suffering—a much more ancient duty of medicine than is the duty to prolong life[10] and one much more enduring—moves into the foreground of obligation when decisions not to resuscitate are made. Once a DNR decision is made, comfort measures become the primary goal.[11,12] This is an important point: all too often patients who have had a DNR order executed on their chart are avoided by their physicians as well as by other members of the health care team. Such abandonment is ethically improper; it is not that nothing can be done, but that the something that can (and must) be done is to bring comfort rather than to sustain life. In the last weeks, days, or hours human contact and comfort are perhaps especially important. Physicians have the obligation to make sure that all concerned understand the intent of the order fully; far from counseling neglect or saying that "nothing can be done," do not resuscitate orders shift the goal to comforting and caring. It may be advisable, in case of doubt, to append to the DNR order a statement clearly emphasizing that all possible comfort measures must be taken.

In most instances in which resuscitation might be technically successful, decisions to write DNR orders should be made jointly with the patient. The alternative—acting without the patient's consent or knowledge—violates the basic respect due others and is crass paternalism. Preferably such decisions are made long before an illness becomes terminal. Discussing the matter only with the family merely spreads paternalism. Wives, husbands, or other loved ones are not entitled to make decisions for competent patients, much as these others are needed in the process of reaching such decisions. Properly families help and support patients in their decision, but they do not speak for them (see below).[13]

There are, of course, rare cases when conscious patients cannot be consulted. But here the burden of proof (why such patients should not be involved) is on the caregiver who fails to consult the patient. The belief that discussing such matters is burdensome to the patient has been shown to be a fallacy.[14]

Often, and preferably, decisions about "how far to go" have been made long ago when, perhaps, a living will has been written by the patient and discussed with the caregivers. Making decisions beforehand is preferable because it provides an optimal opportunity for the patient to make an autonomous choice (see Chapter 7) and because it allows a dialogue among physician, patient, and family which permits a squaring of moral views. During such a dialogue, physicians can and must make sure that patients really understand the consequences of their choices rather than making such choices with little or with biased information. It is here that a discussion of what it means to be on a ventilator or what it means to be defibrillated is not only in order but essential. In this day and age, lay persons, often conditioned by the media, frequently have a warped idea about such matters. The fear of being on a ventilator may be grounded in the assumption that once this device is used it will be permanent.

When such decisions have not been made beforehand, and when circumstances are such that patients might reasonably have doubts about the prolongation of their life, a compassionate discussion about such matters is one of the physician's obligations. It is the physician's obligation because the alternative of substituting his or her own, or the family's, judgment for the patient's is a crass exercise of paternalism and disrespects the basic autonomy of another.

Living wills have become popular. These documents, in variable detail, set out a patient's wishes long prior to the time when he or she is disabled. Almost universally, such documents are phrased in such a way that health professionals are instructed to forego certain measures (resuscitation, ventilation, etc.) if the patient is judged to be "beyond hope." This gives comfort to the health professionals who must decide, often helps reinforces a patient's will to the family, and assuages the family's feelings of guilt if they agree not to press on. But it still leaves the final decision of when the patient is and when he or she is not beyond hope in the physician's hands.

When possible, families should be involved in such critical decisions. Properly the role of the family is to advise patients or to act as their sounding board. Families may support or disagree with a viewpoint or decision; family members may counsel, advise, cajole, and argue. But normally the family acts through and not for the patient. Unless patients are unconscious and their previous choice in such circumstances is unknown, or unless patients are clearly incompetent, the final decision must be made by the patient.[13] When patients are incompetent, unconscious, or clearly incapable of making informed choices and when no prior wishes are known, the family is involved in such decisions because it is assumed that they are most familiar with the patient's world view and that they truly have the patient's best interest (defined on the patient's terms) at heart. Family here is used in the broadest sense of family: not merely kinship but a sense which includes those others closely associated with the patient and, therefore, likely to have the patient's best interest at heart and to be most familiar with his or her worldview. Judgments as to what ethically (not legally) constitutes "family" in that sense, are judgments which physicians and other health care professionals will find most troublesome to make but which, nevertheless, they will have to make to the best of their ability.

These days resuscitating patients has, on the one hand, lost much of its original appeal, and, on the other, has been mindlessly applied even to cases in which doing so has not the slightest chance of success.[9] Often our enthusiasm to restore the heartbeat or to support respiration even in cases in which success is possible, is tempered by the fear of "creating a vegetable." This unfortunate fear is largely based on essentially anecdotal experience. At the very least, resuscitation "buys time" for deliberation.

Well-thought-out DNR orders are a necessary part of medical practice. But failing to resuscitate a patient who might have lived a few more years of a full life because of a fear that doing so might result in an irreversible vegetative state is a tragedy. First of all, as has been shown, creating such vegetative states is rare.[15] Secondly, having tried and having been unsuccessful does not compel one to continue. The decision not to continue treatment can, in such cases, be appropriately made (see the section on "acognitive states" below). Here, as is so often the case, failure in some is the price paid for success in other cases.

DECISIONS NOT TO LEAVE HOME

Decisions not to leave home are made more and more frequently today.[16] Under proper conditions, these decisions represent a reasoned judgment made by patients in concert with their families and caregivers not to seek hospital care but to remain and die at home. More is involved here than is involved when patients ask not to be resuscitated. Since patients who decide against institutionalization remain at home, their families and loved ones are intimately and critically involved: it is the patient who chooses to remain at home, but it is the family and other caregivers who provide the necessary conditions so that remaining at home is possible. Decisions to remain at home are, therefore, invariably communal decisions involving a number of people joined in and working in a common enterprise.

Decisions to remain at home are more complex than decisions not to resuscitate for yet another reason: although in both of these decisions technical intervention that would not serve the best interest of the patient as determined by him/herself is ruled out, decisions not to leave home are made in a quite different milieu. DNR decisions are

normally made in a milieu in which such a decision is part and parcel
of everyday life and in which the implementation of such decisions is
by persons who are socially accepted as being responsible and accountable for such decisions.[17] When patients remain at home, the family
who must ultimately implement the decisions (by, for example, not
calling the emergency medical squad when an emergency occurs) has
no social credentials to act in such a manner. Families fear that by not
calling for help, even when decisions of this sort are made beforehand,
they will "not be doing the right thing." They have doubts, feelings of
guilt, and, at times, a fear that social disapproval by neighbors or other
members of the family may follow.[17] Helping with such decisions,
therefore, requires even more support and understanding from the
health care team than does the decision not to resuscitate.

In addition, things are not necessarily quite this cut and dried.
While in many instances, the treatment milieu of the home may have a
lot more to offer to the patient than does the hospital setting,[18] unforeseen circumstances can occur. Patients and caregivers may, at the time
that the decision is made, feel that home care would be best. Yet,
patients with advanced cancer or who have for some other reason made
such a decision may be confronted by an unexpected complication.
They may, for example, be in florid pulmonary edema, break a leg, or
have a painful abscess associated with sepsis at a time when removal to
a hospital to alleviate the severe discomfort of such an intercurrent
condition seems advisable. Such a sudden event may, in addition,
cloud the patient's judgment and force caregivers into making decisions for them. If we are to "rehumanize dying" and make what Stollerman calls "lovable decisions,"[19] temporary removal to the hospital
may, in fact, be necessary.[17] Decisions of this sort may be guided by
similar considerations as are decisions to limit treatment (see below).

ACOGNITIVE STATES

The "acognitive state" is defined as a state of biological existence
in which the ability to think, know, and feel is permanently absent.
This definition would include brain death, irreversible coma, and the
vegetative state. A brief technical description follows.

The cerebral hemispheres, necessary for perception, volitional motor function, and thought, in turn depend on the reticular activating
system located in the rostral brain stem. The reticular activating system
provides wakefulness and, therefore, allows cognitive function. Without it, coma ensues. The caudal portion of the brain stem is necessary

for respiration. A patient whose entire brain stem is destroyed is, therefore, comatose and unable to breathe without mechanical assistance. According to our current definition, such patients are brain dead.

One whose hemispheres are destroyed but whose reticular activating system is preserved will have periods of wakefulness but will lack awareness, perception, and cognition. Such patients are said to be in the vegetative state. Patients with a preserved brain stem but a destroyed reticular activating system will be able to control their breathing but will be permanently comatose.[20–23]

When we speak of "brain death," whole brain death is implied.[24] This, according to accepted standards today, is considered to be the equivalent of death since without respirator support cessation of all other vital functions will occur in a very brief time. And at that time, organismic death will ensue. Attempts to redefine death more broadly so as to include acognitive states is conceptually problematic. Such patients are not, in a biological or philosophical sense, dead. They continue to breathe, excrete, and metabolize. Setting criteria for something (death, for example) implies that that something has been defined. As Hans Jonas has so aptly noted: we can either manipulate facts so as to redefine death when, in fact, death has not occurred or we can "squarely face the issue of the rightness of continuing solely by our artifice what may still be called life."[25]

The vegetative state, consisting of an intact reticular activating system but without cortical function, is one of the most difficult. Patients here look "so alive": they frown, grimace, swallow, and blink. The state is analogous to one's placing radio, lights, and window shades on various timers and then leaving the house. Observers outside the house would conclude from the changing lights, shades, and music that someone is at home. But such is not the case. In the vegetative state also, the appearance, but not the fact, of "being home" is preserved. Emotively this presents a terrible burden for the family and for health care professionals. It is, therefore, extremely difficult to deal with.

When the reticular activating system no longer functions but the brain stem is preserved, acognitive patients do not require a ventilator. They are evidently unconscious without signs of wakefulness or volitional response. Such patients are said to be comatose.

When we consider (permanent) acognitive states other than brain death, we must come to grips with why it is that life is being maintained. If we are to eschew the vitalist position—if, in other words, we are to affirm that life serves as a condition for experience and not as a "good" in itself—we will see no ethical imperative to maintain such an existence. On the other hand, neither will we discover an ethical imperative to discontinue all life support. Such patients, since they now lack primary moral worth (since, in other words, they are incapable of being harmed or benefited on their own terms) are no longer the primary objects of concern. Their relatives and the health care team, for whom they are of secondary as well as of symbolic worth, and the community, for whom (as representing a symbol of humanity) they are of symbolic worth, now move to the forefront of decision making. The decision is a communal one, made by the moral agents concerned in the context of the community in which such decision takes place.[26]

Patients of this sort, patients who may be said to have lost primary moral worth, may have another sort of secondary worth. Aside from the symbolic worth for loved ones and community, their organs may have secondary worth to another in vital need for life or function of transplantable organs. It is here that a conflict, resolvable only by the particular values of particular communities, among various forms of symbolic and secondary worth is played out (see Chapter 9).

THE LOCKED-IN STATE

Rarely a combination of lesions can produce a state in which patients are awake, retain the ability to think, but do not retain the ability to communicate in any way. In the "locked-in state" patients have intact hemispheres but lesions of the motor pathways in the pons or midbrain which prevent them from speaking, controlling their facial muscles, or otherwise expressing themselves. They are totally paralyzed, their mentation totally disconnected from their ability to act or to make their desires known. Consciousness is maintained since the reticular activating system is spared. These unfortunate persons can think, feel, and know but can in no way express themselves. They pose incredibly difficult ethical problems. This is especially and poignantly the case when none of their previous wishes relating to life support are known.

DEMENTIA AND LIMITING TREATMENT

Severe dementia (in which all reversible causes have been excluded, in which no reasonable doubt as to diagnosis or prognosis remains, and in which there is an evident lack of meaningful thought processes) is a very troublesome problem. A sometimes long road separates its early stages from the ultimate, lingering nonbeing of the vegetative state. Along this road, various problems and options inevitably will present themselves and will need to be dealt with.[27]

When patients are mildly demented, still able to communicate fairly well, and are still considered competent to make their own choices, no real problem (other than the problem of determining competency, a terrible problem in itself at times) exists. Patients capable of deciding their own good on their own terms must be given the respect due others. Likewise, patients who are no longer capable of making such choices but who have expressed their wish explicitly (by means of a "living will") or by a tacit understanding over the years do not pose an unsurmountable problem: their expressed will, accepted by their physician, forms the framework of their care.

When physicians face such problems in patients in whom no framework of care has been previously established, they are often inclined to obfuscate and to evade facing the issue: against their better judgment, they treat, but often they treat reluctantly and with half measures.[28] Establishing a framework for the care of such patients is, at best, difficult and inevitably leaves a residuum of doubt. Often relatives, by helping physicians understand their patients more fully, aid by acting as acceptable surrogates. At other times, relatives may be absent, disinterested, or materially prejudiced and may, consciously or not, do other than seek the patient's "best interest." A substitute judgment, at best difficult, may then have to be made. Further, and perhaps more frequently, physicians are asked (and are, I believe, asked properly) to guide and advise on treatment decisions: not only to offer an array of available means but also to share in formulating proper ends.

Often physicians deal with cases in which they feel it appropriate to limit treatment but inappropriate to forego treatment altogether. Examples of this are not limited to adult dementia: the newborn whose illness limits life-span to a few months or years (say, children with Werdnig-Hoffman or Tay-Sachs disease); or the severely mentally retarded who will never be able to communicate or evince more than the ability to perceive discomfort, to name but two. The grounds for determining what treatments are, and what are not, appropriate are often not well delineated and, therefore, *ad hoc*. At times, regrettable decisions are made.

In enunciating grounds for making the decision to limit treatment,[12] our obligation to refrain from causing suffering (and to prevent harm) as well as our obligation to sustain life must be considered. In deciding to treat or to forego treating, at least four considerations are appropriate: (1) the immediacy of the threat; (2) the relievability of the suffering caused by the disease; (3) the suffering entailed in the treatment; and (4) the patient's ability for sustained understanding of and cooperation with treatment.[12]

In general and when no provisions to the contrary have been previously established, an acute threat to life is appropriately met by an attempt to reverse the threat. This, for many other reasons, is done to preserve the opportunity for deliberate choice. Doing otherwise denies that option. In order to minimize suffering, diseases which impose a serious burden of suffering on the patient, and whose treatment burden is less than the burden of the disease itself, must be treated. The goal here is primarily the relief of suffering; prolonging life is now a secondary consideration. When treatment itself is severely burdensome, physicians must reexamine their projected goals and determine whether the burden imposed seems, all things considered, to be justifiable. Such decisions must be made in the context of the specific situation. Patients no longer capable of sustained understanding and, therefore, incapable of cooperation are easily frightened. Often, in order to accomplish treatment, they must be tied down or otherwise restrained. Such patients may easily forgive or forget the imposition of brief and relatively slight discomfort but may have their last days darkened by fear and terror when the reason for imposing severe or prolonged discomfort is not understood.

What then, in a demented or otherwise mentally severely impaired but yet conscious patient, is the difference between, say, treating pneumonia or operating for appendicitis and starting dialysis or doing coronary bypass surgery? Using the criteria mentioned above may help. Treating a severely senile or severely mentally defective patient for pneumonia (or taking out his or her appendix) may be justified because pneumonia (or appendicitis) (1) poses an immediate threat at a time when the patient still has a reasonable short-term ability to profit from life, (2) entails relievable suffering; and because treatment, (3) involves little prolonged suffering, and (4) does not require enlisting the patient's sustained cooperation or understanding to accomplish the goals of therapy. Starting patients on long-term dialysis (or doing bypass surgery), on the other hand, may not be justified because (1) the threat may or may not be immediate, (2) suffering is relievable in other ways, (3) the proposed treatment entails considerable suffering which, furthermore, the patient cannot understand, and (4) the patient's cooperation is necessary for success.

Asking ourselves such questions and seeking to work out answers in community with others concerned for and with the patient may be troublesome. The alternative (not asking these questions or seeking these answers or appealing to predetermined principles rather than

using these principles as guidelines along the road to decision making)
has the appeal of simplicity but yields unsatisfactory results if one
assumes that a sense of humanity and compassion is a necessary part of
moral medical practice. In specific situations, specific judgments will
depend upon an understanding of the patient, the context, and the
community in which such decisions are made.

WITHHOLDING FLUIDS AND NUTRITION

Even when physicians are willing to write DNR orders or to limit
treatment in the hopelessly ill, controversies about withholding fluids
and nutrition persist. This is because a fundamental distinction between "caring" and "treating" has been made. Health professionals may
often be willing to stop treatment but find themselves poorly equipped
emotionally to abandon what they perceive to be care.[29] The symbolism of caring[30,31] denotes an activity which is more human than it is
professional: all humans care or at least ought to, but only a few treat.

Intuitively, traditionally, and linguistically, we differentiate between caring (a human and not necessarily active sustaining) and treating (a professional and generally active task). Professionals willing to
stop treatment are unwilling to divest themselves of their basic humanity by—as they may see it—stopping to care. Caring, however, can and
should never stop. We care for people by giving them comfort (that is,
when they are able to be benefited or harmed in themselves and are,
therefore, of primary moral worth); at times, we care for persons whom
we can no longer benefit or harm because by so doing we can bring
comfort to others to whom such persons are of value (i.e., the patient,
now no longer of primary moral worth, retains secondary and symbolic
worth, and, therefore, caring for him or her remains an obligation).

When we, however, care for patients, we must be very clear as to
what we are about. Keeping patients clean, taking care of excreta, washing and dressing them, and preventing or treating decubital ulcers all
seem essential.[24] It is not that insentient patients can know or feel the
difference; not that they can benefit or suffer. Other considerations
demand such care. Respect for the family enjoins that the body of their
loved one be kept presentable and free from the appearance of suffering. The hygiene of hospital ward or nursing home requires meticulous
standards of cleanliness so that infection does not spread. Symbolic
value and aesthetics insist that the human form not be neglected and
allowed to become offensive. Above all, respect for oneself exacts this
task—we cannot allow ourselves the inhumanity of dealing any less

than this with a symbolic representation of ourselves. But caring includes the notion of concern for the welfare of others and protection of
their interests. It is not a blind obeisance for the sake of form.

Nutrition and fluids are certainly needed for biological survival.
When patients, no matter how ill or demented, derive comfort from
such measures or are made uncomfortable by their lack, no one can
doubt that the administration of nutrition and fluids is a moral necessity. However, when patients are acognitive and unable to derive comfort
from such measures, the issue is less clear. There are some who appeal
to an inchoate and atavistic sense of humanity when they state that
under such circumstances these measures still are ethically
needed.[31–34] They feel that supplying food and water to our fellow
creatures is a basic expression of humanity and love and one that we
can ill afford to lose. Furthermore, there are those who fear that allowing health care facilities and health care professionals to withhold fluid
and nutrition from their patients would be socially disruptive: it would
distort the existing relationship between health professionals and
health care institutions and their patients and be contrary to "the integrity of the medical profession as a learned and ethical" one. Such people feel that "in medicine the ultimate value is life," and life must be
supported.[34]

The way the question is framed and understood makes a great deal
of difference to our ultimate decision in the matter. If we look at fluid
and nutrition given by nasogastric, gastrostomy, or enterostomy tube as
"supplying" basic elements of life, and if we frame the question as
"denying" this, we may obtain a far different answer than if we frame
the question as not "forcing" such feedings. Offering the basic elements
of life to persons who may or may not avail themselves of it is a far
different matter than forcing helpless patients to accept our ministra-
tions. No one has proposed that fluids be "denied": what has been
proposed, and what is up for debate, is the propriety of not forcefully
administering fluids and nutrition to the permanently unconscious or
to those terminally ill patients who no longer wish to receive fluids or
nutrition or to those evidently burdened by it.

There is, however, another and more serious problem. Some patients still retain some capacity to experience, but their world is constricted until suffering seems to be their only experience. The elderly
patient totally demented but yet capable of feeling pain, the cachectic
terminal cancer patient whose movement is restricted by intravenous
lines and feeding tubes, and the terminally ill patient who simply says
"leave me alone, I want to die" are examples. Some such patients lie in
their beds in a fetal position and their only response to stimulation

appears to be a groan of pain. Inserting devices to feed such patients usually necessitates restraining them and very evidently causes considerable discomfort. When our attempts to supply fluids and nutrients burden the patient's last days, such attempts no longer, in truth, are ways of caring.[29,35,36] Instead, such attempts may become an officious and unwarranted assault. At the very least, the notion of caring should encompass the notion of not causing pointless suffering.

Providing nourishment and fluids to the dying can be a human and a humane duty, a useless obeisance, or an officious assault. When patients are acognitive and permanently incapable of feeling pleasure or pain, speaking of "maintaining their comfort" is, indeed, nonsense. Some feel that stopping fluids and nutrition under such conditions is morally permissible.[37–41] However, while ethically permissible, it is certainly not required.[29] Such patients, now no longer of primary moral worth, maintain a high degree of secondary as well as symbolic worth to their loved ones as well as to the hospital context and to the community. When failure to supply fluid and nutrients seems morally, humanly, or aesthetically offensive to the family, friends, or members of the health care team, there is no reason why support cannot continue until, perhaps, in the fullness of time opinions slowly change.[26] There is no reason why, when support seems cruel or offensive, it cannot be stopped.

Things, however, stand differently when terminally ill patients are burdened by our attempts to continue feeding them or infusing fluids. In terminal patients, our overriding duty to comfort and, above all, to refrain from causing pain would suggest that forcing nutrition and fluids under these circumstances is difficult to defend. The nature of the case and the context in which it is embodied will decide our choices in specific situations.

SUICIDE

Physicians not rarely are confronted by suicidal patients or by patients who have attempted to kill themselves and are then brought to the emergency department. Sometimes patients are dead on arrival at the emergency room and the physician must decide whether to call or not to call a case "suicide." At other times, physicians will be asked by terminally ill patients seeking to end their own life to give help or advice.

Historically our attitudes toward suicide and toward voluntary active euthanasia have had much in common. (For a brief history of attitudes toward suicide, see the section on euthanasia which follows.) In suicide, persons, for whatever reasons, decide voluntarily to end their own life; in voluntary euthanasia, another assists in carrying out the person's wish. Common to both is that the decision is made by the person who ends up dead.

If man is to be granted an autonomous will and the right to carry out those actions in accordance with it which do not negatively impinge on others, then extinction, at least under some circumstances, cannot be argued to be wrong. The wrongness of suicide, then, must inhere in the harm that one's suicide brings to another. In fact, the harm done to others is the way in which arguments in opposition to suicide have usually been couched. Such others may be relatives, friends, those others (patients, for example) who depend upon us, society at large, or, ultimately, God. Although the wrongness of suicide has also been argued on grounds of violating duties to oneself,[42,43] this argument is too long and too involved to find place here.

Patients who attempt to commit suicide are usually brought to the emergency department at a time when little about their motivation is known. In acting in such situations to save a life, physicians generally intervene not because they themselves feel suicide to be wrong but because data are sparse, and the time needed to analyze such data is insufficient. Respect for a patient's autonomy would prevent one from interfering with a suicide's deliberate decision which is not causing demonstrable severe harm to another; regard for beneficence, however, would incline one to "buy time" so that a proper analysis of circumstances can be made. Suicide is often an impulsive act, and frequently patients who have attempted suicide are only too glad to have been stopped. Physicians who intervene to save a life rarely have either adequate time or sufficient data to make a deliberate choice: the decision to save a life under such circumstances is made because to do otherwise forecloses all options. Patients who are foiled in their attempt can, if they are so inclined, try again.

When physicians know the circumstances surrounding a suicide, things may be different. A patient who takes an overdose of a potentially lethal drug because he or she is hopelessly ill and has no chance for improvement presents quite a different problem than does a patient whose motivation was unknown or a patient who made a capricious or impulsive choice. Here physicians will often be inclined to respect the patient's wishes and may decide to forego treatment.

Patients who have terminal cancer or another terminal condition not rarely ask their physician for the means of suicide. Such requests are often met with a brusque refusal or by an appeal to the law.[5] Physicians who believe that suicide or helping another commit suicide is immoral cannot in good conscience comply with such a request. But neither can they hold their patients hostage to their own idiosyncratic beliefs. A compassionate approach to such patients is necessary if physicians are to act in a more than merely explicitly "moral" (according to their own lights) fashion.

When a person is brought dead to the emergency room, especially after an accident, there is sometimes legitimate doubt as to what really happened. Physicians have a fair amount of latitude in deciding whether to call such deaths accidents or suicides. To say that physicians must simply determine what is and what is not most likely, begs the question. Suicide still often carries a stigma, and a decision that a death was or was not a suicide may cause considerable trauma to others. Physicians must act on what appears likely and may be well advised to throw compassion into the balance. Individual decisions in specific cases will be a composite of many factors and compassion must play its part in such decisions.

Active and Passive Euthanasia

Many if not most physicians have come to accept that there are circumstances when no further treatment to prolong life is defensible. Under some circumstances when life is only a heavy burden and no hope at all remains, to do otherwise is to practice what Pellegrino and Thomasma have so aptly termed a "kind of therapeutic belligerence."[44]

When we speak of passive euthanasia, we speak of the deliberate omission of an act which, under normal and expected circumstances, would reverse a condition and prolong life. It is "letting nature" take its course. The disease, not the doctor, has killed the patient. Refraining from treating septic shock in a patient hopelessly riddled with metastatic cancer would be one example; and there are many more. Often what we are doing is unclear. When we refrain from resuscitating someone who we think could be resuscitated, disconnect a ventilator from a patient whom we know to be dependent on it, or stop supplying fluids and nutrition to a vegetative person, we may or may not call such an act, or such a failure to act, passive euthanasia.

On the other hand, active euthanasia refers to the deliberate taking of a life by active means. Active euthanasia, as used here, must be (1) deliberate, (2) the stopping of a life which, without such an action, would have continued, and (3) under circumstances in which the death of the individual is reasonably felt to be inevitable, shortly at hand,

and, above all, in which the period until that death is filled with relentless suffering. When active euthanasia is discussed, three different questions must be answered. The first question deals with the ethical permissibility of active euthanasia. (Is killing a person under our definition ever a morally allowable act?) If that question can be answered, at least in some circumstances, in the affirmative, then the next question deals with the probity of involving health professionals in such an act. The third question deals with the advisability of legalizing such a step. These are separate (even if not entirely separable) questions.[45]

Most physicians have come to see that in hopeless circumstances, treating merely to delay the shortly inevitable is often not justifiable. Treatment decisions of this sort properly accord with the patient's wishes and, preferably, are decisions mutually agreed upon long before. Only when no such arrangements have been made should surrogate or substitute decision making be considered. Decisions not to treat merely to prolong the life of a patient who is terminally ill and in pain may or may not be justified. The decision here is largely a personal one depending on the patient's values, plans, and goals. A patient near the end of life and in pain may, nevertheless, choose to prolong life for personal reasons: say, to see a daughter graduate or a son get married. Under a similar medical condition, another patient may choose to forego all treatment. Physicians cannot properly make these decisions based on the medical condition alone without ascertaining their patient's wishes. At times, physicians will be asked their advice and should, under ordinary circumstances, give it as part of their ongoing obligation. At other times, patients may choose not to make a choice, leaving such a choice up to the physician. While physicians may feel that this imposes a heavy burden which they are loathe to assume, such a decision, when properly made by a patient, nevertheless, needs to be, perhaps with a heavy heart, respected.

There are many situations in clinical practice when limiting some but continuing other treatments is clearly indicated. Deciding to treat fully or to abandon treatment altogether is generally a far more clear-cut decision than the decision that some but not other treatment to prolong life is in order.[12] Decisions of this sort, made in concert with patients or, when that is not possible, with surrogates, can follow guidelines but must be made fully cognizant of the texture of individual cases (see section on limiting treatment above).

Historically attitudes both toward suicide and euthanasia have varied. In ancient Egypt suicide was clearly proscribed: those who committed suicide were felt to have cut themselves off from the gods.[46] Yet physicians were not only not expected but were indeed morally felt to be ill advised to treat the incurably ill. Greek attitudes were complex. In the Platonic dialogues there is an evolution in thinking about suicide and euthanasia until, in the *Republic*, qualified approval in cases of lingering and hopeless illness is given. The proscription against administering poisons in the Hippocratic corpus may have been as much directed towards preventing physicians from participating in political intrigues as it was against the killing of patients.[47] Most physicians, moreover, were not Hippocratic physicians, and there is good evidence that the use of poisons to assist consenting patients in ending their lives was frequent.[46,48] Aristotle in the *Nichomachean Ethics* rejects suicide altogether. The Epicureans and Stoics approved of suicide and active euthanasia in cases of hopeless or painful illness or when "one's powers were waning."

Greek physicians, and physicians until recent times, were seen as obligated to (1) ameliorate disease, (2) provide comfort, and (3) desist from treating the hopelessly ill.[10] These obligations neither precluded nor included helping patients to die. The Church firmly opposed suicide and euthanasia. In the medieval era, when most physicians were priests and when a physician's first obligation was to see that patients had been "shriven" (given last rites) so that their souls were safe, suicide and active euthanasia were, of course, strictly forbidden. The first departure from this point of view came with Sir Thomas More's *Utopia*, in which this very pious Catholic scholar envisioned a system in which patients afflicted with conditions entailing hopeless and severe suffering would not only be permitted but actually encouraged and helped to commit suicide.

In more recent times, the attitudes towards suicide and euthanasia have begun to change. John Locke, himself a physician, still felt that suicide and active euthanasia were wrong, basing this on the "inalienability" of certain rights: unlike other property, the right to which could be waived, life belonged to God and could, therefore, not be taken. Hume, on the other hand, argued eloquently for the propriety of suicide. Kant, as has been mentioned, categorically opposed suicide. Utilitarian approval of suicide and euthanasia is parasitic on their worldview which approves actions which bring about the greatest good or, at least, do the least harm.

In medicine, the change in attitudes encountered two opposing forces. On the one hand, medicine since the 16th century added the obligation to save life to its other obligations. Preserving life at all costs more and more became a modern obsession.[10] On the other hand, as religious thinking played a lesser role in everyday life, as considerations of autonomy moved more and more to the fore, and as technology made things heretofore impossible possible, questions about preserving life under all circumstances began to be raised.

Much has been made of the difference between allowing death to occur by refraining from treating a treatable condition and causing death by active means. Codes of medical ethics have traditionally stressed this difference. Physicians, even when they no longer feel compelled to support life, are justifiably, we feel, hesitant to cause death. This is not not only an ethical issue: under the law, killing the dying patient by active means is still first-degree murder.

Serious questions have been raised about the distinction between active and passive euthanasia, between what has been called "killing" and "letting die."[1,49] Under most circumstances, physicians will not be faced with the issue of permitting intolerable pain to persist or ending their patient's life. In almost, but not all, circumstances today, pain can be successfully obtunded and this, even if it hastens but does not directly bring about death, is considered generally acceptable.[50] But not all circumstances are circumstances of intolerable pain, and not all pain is entirely relievable. The nagging question, "Is it always and under all circumstances wrong to kill?" remains.

Those who claim that there is always a difference between killing and letting die base this claim on two things. First of all they claim that killing is quite different from allowing death to occur because one can always refrain from a voluntary action (killing) but one cannot prevent all death. Secondly, they claim that simply allowing something to happen gives an opportunity to another to prevent it, while causing it to happen is a more sure-fire thing.[51] Both of these arguments, as Rachels has pointed out, are severely flawed.[1] In dealing with active vis-à-vis passive euthanasia, the point is not that one cannot prevent all death but that one has deliberately chosen not to prevent a specific preventable one. The question, furthermore, is not that another may do what one has neglected to do (for example, institute a treatment which one has deliberately refrained from) but that one has deliberately chosen not to intervene in a situation in which under ordinary circumstances one would be obligated to do so.

Those who affirm that there is a clear moral difference between killing and letting die regardless of context will find that dealing with practical considerations may be troublesome. Consider, for instance, John, hopelessly trapped under a burning vehicle and pleading with his friend who has a gun to shoot him. Would his friend be acting more morally by allowing John's agonizing death or would shooting his friend be a more morally acceptable act? The answer that killing is, under all circumstances, wrong is an absolutist answer ignoring intention and context. If a resolution is sought by trying to find a morally acceptable ("praiseworthy") course of action, none will be found; if, on the other hand, one seeks an answer which, in the circumstances thrust on us, tries to chart the least objectionable (least "blameworthy") course of action, a beginning may be made (see also Chapter 3).

Often the way we linguistically and conceptually "stack the cards" determines whether we call a given act killing or letting die.[45] When we turn off Mrs. Smith's ventilator, or refrain from treating a vegetative patient's pneumonia, the distinction is far from completely clear. A *prima facie* duty not to cause death remains. Killing patients, under all circumstances, is a wrong even if, at times, it seems like a lesser wrong and, therefore, in the human condition a wrong we cannot always evade.

It has been argued that causing a person's death not only seems intuitively wrong: allowing it to be a legally acceptable option may introduce an intolerable opportunity for mischief and may, in fact, brutalize society and demoralize the health care team. On the other hand, allowing intolerable pain and suffering to occur, while, perhaps, not giving the same opportunity for mischief, likewise demoralizes the health care team and brutalizes society.[45]

The way we frame questions often goes a long way toward determining the answer.[45] If we frame the problem as one of "killing," we may be inclined to give a quite different answer than if we frame it as "relieving suffering." And yet refraining from treating intercurrent disease in a terminal and agonizing condition, thus allowing death to occur, or deliberately giving too much of a drug and killing such a patient can be viewed in either of these ways.[45]

While refraining from treating is, at least in some circumstances, acceptable to most physicians, many health professionals find participation in active euthanasia to be reprehensible. The idea of killing under all circumstances affronts their sensibilities. The issue, as was put in a recent paper, "touches medicine at its moral center."[52] The feeling that "if physicians become killers, or are merely licensed to kill, the profession will never again be worthy of trust and respect as healer and comforter and protector of life in all its frailty" is a cogent and powerful one.[52] Physicians and other health professionals are dedicated to life and to its preservation. Society in its social contract with medicine presumes this obligation.

Participation by physicians in capital punishment is compared by analogy to active euthanasia. Superficially, the analogy is apt. Physicians, under our vision of the social contract which informs the physician-patient relationship, must under all circumstances seek the patient's good and never the patient's harm. It is clear that, since the options are unpredictable and wide, the criminal's good (even should he or she conceive otherwise) may not be served by execution. Physicians must never, come what may, utilize tools (conceptual or actual) acquired in the process of medical training for their patient's detriment.[53] But in the terminally ill and horribly suffering patient, that is not the case: since options are foreclosed, the only choice may be between a slow and agonizing, and a briefer and less terrible, death. What serves the patient's "good" in such a situation is far more open to question.

Physicians who frame the question as "killing" will act differently from those who choose to frame it as "relieving suffering."[45] The choice of those who frame the question in either way and who try to balance one against the other still will depend upon their own priorities: those who place priority on the relief of suffering rather than on the injunction against killing will act quite differently than those otherwise inclined. The decision of a physician or other health professional, when it comes to active euthanasia, is a highly personal one.[45]

The decision to allow—or not to allow—the active termination of life is a legal one. Ethics can and properly must light the way. It is a decision made by the community, and, rather than being clearly "right" or "wrong," it is informed by the evolution of the communal ethos. Communities which, for example, decide to permit the active termination of life will have to be mindful of the tremendous danger for mischief and malfeasance that such decisions may pose. The Nazi example is still close at hand. Physicians and other health professionals will have to come to terms with their own beliefs and will, in the fullness of their conscience, have to act accordingly in making judgments in individual cases.[45]

Talking to Patients

Physicians find that talking to patients whose prognosis is poor or for whom no further therapeutic intervention is possible very difficult. Not rarely physicians, at times consciously but more often unconsciously, avoid such patients and, when they must be with them, avoid the issue by resorting to idle chatter or pointless jocularity (a thing quite distinct from humor). At the very time that patients need communication most, communication is cut off. This is not a problem unique to health professionals. It is a problem which involves the family who, likewise, are loath to address the problem head-on and who "to be kind" hide behind optimistic platitudes, half-truths, or out-right lies. And yet studies have shown time and again that patients generally want to be involved, want to share, and want, above all, to communicate.[14]

Physicians often do not involve patients in critical matters: often they fail to tell them the truth about their prognosis, and frequently they fail to involve patients in critical life-and-death decisions.[54–57] When this happens, the physician-patient relationship becomes a game of charades. Often such a failure to communicate demoralizes the other members of the health care team. Nurses, asked by patients who find communication with their doctors cut off, find themselves in a terrible quandary: they can tell the patient the truth, knowing that this may bring about the physician's anger as well as perhaps otherwise "get them into trouble"; they can join in the game of charades; or they can simply lie to the patient. Physicians as the acknowledged heads of the health care team owe an obligation not only to the patient but likewise to the other members of the team.

On the other hand, while patients, because of the respect humans owe one another, ought not to be lied to, telling the truth comes in many shades and gradations. Patients can only be told what patients are ready to hear; they will turn a deaf ear and literally deny being told if told at a time when they are not receptive. I well remember a lady who was told about her diagnosis of cancer at least four times by her physician, and each day would ask again and simply deny having been told. Sick people are not, as Eric Cassel put it so beautifully, simply well people carrying "the knapsack of disease."[57] They are people in whom a whole host of changes and adaptations are and have been taking place. Simply assaulting patients with the truth is hardly the proper thing to do.

Patients must be gently led to receive bad news. The manner in which this is done varies with the personality of each patient, each physician, each situation, and with the peculiarities of a specific patient-physician relationship. It depends on the physician's assess-ment of the situation (an assessment which can receive invaluable help from the other members of the health care team as well as from the family) and defies a stereotypic approach. Human understanding, rather than technical knowledge, is what is needed, and humor, as always, has its place. Physicians have to be as sensitive to the patient's implied wishes as they are to the "letter of the (moral or legal) law." Shoving the facts down the throat of a helpless patient who may derive some lasting comfort from deception is "moral" in no more than a very aseptic sense. The physician has to "size up the patient" (a comment made by Eric Cassel to Prof. Jonas some time ago[58]) and deliver a judgment as to the patient's desire and capacity for truth.[59]

Under most circumstances, most patients, eventually, must be told the full truth. Respect demands as much. The truth, however, has to be gently given. Physicians must allow ample time to share what they perceive to be the truth as well as what they know to be their ignorance and uncertainty, with the patient. A hurried approach to patients under these circumstances violates the duty of respect as much as does not telling the truth at all. Physicians are well advised to defer such conversations to a time when they are not pressed for time, not "due at the office in five minutes," and not visibly harassed by conflicting demands. Sitting on the patient's bedside, perhaps sharing a cup of coffee, perhaps touching a shoulder or an arm, all are appropriate maneuvers which can convert the process from one of mutual pain to one of a sharing of mutual mortality.

Patients may ask not to be told. This does not occur frequently but it does occur. If it occurs, and if it seems to be a truly autonomous decision, the request must be respected as must other such decisions. An ample opportunity for patients to change their minds must be given but the patient who in effect "leaves everything up to the doctor" and does so knowingly has made a deliberate choice. Physicians who cannot live with such a choice (and some may not be able to) are well advised to communicate this to their patients and to reach with them a shared agreement of how to proceed: it may be that the patient delegates a family member; it may be that the physician may have to obtain consultation or turn the case entirely over to another.

On the other hand, relatives may beseech physicians not to tell the truth to their patient. Wives may "forbid" the physician to tell their husband of metastatic cancer or even threaten suit (the fact that patients threaten suit does not mean that they will sue, that they, in fact, can find cause to sue, or that, ultimately, they can hope to win such a suit). They may plead that they know their husband well and that he "couldn't stand to know." In general, physicians are ill-advised to follow such counsel. First of all and in most circumstances, who will and who will not be told should be explicitly or tacitly at least agreed upon long before the need arises. Secondly, when circumstances have made this impossible, the physician's first obligation is to the patient: unless physicians know in individual cases that something about a specific patient makes the administration of truth ill advised, they are obligated to tell it. Streptococcal disease is treated with penicillin except in the very unusual case when penicillin is contraindicated because of some special condition (allergy, for example) peculiar to the particular patient. Truth telling, in the moral sphere, has a somewhat similar standing. Physicians must "size up their patients" (guided, perhaps, by the patient or the family but certainly not dictated to by them) and reach a decision about how much, how quickly, and above all how to share bad news.

ECONOMIC CONSIDERATIONS

Ordinarily, and within our current vision of the physician-patient relationship, physicians in dealing with individual patients cannot put the cost or inconvenience of a given procedure above their individual patient's good. The fact that such a statement must somehow be integrated into the totality of a community whose resources are not infinite likewise is beyond rational dispute. This is not the place to deal with possible ways of integrating these two problems with each other (please see Chapter 12 for a discussion of the problem).

Vast resources are often expended at the end of life. We are a crisis-oriented society. The very same patients who had no access to routine medical care, who could not afford immunization or often even food and warmth, are the object of vast, often heroic efforts when they are found to be critically ill or on the verge of dying from starvation or exposure. Even patients who have had decent medical care throughout life and who have lived in reasonably comfortable circumstances often use up enormous amounts of effort and material at the end of life. Some, but not all, of this is unavoidable.

This is not the place to speak about limiting exotic interventions which may marginally benefit individual patients. Largely these are issues of macro-allocation that must and will be (briefly) addressed elsewhere. There is, however, a great waste of resources occurring in all of our hospitals and this waste consumes large amounts of time, effort, and money: it is the use of resources for patients known to be beyond hope. I speak here of the brain dead kept on a ventilator, of the irreversibly vegetative or comatose, of the infant with extensive grade-4 intracranial hemorrhage who will never be able to lead a sentient existence, and of many more tragic states. The problem is not, as has so often been charged, a problem of the elderly. It involves all age groups. I do not speak of those who, at whatever level, retain a capacity to enjoy existence but rather of those beyond hope who are incapable of being benefited although, at times, they retain the capacity for being harmed. Such patients consume a vast amount of resources in their tenure on earth. These resources cannot be measured only in money, material, or space:

much more is involved. Resources include the energy, hope, and love of relatives and friends as well as those of the health care team. Once all hope is gone, it seems morally indefensible to consume such resources in the empty discharge of an empty duty while others starve.

Hardin compares modern civilization to herdsmen sharing a commons.[60] As conditions become more crowded, herdsmen seeking only their private good by increasing their herd jeopardize the commons. "Freedom in a commons brings ruin to all." In our commons, interminally consuming limited resources beyond the hope of reasonable gain seems only questionably justified. Hiatt voices concern for three types of demands on medical resources[61]: (1) those that pose a conflict between the society and the individual, (2) those for potentially preventable conditions, and (3) those of no value. Using up material as well as other resources to maintain patients at the end of life who are insentient (or who are beset by unrelievable and unending pain and who do not wish their life prolonged) is, at the least, ill-advised and to the detriment of all concerned.

REFERENCES

1. Rachels, J., The End of Life, Oxford University Press, New York, 1986.
2. Carrick, P., Medical Ethics in Antiquity, D. Reidel, Dordrecht, The Netherlands, 1985.
3. Lattimore, R. (trans.), The Odyssey of Homer, Harper & Row, New York 1967.
4. Plato, Phaedo (W.H. Rouse, trans.), in: Great Dialogues of Plato, (E.H. Warmington and P.S. Rouse, eds.), American Library, New York, 1956, pp. 460–521.
5. Cullman, O., Immortality of the soul or resurrection of the dead, in: Immortality and Resurrection (K. Stendhal, ed.), Macmillan, New York, 1965, pp. 132–164.
6. Loewy, E.H., Oh Death, where is thy sting? Reflections on dealing with dying patients, J. Med. Humanities Bioethics 9(2):135–142, 1988.
7. Pearlman, R., and Speer, J., Jr., Quality of life considerations in geriatric care, J. Am. Geriatr. Soc. 31(2):113–130, 1983.
8. Pellegrino, E.D., and Thomasma, D.C., For the Patient's Good: The Restoration of Beneficence in Health Care, Oxford University Press, New York, 1988.
9. Blackhall, L.J., Must we always use CPR? N. Eng. J. Med. 20:1281–1284, 1987.
10. Amundsen, D.W., The physician's obligation to prolong life: A medical duty without classical roots, Hastings Center 8(4):23–31, 1978.
11. Pariser, J.J., Comfort measures only for DNR orders, Conn. Med. 46(4):195–199, 1982.
12. Loewy, E.H., Treatment decisions in the mentally impaired: Limiting but not abandoning treatment, N. Engl. J. Med. 317:1465–1469, 1987.
13. Loewy, E.H., Patient, family, physician: Agreement, disagreement, and resolution, Family Med. 18(6):375–378, 1986.
14. Kübler-Ross, E., On Death and Dying, Macmillan, New York, 1969.
15. Bedell, S.E., Delbanco, T.L., Cook, E.F., et al., Survival after cardiopulmonary resuscitation in the hospital, N. Engl. J. Med. 309:569–576, 1983.
16. Stollerman, G.H., Decisions to leave home, J. Am. Geriatr. Soc. 36:375–376, 1988.

17. Loewy, E.H., Decisions not to leave home: And what will the neighbors say? *J. Am. Geriatr. Soc.* 36:1143–1146, 1988.
18. Rossman, I., The geriatrician and the homebound patient, *J. Am. Geriatr Soc.* 36:348–354, 1988.
19. Stollerman, G.H., Lovable decisions: Re-humanizing dying, *J. Am. Geriatr Soc.* 34:172, 1986.
20. Pallis, C., ABC of brain stem death, *Br. Med. J.* 285:1409–1412, 1982.
21. Plum, F., and Posner, J., *The Diagnosis of Stupor and Coma* (3rd ed.), F.A. Davis, Philadelphia, 1983.
22. Daugherty, J.H., Rawlinson, D.G., Levy, D.E., et al., Hypoxic-ischemic brain injury and the vegetative state: Clinical and neuropathological correlation, *Neurology* 31:991–997, 1981.
23. Plum, F., and Posner, J.B., Disturbances of consciousness and arousal, in: *Cecil's Textbook of Medicine* (18th ed.), (J.B. Wyngaarden and J.B. Smith, eds.), W.B. Saunders, Philadelphia, 1988, pp. 2061–2076.
24. President's Commission for the Study of Ethical Problems in Medicine and Biomedical and Behavioral Research, *Deciding to Forego Life-Sustaining Treatment*, U.S. Government Printing Office, Washington, 1982.
25. Jonas, H., The right to die, *Hastings Center* 8(4):31–36, 1978.
26. Loewy, E.H., Do we have a moral duty to sustain the permanently acognitive patient? in: *Ethical Dilemmas in Modern Medicine: A Physician's Viewpoint* (E.H. Loewy, ed.), Edwin Mellen Press, Lewiston, NY, 1986, pp. 203–236.
27. Loewy, E.H., Moral considerations in dealing with dementia, in: *Ethical Dilemmas in Modern Medicine: A Physician's Viewpoint* (E.H. Loewy, ed.), Edwin Mellen Press, Lewiston, NY, 1986, pp. 237–262.
28. Hilfiker, D., Allowing the debilitated to die: Facing our ethical choices, *N. Engl. J. Med.* 308:716–719, 1983.
29. Loewy, E.H., Nutritional support in the hopelessly ill, in: *Ethical Dilemmas in Modern Medicine: A Physician's Viewpoint* (E.H. Loewy, ed.), Edwin Mellen Press, Lewiston, NY, 1986, pp. 305–324.
30. Capron, A.M., Ironics and tensions in feeding the dying, *Hastings Center* 14(5):32–35, 1984.
31. Ramsey, P., *The Patient as Person*, Yale University Press, New Haven, 1970.
32. Meilander, G., Removing food and water: Against the stream, *Hastings Center* 14(6):11–13, 1984.
33. Callahan, D., On feeding the dying, *Hastings Center* 14(6):22, 1984.
34. Derr, P.G., Why food and fluids can never be denied, *Hastings Center* 16(1):28–30, 1984.
35. Wanzer, S.H., Adelstein, S.J., and Cranford, R.E., The physician's responsibility toward hopelessly ill patients, *N. Engl. J. Med.* 310(15):955–959, 1984.
36. Lynn, J., and Childress, J.F., Must patients always be given food and water? *Hastings Center* 13(5):17–21, 1983.
37. Towers, B., Irreversible coma and withdrawal of life support: Is it murder if the IV line is disconnected? *J. Med. Ethics* 8(4):203–205, 1982.
38. Steinbock, B., The removal of Mr. Herbert's feeding tube, *Hastings Center* 13(5):13–16, 1983.
39. Green, W., Setting boundaries for artificial feeding, *Hastings Center* 14(6):8–10, 1984.
40. Annas, G.J., Do feeding tubes have more rights than patients? *Hastings Center* 16(1):26–28, 1986.

41. Paris, J.J., When burdens of feeding outweight benefits, *Hastings Center* 16(1):30–32, 1986.
42. Kant, I., *Foundations of the Metaphysics of Morals* (L.W. Beck, trans.), Bobbs-Merrill, Indianapolis, 1978.
43. Kant, I., Suicide, in: *Lectures on Ethics* (L. Infield, trans.), Peter Smith, Gloucester, MA, 1978, pp. 148–154.
44. Pellegrino, E.D., and Thomasma, D.C., *For the Patient's Good: The Restoration of Beneficence in Health Care*, Oxford University Press, New York, 1988.
45. Loewy, E.H., Healing and killing, harming and not harming: Physician participation in capital punishment (in preparation).
46. Amundsen, D.W., History of medical ethics: Ancient near-east, in: *Encyclopedia of Bioethics* (W.T. Reich, ed.), Macmillan, New York, 1978.
47. Carrick, P., *Medical Ethics in Antiquity*, D. Reidel, Boston, 1985.
48. Gourevitch, D., Suicide among the sick in classical antiquity, *Bull. Hist. Med.* 43:501–518, 1969.
49. Rachels, J., Active and passive euthanasia, *N. Engl. J. Med.* 292(2):78–80, 1975.
50. Pius XII, The prolongation of life, *Pope Speaks* 4(4):393–398, 1958.
51. Trammel, R., Saving life and taking life, *J. Phil.* 72:131–137, 1975.
52. Gaylin, W., Kass L.R., Pellegrino, E.D.,et al., Doctors must not kill, *J.A.M.A.* 259:2139–2140, 1988.
53. Loewy, E.H., Healing or killing: Health professionals and execution, in: *Ethical Dilemmas in Modern Medicine: A Physician's Viewpoint*, (E.H. Loewy, ed.), Edwin Mellen Press, Lewiston, NY, 1986, pp. 107–132.
54. Bedell, S.E., and Delbanco, T.L., Choices about cardio-pulmonary resuscitation in the hospital: When do physicians talk with patients? *N. Engl. J. Med.* 310(17):1089–1092, 1984.
55. Lo, B., Saika, G., Strull, W., et al., "Do not resuscitate" decisions: A prospective study at three teaching hospitals, *Arch. Intern. Med.* 145(6):1115–1117, 1985.
56. Youngner, S.J., Lewandowski, W., McClish, D.K., et al., "Do not resuscitate" orders: Incidence and implications in a medical intensive care unit, *J.A.M.A.* 253:54–57, 1985.
57. Cassel, E., *The Healer's Art: A New Approach to the Physician-Patient Relationship*, J.B. Lippincott, Philadelphia, 1976.
58. Jonas, H., The right to die, *Hastings Center* 7(4):31–36, 1977.
59. Cassel, E., The function of medicine, *Hastings Center* 7(6):16–19, 1977.
60. Hardin, G., The tragedy of the commons, *Science* 162:1243–1248, 1968.
61. Hiatt, H.H.L., Protecting the medical commons: Who is responsible? *N. Engl. J. Med.* 293(5):235–241, 1975.

CHAPTER 11

Problems at the Beginning of Life

When problems involve children we tend to look at them in a different way than we look at similar problems involving older (and especially elderly) patients. Reasons for this attitude are briefly examined. Specific problems occurring at the beginning of life are discussed. Abortion is examined in its historical and philosophical setting. The problem of abortion is used to examine the probity of legislating the moral beliefs of one particular group and thereby restraining the rest of the community. Other problems examined in this section are problems of defective newborns, the use of anencephalics as organ donors, informed consent in the pediatric age group, surrogacy, forced C-section, and fetal abuse. The economic aspects of these problems are very briefly considered.

INTRODUCTION

Questions dealing with ethical issues at the beginning of life are often viewed differently than are questions at life's end, even when such issues deal with analogous problems. There are a number of reasons for this. Unconsciously we tend to associate youth with hope and with unfulfilled but fulfillable opportunities, whereas we associate old age (or often just older age) with decline and hopelessness. We invest the young with a range of symbols (youth as a symbol for innocence and future) and metaphors (youth as springtime and hope) quite different from the symbol and metaphor we use for later years. Such symbolism and metaphor easily get in the way of rational thought. When we encounter the anencephalic infant or the child with Werdnig-Hoffman disease, youth is not the question: the absence of cortical function, or the fact that life span is severely limited, is. We find the absence of cortical function or the hopelessness of illness intolerable in one that young. And often, and against all reason, we tailor our ethical judgments accordingly. Even when we deal with patients later in their life (say, a 30-year-old lady dying of breast cancer), youthfulness, against all reason but consistent with symbol and metaphor, obtrudes into our ethical judgments. Having a devastating illness and being young (even very young) does not alter the medical facts as the necessary facts on which ethical judgments must be based; it merely makes the situation more tragic and more difficult to cope with.

This chapter deals with a melange of problems at the beginning of life. We attempt to grapple with some of these issues, as exemplified by the problem of abortion, by clinical questions in the care of severely defective newborns, and by the quandaries of informed consent in infants and children. These represent the more common issues faced at this period of life. In addition, we briefly touch on some of the problems posed by surrogate motherhood and by the use of women merely as fetal containers.

THE PROBLEM OF ABORTION

This troublesome issue is made troublesome above all because of its religious overtones and because of the emotive response it brings forth in many people. No attempt is made here to deal with the issues of religious morality: i.e., no effort is (or, in fact, reasonably can be) made to apply reasoning to religious strictures (see also the Preface, and Chapters 1 and 2). In what follows, we attempt to examine the history of the problem, to outline some of the points made about abortion by secular ethics, and will address the troubling and separate issue of legislating moral codes peculiar to specific enclaves to entire communities.

Historically, our attitudes toward abortion have varied. Law and usage have, at times, prohibited abortion for three reasons: (1) to protect the mother's life; (2) to protect an unborn life for its own sake; and (3) to protect the community or state. As technology has progressed, protecting the mother's life by prohibiting abortion made no sense. Under modern circumstances, protecting the unborn is the usual reason given. Nations plotting war (Nazi Germany, as an example) often have an interest in creating as many able-bodied men as possible and, therefore, an interest in protecting the unborn. At other times, the interest of the state in protecting the life of its members is appealed to. Such an appeal, however, begs the question since it fails to stipulate criteria for the kind of "life" entitling its bearer to such protection. The interest of the state in protecting all life is obviously far from absolute. States arm their police, prepare for or wage war, and execute criminals.

Among the Greeks, the father's right to decide his children's fate was upheld throughout the "golden ages."[1] In the Hippocratic tradition, physicians were enjoined against performing abortion just as they were prohibited from "cutting for stone." This stricture may reside in the fear of discrediting the physician through causing the death of the patient by a hazardous procedure (or, in the case of cutting for stone, of causing sterility), or it may be part of an essentially Pythagorean viewpoint, which informs so much of the Hippocratic oath.[2,3] Abortion done by midwives was not prohibited. Most physicians in ancient Greece, furthermore, were not Hippocratic physicians nor were they bound by an oath which apparently only a few took.[2,3] The practice of abortion, done by midwives or by physicians, was apparently widespread.[2]

Aristotle's influence on attitudes toward abortion in and outside the Christian Church has been profound. Briefly speaking, he held that the embryo was initially vegetative (nonanimated) and only later became "animated" as it was entered by the soul. Killing the nonanimated fetus was an act of destroying life but not murder; killing the animated fetus was an act of murder.[4-8] Aristotle equated animation with "quickening," and this criterion has been persistently appealed to.

Aristotle's concept profoundly influenced the early Christian Church. The critical question—"When does the soul enter the body?"—was usually answered along Aristotelian lines. Today's question—"When does personhood begin?"—asks the same question in secular terms. A very few early theologians (in the third century, Tertullian, for example) felt that the soul entered at conception, but they were in the minority. Most theologians agreed with St. Augustine (fifth century): killing the ensouled was murder; killing the unensouled was not. In the 13th century Pope Innocent III decreed that a priest who had been "party to a miscarriage" after quickening must refrain from serving mass, but one involved beforehand could continue to do so.

In the 13th century, St. Thomas Aquinas affirmed what is still the Catholic view today: killing an ensouled fetus is murder. What has changed is the view of ensoulment: Pope Clement VI in 1708 fixed the date at which Mary's soul entered her body as being 9 months before her birthdate, but abortion prior to quickening was not officially condemned. In 1854, in fixing the date for the feast of the Immaculate Conception, Pius IX reaffirmed that the soul of Mary entered her body at conception, and in an 1869 pronouncement the distinction between the ensouled and the unensouled fetus was removed. All souls entered at conception, and, therefore, abortion was murder. The fact that papal infallibility was promulgated the same year complicated the issue.

The technical advances of the 19th and 20th centuries, the greater understanding of infection and the development of safe anesthesia, enabled abortion to become a practical alternative rather than being a desperate last move. The risk of abortion to the mother when done in a proper medical setting no longer could serve as an excuse to outlaw abortion. Abortion was practical and safe, but was it ever morally permissible and, if so, when, where and why? Laws, both in Europe and America, created a situation in which the well-to-do and well-connected had relatively easy access to safe abortion services; the poor and ignorant continued to frequent back-alley abortionists. Death or, at times, desperate illness were the frequent consequences.   Gradually, laws and attitudes changed.

Since "rights" are usually held to be virtually absolute, since they are usually regarded as "trump cards" of moral reasoning, and since, therefore, an appeal to such "rights" is meant to settle the question, turning to "rights" of mother or fetus in such instances does not help.[9] If, however, instead of trying to adjudicate claims to clashing "rights," we look at "interests," a more flexible point of view results. A flexible point of view, of course, is the very thing that those who oppose abortion under all and every circumstance would contest. Flexibility is not possible when absolute positions are taken (for a more thorough discussion of "rights" and "justice," see Chapter 12).

In the view of those absolutely and completely opposed to abortion under all and every circumstance, the "right" of the unborn child (no matter how unformed) is inalienable. There are, in fact, not many who would hold such an absolute view. When confronted with a situation in which a 12-year-old girl's life is threatened by a pregnancy which was the result of incestuous rape and who now carries a fetus known to have a dominant gene for a psychiatrically devastating and horribly painful condition, many of those who previously affirmed their absolute opposition would falter. But absolutism of this sort does not permit faltering: the moment an exception is granted, the edifice of the "absolute" falls. For the purposes of this discussion, we shall assume that an absolute opposition to abortion under all and every circumstance cannot be justified except by an appeal to religious principle. If abortion were absolutely precluded on secular ethical grounds then, among other things, no rational discussion of the conflict would be needed or possible. Abortion would be wrong, and that would end the discussion.

In most pregnancies the interest of mother and fetus coincide; only in the unusual case does a conflict of interests exist. Such conflicts, then, are in need of moral adjudication. Making the interests of either binding under all circumstances settles by arbitrary fiat rather than by moral deliberation. Interests may clash in two ways: (1) the mother may wish to terminate the pregnancy "against the interest of the fetus" or (2) the mother, for whatever reason, may refuse to terminate a pregnancy when its outcome would be "against the fetus' interest." This latter situation, which has led to "wrongful life" suits, presupposes that persons have a legitimate interest in being born unhampered by serious congenital defects.[10] Such views are based on the further belief that it is preferable not to be born than to be born severely defective. In a sense, such a belief is analogous to the belief that it is better to be dead than to live life in certain ways. The issue of "wrongful life" is, however, an issue that has rarely come up and which is too complicated to be included here.

In dealing with the ethics of abortion, the two views forming the boundaries of the argument are: (1) the fetus from the moment of conception is, under all and every circumstance, of equal intrinsic value as the mother, and its destruction is, therefore, murder; and (2) the fetus is merely a part of the mother's body and may be dealt with as such without any moral concerns.

The first presupposition, that the fetus' life is of equal intrinsic value as that of the mother and that, therefore, its destruction is murder (and that such a murder is the moral equivalent of murdering the mother), rests on several premises: (1) the fetus is human life and, therefore, "sacred"; (2) the fetus is "innocent" and, therefore, deserving of full protection; (3) the potential of being a person (the potential for being of primary moral worth) endows it with the same rights as if it were a person (or of actual primary moral worth). The second presupposition, that which holds that the fetus is merely its mother's body part, denies all of these arguments. Moderate positions are often drowned out by the ensuing rhetoric and are further threatened by a stridency which threatens to enshrine personal morals as universal law.[11]

An argument that the fetus is not human life biologically does not hold water. The chromosome count is correct, and a sufficient number of other criteria for both "life" and "human" are met to leave no doubt as to this. That, however, is insufficient to endow an entity with primary or even secondary worth. A tissue culture of colonic mucosa growing in an incubator meets similar criteria for human life and yet could not sanely be considered as inviolable. It is, therefore, not just life (we kill animals and eat spinach) and not just human life (we throw out tissue cultures) which some would hold sacred. What, it seems, we hold as having *prima facie* rights against wanton destruction are entities endowed either with primary worth (those of value now or in the future again to themselves) or of secondary or symbolic worth (those of value to another in themselves or as representative of something held to be of value) (see also Chapter 2).

The argument from innocence is easier to deal with. The term "innocent" is a technical term first used by the Church in sorting out "justifiable" reasons for killing. Early Christianity saw all killing as wrong, even killing in war, as punishment, or in self-defense. The Roman Empire certainly could not countenance the right of citizens to refuse to fight in its armies. If Christianity were to be fully accepted, and if it were, as it ultimately did, to become a state religion, that dilemma had to be addressed. The language of "innocence" was invoked: "innocent" persons could not be killed; those who were not "innocent" could be. Only those who were not engaged in fighting in an unjust war or those who had not broken a just law ("just" being, of course, in either case defined by the state) could be held to be "innocent." Killing the noninnocent was, regrettably, a permissible act.[12] Curiously the interdiction against killing in self-defense persisted up to the time of Augustine. When, therefore, "innocence" is invoked in the abortion debate, it inevitably carries this historical baggage.

Innocence, applied to a fetus, is a peculiar concept. In general, innocence as opposed to guilt implies either that (1) an opportunity to do something has not been taken or (in a far more obscure sense) (2) that something was never done because there had been no opportunity. I can, for example, be innocent of murdering my wife if (despite opportunity and desire) I have failed to do so; or, I can be innocent of murdering Charlemagne since I never had the opportunity to do so. The first example of innocence might hold me exempt from punishment; the second would make even the idea of punishment incoherent. The fetus, in the first sense, lacked opportunity and in the second has failed to earn any special rights. (In a religious sense as "being innocent by virtue of being free of original sin," the fetus is no more free than is the infant: the difference, of course, is that the infant has, for the Christian hopefully, been baptized.) In its original Church meaning, as not having broken an unjust law or not fighting in an unjust war, the fetus is "innocent", but it is innocent by virtue of lacking the opportunity and not by virtue of having made a deliberate choice. Innocence seems to add little to a fetus' moral worth.

The argument from potentiality (resting, as it does, on the zygote's probability for being) is noteworthy.[13] The human zygote most certainly is a form of human life with the potential for being of primary moral worth (in the usual case, it is of secondary and of symbolic moral worth because of the immense value to the parents, but when abortion is the issue this is not the case). It is, in that respect, similar to an acorn, which has the potential of being an oak.[14] But, as Thompson has pointed out, "it does not follow that acorns are oak trees or that we had best say they are."[14] Zygotes, among other things, have the potential for being spontaneously aborted, for being malformed, as well as for becoming villains or saints. Further, a chimera may result from two or more fertilized eggs and the product may be multiple persons.[15] Potential to be, then, is for being many things, and it is unknowable. Potentiality (that the fetus has the potential for being of primary moral worth is, it seems, beyond reasonable dispute) certainly carries more moral weight than does the lack of that potential. The obvious question, however, is whether such moral weight is as entitling under most circumstances as is that of an actual entity unquestionably endowed with primary worth.

Comparisons between the fetus and an anesthetized or temporarily comatose patient are sometimes made because in both sets of circumstances a potential for sentient being exists. The difference between these two situations, among others, is that in the anesthetized or temporarily comatose new sense experience will be integrated into preexistent memory; in the fetus, prior to function of the neocortex at least, no preexistent memory exists. Anesthetized or comatose persons can be said to have had a preexisting vested interest in resuming their life with its biography, its unrealized plans, hopes, and aspirations, and, therefore, in their recovery, which fetuses do not have. Anesthetized or comatose persons have an identity beyond the spatiotemporal continuity of the physical body: their identity concerns continuity and connectedness of personality, memory, and other mental phenomena.[16] They "have a life" in addition to "being alive." In fetuses, this is not the case.

The presupposition that the fetus is merely a part of the mother's body to be disposed of without moral concerns ignores rather than refutes the previous arguments. By virtue of its potential, the fetus is uniquely different from other body parts. Distinct from them, it has a potential for being which merits concern; the colon, lacking this, does not. Wanton destruction of the colon may harm its host; wanton destruction of the fetus concerns both the host and, in an inchoate way, the fetus. There is, therefore, a legitimate and growing prima facie reason for not destroying the fetus that does not apply to other body parts.[17]

If the right (or interest) of the fetus not to be destroyed is seen as a *prima facie* right (or interest), it must be adjudicated against other claims. The force of the fetus' claim, as well as the force of the mother's, depends on the existential status of the claimants. The claim of the fetus gains in force as the central nervous system develops. This is the case because until sufficient development is present, the notion of present benefit and harm (the notion, that is, of being currently of primary moral worth) cannot rationally be upheld. At 8 weeks, brain waves begin to develop, and it is here, some suggest, that a life worthy of protection emerges.[5,18] The emergence of brain waves, however, does not denote the possession of faculties but, rather, the physical potential for their development.[5] Thus there seems to be a slowly growing force to a claim for life which reasonably starts at conception as a rather weak *prima facie* condition against being frivolously destroyed and grows, especially after the CNS proceeds to function. The CNS and its function form, according to that point of view, the necessary condition for the emergence of primary worth but do not constitute it. As the fetus grows, ever weightier reasons to set aside that *prima facie* right would seem necessary.

If one examines the issue, one is forced to come to two alternative conclusions: either (1) abortion under all and every circumstance is morally wrong or (2) there are instances in which abortion (albeit it still far from a praiseworthy act) can clearly be seen to be the lesser of two evils. If one subscribes to the second alternative, what remains is to enunciate those conditions under which maternal interests are weightier than are those of the fetus. One can, for example, retreat from an absolutist position and permit abortion when maternal life is threatened. This, in itself, is already a concession to the second stance.

Attitudes toward the ethical permissibility of abortion will vary depending on the person making this judgment. If one is to look at the matter in a nonabsolutist way, denying that either the mother's right to control her own body at all times or the infant's claim to have the right to live is absolute, one will be forced to apply certain criteria. As with end-of-life issues, one will have to differentiate between being alive (a biological statement) and having a life (a biographical statement denoting a capacity for hopes, aspirations, and social interconnections). Furthermore, one will have to acknowledge that while fetuses certainly are alive, they, at least early on, do not have a life (although they potentially do). Early on, at the very least, fetuses are not of primary moral worth (although they have the potential to be of primary worth) while pregnant women are. The moral worth of fetuses inheres in (1) their potential, (2) their secondary worth (which may be positive or negative) to the mother and perhaps to others, and (3) their symbolic worth as

future members of humanity. Deciding to participate or not to participate in an abortion becomes a personal balancing act in which such
considerations must be weighed and sifted.

An important issue remains: can communities, or majorities within them, enunciate a moral position outlawing abortion and, accordingly, promulgate binding laws? Should abortion, in other words, be a
political football subject to the rule of a (possibly slim) majority or,
perhaps, should such decisions be left to private conscience? And is
such private conscience to be given free reign at every stage of pregnancy or only at certain times or under certain conditions?

Communities, in making rules, must safeguard the interests of all
their members. In making judgments about abortion, communities may,
for example, decide to leave the issue up to the mother and to the
health care professional early in pregnancy and hedge abortion with
increasingly greater restrictions as the pregnancy proceeds until, once
viability is attained, abortion is only possible to safeguard the seriously
threatened life of the mother. Such judgments, then, are predicated not
upon an absolute view of rights and wrongs but rather on a realization
of a changing situation in which fetal interests (and, therefore, communal interests in safeguarding fetuses) grow. Judgments of this sort, furthermore, are subject to change. Flexibility would allow new evidence
and new technical developments to affect the communal ethos from
which, after all, such judgments emerge.

The argument that outlawing abortion is analogous to outlawing
slavery (that is, that abortion at any stage of pregnancy is an evil which
is clearly enough an evil so that outlawing it becomes a legitimate
communal concern) has often been made. Some argue that since many
within a community felt slavery to be morally permissible, outlawing
slavery has a similar standing to outlawing abortion. Abolitionists and
"right-to-lifers" are seen to be similarly concerned with advancing moral views and with safeguarding individual "rights." Slaveholders and
those who would leave abortion to individual choice, are likewise
equated in this calculus. On the face of it, the argument has logic: if we
equate the black man or woman with the embryo, the conclusion follows. But the argument is flawed. The basic assumption equating the
status of slaves with those of embryos cannot withstand closer scrutiny.
Slaves evidently have actual, rather than merely potential, primary
moral worth; fetuses (at least early on) do not. Slaves (or disadvantaged
persons) can suffer. They actively feel the whip (or sense the discrimi-
nation against them) and they know the pain of slavery or disadvantage; fetuses do not. Slaves, furthermore, are part of the community
which holds slaves. They have the immediate ability to participate in

judgments but are artificially disenfranchised. They stand mute. The muteness of the fetus is of a different order.

Outlawing slavery is necessary to safeguard actual others who may come to harm. It is of the same order as laws against speeding, spitting on the sidewalk, or murdering teen-agers. Outlawing abortion, on the other hand, is predicated on an unique and not demonstrable belief system which claims actual value for potential attributes. It is of the same moral order as attending church, keeping the Sabbath, or having sex with another consenting adult. Enforcement of such matters legitimately belongs within the social sanction of specific groups or belief systems. The community that enforces such belief systems in legal form arguably disrupts its own peace.

SEVERELY DEFECTIVE NEWBORNS

Some years ago a child with Down's syndrome and pyloric obstruction was born at Johns Hopkins Hospital. The parents, after considerable agony, refused surgery. Consistent with their wishes, the baby was not given nutrients or fluids and was allowed to die.[19] Similar cases in future years—some with Down's syndrome, others with far more severe mental and/or physical deformities and with various degrees of hopefulness or hopelessness—became ever-more-troubling issues. The recommendation that such decisions should be jointly and solely handled by physicians and parents[20] not only confronted communal sensibilities but also ran the severe danger of being capricious or arbitrary; the attempt of the government, essentially by "dumping" all such defects into a single pigeonhole, to settle the issue by fiat likewise proved unworkable and extreme.[21–24]

This issue is indeed one exacerbated, if not created, by modern technology. Until fairly recently, most children with severe defects either succumbed to their primary defect or died as a result of a number of relentless and untreatable intercurrent illnesses. Today's technology has made many of these conditions treatable without in any way affecting the underlying basic problem. Settling such problems by developing dogmatic formulas on the one hand (and thus to reduce moral decision making to a cookie-cutting approach) or settling such cases purely on the whim of those immediately concerned without reference to guidelines (and thus to leave such weighty decisions to a process in which the benefit of the patient may be given short shrift) is superficially tempting but begs the particular question. A middle course more conducive to finding just answers needs to be developed.[25]

The problem has at least several presentations: (1) those in which children are mentally presumably normal but suffer from severe (albeit, perhaps, partially correctable) physical handicaps (neural tube defects are the main example); (2) children with a life-threatening defect as well as a permanent irremediable handicap (Down's syndrome with duodenal atresia would be an example); (3) infants born perhaps apparently normal but inevitably destined to die of a relentlessly progressive degenerative condition with or without severe discomfort long before reaching an age of more than a few years. Such infants may maintain normal mentation throughout their period of decline (as, for example, Werdnig-Hoffman) or may be fated to have their initially normal mentation as well as their physical state deteriorate (as, for example, Tay-Sachs); (4) the severely premature, hopelessly respirator-dependent newborn with, perhaps, severe intracerebral bleeding; and (5) newborns with little or no higher cortical activity (the anencephalic or the near-anencephalic child). At first glance, there seems little in common among these considerations. In all of these cases the prognosis is bad, but it is bad in different ways and for different reasons.

In the first instance, unless complicated by other cerebral conditions, the problem is almost purely physical. But, at times, the physical part cannot be ameliorated without prolonged, often severe and persistent suffering. Chances for leading a normal life range from slim to fair, depending upon the particular condition encountered. In the second case (Down's syndrome with, say, duodenal atresia), the prognosis of the underlying disease is quite acceptable provided the rather easy-to-repair defect is, in fact, repaired. In such cases, one is left with a child able to feel pleasure and pain even though not at a level we are wont to consider normal. There can be no question that such children, since they are capable of being benefited and harmed, are of primary moral worth and that considerations of their secondary worth (their value to others) must take a back seat. What is more questionable is the parents' responsibility to undertake the care of such children without community support.

In the third example, infants are mentally normal initially, but either their mentation or their physical state will rapidly and relentlessly decline until they die. Although both Werdnig-Hoffman and Tay-Sachs children will die an early death, children with conditions such as Werdnig-Hoffman will be able to feel pleasure, or at least pain, and maintain primary worth up to the very end; those with conditions like Tay-Sachs will not. In effect, children who maintain their mentation up to the very end must, for that reason, be considered quite differently than those who do not. When the ability to feel pleasure and pain is maintained, parents stand in place of the child in helping to determine what is in his or her best interest (they, in other words, act as surrogates, and the child's best interest remains central); when, however, the ability to be benefited or harmed no longer is present, the "best interest" of the child assumes symbolic significance.[26] Arguably, parents and the best interest of the parents and of the rest of the family now move much more into the center stage of ethical decision making.

In the fourth instance, encountered all too often in the neonatal nursery, an inevitably hopeless condition, often with little or no mentation, is present. There are gradations of this. When the ability to feel pleasure or pain in adults is severely and permanently limited in the face of little chance for physical recovery, attempts to maintain their existence are seriously questioned and are often abandoned (see Chapter 10). In children, emotive and symbolic considerations in analogous cases often sway us to make starkly different (and, at times, difficult to defend) judgments.

In the fifth instance (that of the anencephalic infant) there is no hope for physical survival and no mentation. Such children, in our terminology, lack primary moral worth, albeit that secondary and symbolic worth endures. A situation analogous to that of the vegetative state exists (see Chapter 10). Dealing with such infants differently merely because they are infants is rooted in emotive and symbolic considerations. (The problem of using such infants as organ donors is briefly addressed below.)

In dealing with problems concerning impaired infants, then, a number of problems exist. First of all, such infants cannot give or withhold consent; decisions inevitably are made by surrogate judgment (in which the parents, acting as surrogates, speak for the children) or by substitute judgment (in which health professionals, or the courts, substitute their own judgment). In adults, there is a sharper differential between surrogate and substitute judgments: surrogates, by virtue of acting as surrogates, are felt to have closer ties with the patient's prior worldview, and such surrogates, therefore, would be more likely to judge through the eyes of the patient's values; substitute judgments, perforce, are based on the judgment of strangers who inevitably will choose through their own values. The infant's values and worldviews are inchoate, unknown, and unknowable; their probable judgments are opaque. The difference between surrogate and substitute judgments, therefore, is more blurred and tenuous.

Secondly, when judgments are made for infants, they are embodied in a set of preconceived emotional and symbolic considerations quite different from those which operate in adults, especially in elderly adults. It is often difficult to keep the disease and the patient's actual condition and prognosis, rather than the age of the patient, in mind and to judge accordingly.

Thirdly, the calculus between risk and benefit is even more obscure: we tend to judge benefit and pain from our own vantage point. Pain, on the one hand, may be easier to endure by us by virtue of being understood; for the infant or young child, lack of ability to understand and, therefore, terror may also enter the equation (see also the section in Chapter 10 dealing with limiting treatment in demented patients).

Fourthly, predicting success or failure is extremely difficult in the neo-natal period. Viability varies as technology changes and the definition of what is and what is not "viable" is, in itself, a difficult one. If by viability one means biological survival, it is one thing; if viability is taken to mean biological survival permitting an acceptable life, it may well be another. Here more than in most other places, the "ethics of uncertainty" must be taken into account.[26]

The current Baby Doe regulations were historically first made to prevent arbitrary nontreatment of defective newborns. Initially, this regulation forced the treatment of all defective infants no matter what the defect and for as long as treatment was technically possible. The wishes of the parents or the opinions of health professionals were quite irrelevant. Hospitals were forced to post the telephone number of a "hot line," and anyone was encouraged to report the "mistreatment" of such an infant. Flying squads were set up, and hospitals could, at any time, be inspected and their routine disrupted by federal officials. The results were disastrous, and the courts eventually declared this venture to be unconstitutional.

The regulations today have been somewhat modified.[26] Instead of being tied to civil rights considerations, they are now tied to federal funding and controlled by the states: states that wish to participate in funding must comply. At the present time there is some optionality, although there is still the danger of unwarranted intrusion: in making decisions neonatologists ostensibly may not consider the child's probable future impairment and quality of life.[26] Neonatologists, in general, have been very sensitive to this issue. In a recent large-scale survey, neonatologists felt that the regulations even today not infrequently result in unwarranted, useless, and, at times, even cruel treatment.[27] Quality-of-life issues and considerations dealing with the future impairment and function of such children, far from being prejudicial to the cases being judged, are their essence.

Informed Consent in Children

Although the validity of parental consent for children has been taken for granted, absolute parental freedom to make final judgments for their children has been found to be increasingly problematic. If, of course, one were to presume that parents inevitably choose in their child's best interest and if one, under all circumstances, allows the parents alone to define that interest, no problems exist.

But do parents always have their child's best interest at heart, and do they always know what that interest is? What if parents have their own agenda (if, for example, they stand to benefit from a life insurance policy on their child's life or, far more subtly, if they have to make judgments which must balance the interest of a severely impaired child against that of other normal children)? What if the parents see it against the child's best interest to be transfused (because in the parents' viewpoint such transfusion spoils the chance of going to Heaven for their child) or see it concordant with their child's interest to allow the child to become a subject of nontherapeutic experimentation?[28]

Not least, how to define "a child" and how to adjudicate the "child's" proper role in deciding what should and what should not be done is highly questionable if only because the legal question ("when is a child a child") is only feebly connected with the growing autonomy of developing adults. Looking at autonomy in the 3-, the 10-, and the 15-year-old in the same way is patently ridiculous. The "mature minor" rule, a rule which permits medical treatment without parental consent under certain circumstances after age 15,[29] and other statutes covering "emancipated minors" (which vary from jurisdiction to jurisdiction) give a partial solution at what is inevitably an arbitrary cut-off point but otherwise beg the question. Maturing, it would seem, is neither an all-or-nothing proposition nor altogether predictable by age. Ethically, the best that we can do is to judge individual situations on their own merits using arbitrarily fixed groupings merely as statistical guideposts on our way.

Parental rights over their children are not absolute: parents are not at liberty to destroy, maim, or neglect their children. The interest of the state in protecting individuals does, at least as far as physical abuse is concerned, act to safeguard children. The question, "Can anyone give proxy consent for another which is not in that other's best interest?" is not easily answered, for it leaves the interest of that other necessarily undefined.[30]

While parents, in our society, are not at liberty to destroy their children, their power over such children nevertheless goes very far.

Parents, for example, can have their children operated on for religious reasons alone (circumcision is, perhaps, the most frequent example). They are free to inculcate their children with rather injurious points of view and teach them rather devastatingly destructive things. Parents, for example, can bring up their children as flagrant racists and teach them the gentle art of handling submachine guns without running the risk of community interference. As always, it is a problem of balancing communal and personal obligations. It is, however, a problem with a twist: a third party is involved.

When it comes to making determinations for infants or very young children, "interests" as viewed in our community must conform to societal norms. Parents are not at liberty (legally, at least) to abstain from consenting to clearly life-saving procedures. A difference between the right to assent to a procedure clearly for another's benefit (transfusion or appendectomy, for example) and the right to refuse such a procedure for another and risk, or bring about, certain death has been made.[31] Physicians, when confronted with situations in which a child's parents refuse to permit a clearly life-saving procedure in very young children, have historically been able to obtain a court order or, if a pressing emergency exists, to proceed without a court order until such an order can be obtained.[31]

A child's refusal to permit life-saving treatment—especially when that child is of more mature years and has been further matured by experience, when the illness itself is not reversible, or when treatment has only a slim chance or is excessively burdensome—is an agonizing one. In the adolescent, the decision properly is one in which the patient maximally participates[32]; in younger children, it is often one in which participation becomes more and more problematic. But here, as in all other pediatric issues in which children able to express themselves coherently are involved, the decision is, at the very least, a communal one in which the child is a partner in the communal enterprise of decision making and not an inanimate object to be acted on by others.[33–35]

Experimentation in children is even more problematic. Ramsey[36,37] has argued that "consent as a canon of loyalty" precludes the use of children for experimentation unless, all other means having failed, such experimentation can reasonably be believed to result in direct benefit to the child. He includes "offensive touching" in the course of experimentation (drawing blood, for example) in this interdiction. Others have taken a more moderate view in which minimally risky and minimally offensive procedures may be permissible, whereas others may not.[28,38,39]

Experimentation in children, obviously, must first of all conform to the ethically acceptable principles of research.[40,41] Beyond this and since children, together with prisoners, the mentally defective and, at times, the elderly, are particularly vulnerable to abuse, further safeguards are essential.[42,43] Unfortunately, some research, research which is often of the greatest importance to future generations of children, can only be performed on children. Recognizing this, the National Commission for the Protection of Human Subjects came up with specific guidelines in such circumstances.[42,44] Guidelines included the requirements that (1) risks must be minimal except in circumstances in which the subject him or herself would have a fair prospect of benefiting, and (2) permission of parents and, where possible, assent of the child are free and informed. Such guidelines fail to answer the moral question in particular cases. They are not mindless rules to be applied in cookie-cutter fashion, and they do require a further analysis and definition of "risk" as well as of "free consent." If taken as guidelines instead of as substitutes for moral reasoning, they may begin to serve well.

ANENCEPHALIC CHILDREN

The issue of using anencephalic infants as organ donors has recently been raised. In part this interest has resulted from the greater success that transplantation in more mature humans has had, and in part it is stimulated by the necessity of extending our frontiers of knowledge further. The parents of such prospective children frequently wish to see at least some perceived good resulting from their personal tragedy; the publicity that the media have given to this issue have helped keep the issue before the public eye. Using such infants has been hailed by some as providing more badly needed organs while, at the same time, being decried by others because of the perceived affront to human dignity of extending the biological existence of a newborn merely for the sake of harvesting organs. The battle was joined when infants of this sort actually began to be used for this purpose.

Using infants (or other humans) who are actually brain dead as organ donors offers few problems to most people today. Such (previous) persons are legally and ethically acknowledged to be dead, and only those who would object to organ transplantation, cadaver usage, or the temporary preservation of biological process until organs can be harvested would object. And those objections are a different story.[45] Anencephalic infants offer a problem because criteria for brain death under a week of age are not firm[46] and because some persons are affronted by keeping such infants on a respirator merely to harvest their organs (see also Chapter 9).

The anencephalic child is not brain dead. It is, however, bereft of the necessary substrate which is acknowledged to underwrite perception. Anencephalic infants, now and in the future, lack the capacity for experience, and preserving such a life as a condition for experience is therefore futile. Such children, in other words, lack the capacity to suffer and, therefore, lack "primary worth" or the potentiality to develop "primary worth" (see Chapter 2). As noted before, a large body of experimental evidence indicates that the capacity to suffer is intimately connected with the presence of a neocortex. It is the neocortex which in those biological organisms known to us, underwrites thought and memory. It is memory (the ability to recognize and to have sustained perception) which underwrites thought, here defined as the integration of external or internal sense perception into memory. And it is the capacity to suffer, underwritten by the neocortex, that endows entities with the primary moral worth which makes them fitting centerpieces for the physician's moral consideration. Anencephalics lack the necessary condition for suffering.

That is not to say that such infants are without value. On the contrary: value here is because of the real and symbolic valuing done by the parents and by the community. Anencephalics thus have "symbolic moral worth" and, for those in need of organs, "secondary worth."

Communities, which value anencephalic and brain dead persons in a symbolic way, also include those members of the community who are in need of organs to sustain their existence. Since anencephalic infants cannot be harmed or benefited in themselves, since by our definition they are not of "primary worth," the ethical question is not as much concerned with such infants as it is with the benefit or harm that our doing or not doing things to such infants has for others. In the first instance, this then would be a question of parental values. When the parents, however, freely agree to the use of their child's organs (and in some instances at least perceive that some good for another may come out of that tragedy to themselves), communal values come into play. Communities, who ultimately must judge the morality and legality of using such infants, now must decide whether they will value symbol or reality more: the symbol of humanity represented by the anencephalic child or the reality presented by members of the community who may live because of that symbol. Valuing symbols more than the reality which they portray can lead to a dangerous undervaluing of reality and, ultimately, to its distortion (see Chapter 9 for a further discussion).

When we deal with anencephalic infants, however, we are not dealing with the brain dead as we do when we harvest organs. These infants have a rudimentary brain stem and have some reflex activity. Inevitably and rather rapidly, however, they deteriorate until they can be supported only by artifice. This is not quite the same as maintaining the brain dead: or is it? In both cases our decision not to support by artifice is grounded on the conviction that such artifice serves only to prolong a state of being that, by no reasonable measure, now or in the future again, can be considered to be self-knowing, self-realizing, and, therefore, to have the capacity for suffering. In such cases, what is being maintained is a highly complex and intricate tissue culture bereft of those things which give it, in itself, meaning. What meaning there is, is meaning for others who themselves are self-knowing and self-realizing. Anencephalics cannot, now or in the future, experience suffering or joy; they lack "primary worth." To fear that maintaining such infants by artifice until donation can be effected might violate the reverence owed to them, is to conflate symbol and reality. Such infants do have value, but it is a value expressed by others (the parents as well as the community) who value. Such infants, in themselves, cannot be benefited or harmed: only the valuers can be. The parents, the community, and the person desperately in need of an organ to maintain life or restore function form the legitimate centerpiece of our concern when it comes to the disposition of such infants.

Members of the community, those with and those without a need for organs, form communities because they share an underlying set of values. Among these values are the symbols they cherish, the conventions they adopt, and the regard they have for each other's weal and woe. The value of living persons whose life may be extended or made more tolerable by transplantation of needed organs must be contrasted with the value of the symbol that the anencephalic or the newly dead represents. Neither the anencephalic nor the brain dead are entities of primary worth but neither are they therefore without any value at all. It is valuing done by others which gives anencephalic infants both symbolic and secondary worth: the valuing done by the parents and the community gives symbolic worth; the valuing done by those in desperate need of transplantable organs gives them secondary worth. If those for whom the anencephalic has symbolic worth are willing to use this symbolism to help another member of the community, the community can have no reasonable objection.

There is one other troubling and perhaps more important issue, which has, perhaps, not been sufficiently raised: that is the question of using newborns, healthy but for the adequate function of a single vital organ, as experimental objects under these circumstances. Where a human track record exists, or at least where a comparable animal model has been shown as workable, such a move may, under very constrained conditions, be justified. Even here, the problem of surrogate informed consent may be a troubling issue. Where, however, a track record is lacking, and where animal models are not sufficient to light the way, such experiments are highly problematic. It is clear that no absolute certainty exists and that progress depends upon a careful forging ahead into the unknown; but reasonable, careful progression of experimentation must and should precede the extension of a procedure to patients. Innovation without this seems ill-conceived. That, to me, is one of the central problems in transplantation from the anencephalic. Experimentation must not be conflated with therapeusis, no matter how devoutly effective treatment is hoped for.

Surrogate Motherhood

Surrogate motherhood—the procedure by which one woman is hired by another to bear children which the first, for whatever reason, was unable to conceive or carry—has become a practical reality and an ethical problem.[47-50] It is a problem because the interests of the surrogate and the mother may strive for the same goal initially but later, in great part because of the influence of biological, emotional, and social forces, diverge dramatically. Payment, it has been shown, plays a significant role in most persons' decisions to be surrogates.[51,52] Inevitably, it is the wealthier who can and do afford to rent the uterus of one who is poorer. Renting out one's uterus, no matter how one feels about contracts, is not the same as renting out one's garage or even one's time and skill to do a job. A good deal more than that is at stake.

Surrogate motherhood, at least in one of its manifestations, is, furthermore, a misnomer.[53] "Surrogacy" is used in at least two different ways: (1) The "surrogate" may be artificially fertilized with the sperm of the father, carries the pregnancy, and then surrenders the child to the biological father (and, presumably, his spouse). "Surrogacy" here is indubitably a misnomer: the mother, in every sense, is the biological mother. (2) The "surrogate" may have another's ovum, artificially or otherwise inseminated by a male, implanted in her uterus. She then carries a fetus in whose genes she does not share. In the sense of not having contributed to the genetic makeup of the offspring, she is not the biological mother; in the sense of carrying the pregnancy and, inevitably, becoming biologically and perhaps emotionally involved, she is.

Here we shall refer to the "surrogate mother" in either instance but caution that the misapplication of the term in the first and the possible, or at least partial, misapplication of the term in the second instance must be kept in mind. As in many other instances, the language in which we frame problems plays a significant role in their final adjudication.

If one views communities as united merely by duties of refraining and sees in freedom an absolute condition (see Chapter 2), one will have little problem seeing in surrogacy a purely personal concern. On the other hand, if communities, instead of subscribing to a purely autonomy-based justice, include beneficence as a necessary ethical condition, such contracts may be more suspect.

Two views of "surrogacy" then are possible. One bases its justification on the right of consenting adults to control their destinies as long as they do not impinge on others. Such a view holds that surrogacy falls into such a category: persons have knowingly contracted together, the contract is valid, it is no one else's business, and that is the end of the matter. Contract laws, here to enforce valid contracts, can be invoked. The other view sees surrogacy as involving far more than merely a contract which is no one else's business. Although it is a contract between consenting adults who do have a right to control their own destiny, such a right is enmeshed in a social matrix of values and not, therefore, inevitably no one else's concern.

Persons who oppose surrogacy, do so because they feel that (1) mothers, during pregnancy, inevitably have a surge of hormones and undergo other changes which more often than not, result in their bonding with the child they carry. When such children must then be given up, severe hardship and, therefore, battles likely to be socially disruptive may occur. (2) Having one woman (almost inevitably poorer) carry the child of another (almost invariably considerably more affluent) is an act of social condescension likely to be communally disruptive. (3) The use of resources to create more life instead of taking care of existing life is ill-advised. There are many children in need of adoption who will never be, and perhaps first ought to be, adopted. Many, furthermore, feel that often a racist agenda motivates the desire to try surrogacy instead of adopting a child in need of a home.

Women, under current laws, are not allowed to sell their babies or, at least, to do so outright. The restrictions against this are restrictions made not only for the good of the infant but, ultimately, to safeguard the community. Those who feel this way feel that organs, blood, and children are different from cars, houses, and even one's labor and that, therefore, they ought not simply to be for sale.

Surrogacy is, perhaps, not quite the same thing. In a community which puts a high value (let alone in a community which puts an absolute value) on personal freedom and choice, especially when it comes to the use of one's own body, making rules that restrict such contracts between well-informed and freely consenting adults is, at the least, problematic. Those who argue for surrogacy largely rely on such an argument. Contracts, on the other hand, exist within the embrace of a social milieu and, at the very least, have to be mindful of it. In communities which put a high value on freedom, making such contracts and enforcing them may not be morally precluded; if, however, such contracts are socially disruptive, or if by making such contracts resources are used that could be otherwise (and in the communal view better) used better in other ways, such contracts may be unwise enough to be problematic.

Forced Cesarian Section and Fetal Abuse

There has been a recent trend to attempt to control the behavior of pregnant women during their pregnancy in order to "safeguard" the fetus. These attempts have taken a variety of forms: the first are enforced C-sections in which women, by court order, are forced to undergo C-sections[54]; the second is the attempt to bring charges of "fetal abuse" against women who are felt to have contributed to the damage done to a fetus during pregnancy.[55]

In one such case a woman, dying of metastatic cancer and carrying a possibly viable fetus, was forced to undergo C-section. This was done on the basis of a court order issued at the hospital's request despite her own, her husband's, and her doctor's vigorous objection. The patient as well as her offspring died.[55] Throughout the country, court-ordered C-sections have become increasingly more customary.[56]

In another case, a pregnant woman delivered a brain-dead infant. She was charged with fetal abuse because she had allegedly not followed her physician's advice against taking amphetamines and having intercourse during pregnancy and had delayed coming to the hospital when she began to have some bleeding. That case was eventually dismissed on a technicality, but the possibility of other cases of this sort has been very much discussed.[57]

Obstetricians formerly felt that their relationship was with the mother. The child, except perhaps for those who under no circumstances would ever abort the mother, was an important, but not a prime, consideration. Some of these feelings have changed today.

Obstetricians often feel as much concern for the fetus as they do for the mother, and apparently sometimes more. In a questionnaire submitted to the heads of maternal-fetal medicine at 57 institutions, 46% thought that "mothers who endangered the life of the fetus should be detained in hospitals or other facilities so that compliance could be ensured"; 47% thought that the precedent for enforced Cesarean sections should be "extended to include other procedures that are potentially life-saving for the fetus"; and 26% advocated "state surveillance of women who stay outside the hospital system in the third trimester."[58] The obstetric literature reflects the concern of practicing obstetricians. The forceful delivery of patients by operative intervention (or even coercing them to do or not to do "as the doctor orders") is becoming more routinely considered and, at times, done.[59–62] The tendency to consider the mother primarily as an incubator for her developing infant is growing.

In looking at these issues, there are two problems: the first deals with whether or not it is unethical for a mother who had decided not to terminate a pregnancy to jeopardize the fetus by doing or neglecting to do certain things; the second deals with the rights of communities to force women to do or not to do things to their own body during the course of pregnancy. These are different questions: the first clearly deals with personal morality; the second with the community's right to enforce its own vision of personal morality on its members. There are clearly instances (murder, for example) when communities do, and we feel should, enforce such visions; there are others when such visions are not sufficiently clear. Enforcement, under such circumstances, becomes quite a different matter (see also the discussion of abortion above).

Women who are pregnant, generally (but not always; some states refuse to fund Medicaid abortions) have the opportunity to terminate their pregnancy. When women choose not to terminate their pregnancy, they voluntarily choose to take on at least some responsibility for a developing other.[63] Members of a community have an obligation to help, or at the very least not to harm, other members of community no matter what vision of community they may share. Such obligations are arguably strengthened when certain relationships are freely assumed: that of physician to patient, professor to student, or father to child are examples. Pregnant women who choose not to abort would seem to share in such a relationship with their developing infant. That does not mean that every moment of their life or every action of their body must be devoted to this enterprise. But it does advance the claim that some responsibility exists and that totally ignoring the good of the offspring is basically an irresponsible thing to do. The extent of this responsibility is, to a large degree, a social vision and one that will show considerable variation from community to community and from individual to individual. But that there is some responsibility is hard to deny.

On the other hand, the obligations women have to their offspring are not entirely analogizable to those of physician to patient or professor to student. Physicians do not have the obligation (at least I have never heard this argued!) to consistently do things to their bodies (other than to get fatigued, perhaps) in order to promote their patient's welfare. No one would seriously consider it to be a doctor's duty to donate blood or to undergo a surgical procedure for the patient's good. Physicians who give blood (or kidneys) to their patients are considered to be doing a supererogatory thing. When women are held to have obligations to their developing offspring, these obligations inevitably must be translated through their own bodies. In the view of some, pregnant women must follow their obstetrician's instructions to the letter even if this means a radical alteration in their life-style: they must take, or refrain from taking, certain drugs or foods, must exercise or not exercise, must undergo or not undergo certain procedures, etc. And they must do this not only because it is "good for the baby" but also because their obstetrician has decided that it is, in fact, good for the baby. Their doctor, for the duration of the pregnancy, becomes the patient's master.

Granting that an obligation toward the developing fetus on the part of the mother exists is not the same as claiming either that this obligation is absolute (that, in other words, women must follow their obstetrician's dictates to the letter) or that such obligations can or should be legally enforced. The law, under ordinary circumstances, cannot compel persons to do things to their bodies that they do not choose to do.[56,57] I cannot be forced to go to bed or not to go to bed at certain hours and I cannot be forced to undergo bypass surgery against my will. Communities can force me not to take illicit drugs but their power, even in that respect, is modified by the right to privacy which I enjoy. Debatably it may be immoral for me not to take a medication which would enable me to be gainfully employed and by so doing (or not doing) deprive my family of a decent livelihood, but legally forcing me to do this is another matter. Some analogies to the issue of "self-causation" when we invoke the patient's responsibility for his or her own disease, exists[64] (see also Chapter 12).

ECONOMIC CONSIDERATIONS

As with "end of life" issues, economic considerations cannot be the primary ethical motivating forces when it comes to decisions between physicians and patients. This statement is historically grounded in our current vision of the physician-patient relationship (see Chapter 4). The physician's obligation to his or her patient, however, does not exist outside the social context and cannot be unmindful of it. At the very least, doing expensive and useless things at a time when resources are sorely needed to accomplish desperately needed and rather modestly priced therapeutic or preventive measures, is problematic. Ways must be found to accommodate the evolving vision of the physician-patient relationship in its social nexus without either radically dismantling one or the other (see Chapter 12). Physicians, in today's society, must serve as advisors to the community as well as physicians to individual patients. Since communities expect this function, and since physicians historically have discharged such functions, the social contract enabling medicine demands as much.

REFERENCES

1. Durant, W., *The Life of Greece*, Simon & Schuster, New York, 1939.
2. Carrick, P., *Medical Ethics in Antiquity*, D. Reidel, Boston, 1985.
3. Edelstein, L., The Hippocratic oath, in: *Ancient Medicine: Selected Papers of Ludwig Edelstein* (O. Temkin and C.L. Temkin, eds.), The Johns Hopkins Press, Baltimore, 1967, pp. 3–63.
4. Dunstan, G.R., The moral status of the human embryo: A tradition recalled, *J. Med. Ethics* 1:38–44, 1984.
5. Kushner, T., Having a life versus being alive, *J. Med. Ethics* 1:5–8, 1984.
6. Engelhardt, H.T., Bioethics and the process of embodiment, *Perspect. Biol. Med.* 18:486–500, 1975.
7. Aristotle, *De Generatione Animalium*, in: *The Basic Works of Aristotle* (R. McKeon, ed.), Random House, New York, 1971.
8. Engelhardt, H.T., The ontology of abortion, *Ethics* 84:217–234, 1974.
9. Churchill, L.R., and Simàn, J.J., Abortion and the rhetoric of individual rights, *Hastings Center* 12(1):9–12, 1982.
10. Annas, G.J., Righting the wrong of wrongful life, *Hastings Center* 11(1):8–9, 1981.
11. Loewy, E.H., Unsticking the sticky wicket of abortion, in: *Ethical Dilemmas in Modern Medicine: A Physician's Viewpoint* (E.H. Loewy, ed.), Edwin Mellen Press, Lewiston, NY, 1986, pp. 155–178.
12. Rachels, J., *The End of Life*, Oxford University Press, New York, 1986.
13. Noonan, J.T., An almost absolute value in history, in: *The Morality of Abortion: Legal and Historical Perspectives* (J.T. Noonan, ed.), Harvard University Press, Cambridge, 1970.
14. Thomson, J.J., A defense of abortion, *Phil. Public. Affairs* 1(1):47–66, 1971.
15. Milby, T.H., The new biology and the question of personhood: Implications for abortion, *Am. J. Law Med.* 9(1):31–41, 1983.
16. Green, M.B., and Winkler, D., Brain death and personal identity, *Phil. Public Affairs* 9(2):104–133, 1980.

17. Warren, M.A., On the moral and legal status of abortion, *Monist* 57:43–61, 1973.
18. Jones, G.E., Fetal brain waves and personhood, *J. Med. Ethics* 10:216–218, 1984.
19. Gustafson, J.M., Mongolism, parental desires and the right to life, *Perspect. Biol. Med.* 16:529–559, 1973.
20. Duff, R.S., and Campbell, G.M., Moral and ethical dilemmas in the special-care nursery, *N. Engl. J. Med.* 289(25):890–894, 1973.
21. Robertson, J.A., Dilemma in Danville, *Hastings Center* 11(5):5–8, 1981.
22. Arras, J.D., Toward an ethic of ambiguity, *Hastings Center* 14(2):25–33, 1984.
23. Campbell, A.G.M., Which infants should not receive intensive care? *Arch. Dis. Child.* 57:569–575, 1982.
24. Annas, G.J., Checkmating the Baby Doe regulations, *Hastings Center* 16(4):29–31, 1986.
25. McCormick, R.A., To save or let die: The dilemma of modern medicine, *J.A.M.A.* 229(8):172–176, 1974.
26. Rhoden, N.K., Treating Baby Doe: The ethics of uncertainty, *Hastings Center* 16(3):34–42, 1986.
27. Kopelman, L.M., Irons, T.G., and Kopelman, A.E., Neonatologists judge the Baby Doe regulations, *N. Engl. J. Med.* 318(11):677–683, 1988.
28. McCormick, R.A., Proxy consent in the experimentation situation, *Perspect. Biol. Med.* 18(1):2–20, 1974.
29. Holder, A.R., *Legal Issues in Pediatrics and Adolescent Medicine*, John Wiley & Sons, New York, 1977.
30. Langham, P., Parental consent: Its justification and limitations, *Clin. Res.* 27(5):349–358, 1979.
31. Shaw, A., Dilemmas of "informed consent" in children, *N. Engl. J. Med.* 289:885–890, 1973.
32. Schowalter, J.E., Ferholt, J.B., and Mann, N.M., The adolescent patient's decision to die, *Pediatrics* 51(1):44–46, 1973.
33. Gaylin, W.A., The competence of children: No longer all or none, *Hastings Center* 12(2):33–38, 1982.
34. Bartholome, W.G., In defense of a child's right to assent, *Hastings Center* 12(4):44–45, 1982.
35. Gaylin, W.A., Reply to Bartholome, *Hastings Center* 12(4):45, 1982.
36. Ramsey, P., *The Patient as Person*, Yale University Press, New Haven, 1970.
37. Ramsey, P., The enforcement of morals: Non-therapeutic research on children, *Hastings Center* 6(4):21–30, 1976.
38. O'Donnell, T.J., Informed consent, *J.A.M.A.* 227:73–75, 1974.
39. Curran, C.E., Human life, *Chicago Stud.* 13(3):279–299, 1974.
40. Levine, R.J., and Lebazqz, K., Ethical considerations in clinical trials, *Clin. Pharmacol. Ther.* 25(2):732–741, 1979.
41. Fried, C., *Medical Experimentation: Personal Integrity and Social Policy*, Elsevier, New York, 1974.
42. National Commission for the Protection of Human Subjects of Biomedical and Behavioral Research, *Report and Recommendations: Research Involving Children*, DHEW Pub. (77–0004), Washington, 1977.
43. Marston, R.Q., Research on minors, prisoners and the mentally ill, *N. Engl. J. Med.* 288(3):158–159, 1973.
44. McCartney, J.J., Research on children: National commission says "Yes, if . . . ," *Hastings Center* 8(5):26–31, 1978.

45. Loewy, E.H., Waste not, want not: Communities and presumed consent, in: *Medical Ethics: A Guide for Health Professionals* (D.C. Thomasma and J.C. Monagle, eds.), Aspen Publishers, Rockville, MD, 1988.
46. Task Force for the Determination of Brain Death in Children, Guidelines for the determination of brain death in children, *Ann. Neurol.* 21:616–617, 1987.
47. Elias, S., and Annas, G.J., Social policy and ethical considerations in noncoital reproduction, *J.A.M.A.* 255(1):62–68, 1986.
48. Warnock, M., Thinking and government policy: The Warnock Commission on Human Embryology, *Millbank Mem. Fund* 63(3):504–522, 1985.
49. Davies, I., Contracts to bear children, *J. Med. Ethics* 11:61–65, 1985.
50. Ethics Committee of the American Fertility Society, Ethical considerations of the new reproductive technologies, *Fertil. Steril.* 46(3) (Suppl.1):1S–81S, 1986.
51. Parker, P.J., Motivation of surrogate mothers: Initial findings, *Am. J. Psychol.* 140:117–118, 1983.
52. Fleming, A.T., Our fascination with Baby M, *New York Times Magazine* 29 March:33–87, 1987.
53. Annas, G.J., Death without dignity for commercial surrogacy: The case of Baby M, *Hastings Center* 18(2):21–24, 1988.
54. Johnsen, D., The creation of fetal rights: Conflicts with women's constitutional rights to liberty, privacy and equal protection, *Yale Law Rev.* 95:599–615, 1986.
55. Annas, G.J., She's going to die: The case of Angela C., *Hastings Center* 18(1):23–25, 1988.
56. Finamore, E.P., Jefferson v Griffin Spalding County Hospital Authority: Court-ordered surgery to protect the life of an unborn child, *Am J. Law Med.* 9(1):83–101, 1982.
57. Annas, G.J., Pregnant women as fetal containers, 16(6):13–14, 1986.
58. Kolder, V.E.B., Gallagher, J., and Parsons, M.T., Court-ordered obstetrical intervention, *N. Engl. J. Med.* 316(19):1192–1196, 1987.
59. Jurow, R., and Paul, R.H., Cesarean delivery for fetal distress without maternal consent, *Obstet. Gynecol.* 63(4):596–598, 1984.
60. Raines, E., Editorial comment, *Obstet. Gynecol.* 63(4):598–599, 1984.
61. Leiberman, J.R., Mazor, M., Chaim, W., et al., The fetal right to live, *Obstet. Gynecol.* 53(4):515–517, 1979.
62. Shriner, T.L., Maternal versus fetal rights—a clinical dilemma, *Obstet. Gynecol.* 53(4):518–519, 1979.
63. Engelhardt, H.T., Current controversies in obstetrics: Wrongful life and forced fetal surgical procedures, *Am. J. Obstet. Gynecol.* 151(3):313–317, 1985.
64. Loewy, E.H., Communities, self-causation and the natural lottery, *Soc. Sci. Med.* 26:1133–1139, 1988.

CHAPTER 12

Problems of Macro-Allocation

This chapter is a brief introduction to some of the problems in macro-allocation. Specifically, it briefly sketches and examines concepts of justice, rights, and needs before going on to examine macro-allocation from a community perspective. The role of the physician as gatekeeper is examined. Approaches to distribution (market, lottery, first-come, first-served and social value criteria) are analyzed. The use of age as a criterion in the distribution of health care is examined. The chapter ends by briefly contrasting the notion of health care as a right and that of health care as a privilege in modern society.

INTRODUCTION

Problems of macro-allocation (see also Chapter 2) have become increasingly important today. Not so much that, as has been so often said, resources are shrinking; rather, as technology develops, the resources needed for the care of patients have escalated, and this escalation promises to continue. Further, the population here and abroad—especially in third world countries with a population justly clamoring for a portion of the good life—is increasing markedly, in part as a result of the action of medical and social science. Not only is the population increasing: the number of elderly living on retirement and, on the other hand, the greater length of time that it takes to prepare the young for their life's work before becoming productive, alter the traditional relationship between those in the work force and those not. There are more persons justly expecting to share in the available resources and relatively fewer involved in actually producing them.

Man's community shapes individual ethics and participates in them. It is the fundamental context, the necessary stage on and in which our actions unfold. Communities, like individuals, have their needs. In a smaller and a larger sense we inhabit a commons which we all share. Preserving this commons necessitates the placing of limits on its members so that they cannot pursue unbridled personal gain mindless of the communal good. "Freedom in a commons brings ruin to all."[1] The medical commons, no less than the greater commons we inhabit, shares in this. Medical resources are not unlimited, and limiting their use for patients, as well as equitably making these resources available to all members of the community who may still benefit, is one of the problems of contemporary society.[2]

Macro-allocation (as we have said in Chapter 2) deals with the way in which resources are allocated to groups of people rather than concerning itself, as micro-allocation does, with problems on a one-to-one basis. Problems of the latter kind (problems which deal, for example, with discontinuing or starting dialysis for a specific patient) necessarily follow a different set of moral rules and have a different history than do the problems of the former kind (problems which, for example, concern the funding of dialysis programs). Necessarily, problems of macro-allocation must follow a utilitarian calculus: decisions here must attempt to promote the greatest good for the greatest number. On the other hand, micro-allocation issues cannot be tackled in quite the same way. Problems in which people deal with each other on a one-to-one basis (in which lives are identified lives) cannot aim for the greatest good of unspecified others but must be attentive to mutual need and historical context. Physicians, for example, in dealing with their patients must, at least in the context of our current and historical vision of the patient-physician relationship, be mindful of their patients' good above all else. Ethical reasoning here follows a much more deontological line.

Macro- and micro-allocation issues, however, are inevitably linked. Ultimately, macro-allocation allocates resources so that micro-allocation can take place and micro-allocation, of necessity, takes place in the context provided by macro-allocation. Since this is undeniably so, the interface between the two has to be carefully looked at. To claim that these two concerns can each follow its own unique set of rules without inevitable conflict is to wear blinders. Analogous to a unified field concept in physics, some unity of law must exist if two systems are to operate smoothly in the same time and space.

In this chapter, problems of macro-allocation can merely be introduced. They are complex, and the literature dealing with such problems (literature which, of necessity, encompasses many fields: economics, law, sociology, medicine as well as ethics, to name but a few) is necessarily vast. Here, I will examine (1) problems of justice and of rights, (2) a definition of need, (3) types of macro-allocation decisions and the community's role in macro-allocation, (4) the physician's role in macro-allocation and physicians as gatekeepers, (5) distributing scarce resources to individual patients, looking at various approaches such as market, social value judgments, lottery, and first-come, first-served, (6) age as a consideration in rationing, and (7) the question of making health care available to all members of a just community.

JUSTICE AND RIGHTS

Justice (see also Chapter 2) central to issues of macro-allocation, is often spoken about as one of the mainstays of ethical behavior. And yet, justice, if it is indeed to "give to each what is his or her due," is ephemeral. We conceive of doing justice in necessarily different ways when we deal with groups (in which lives are statistical lives) or when we deal with the individuals within such groups (which are now identified lives). In dealing with individuals in a one-to-one setting (physicians, for example, dealing with their patients) justice, while necessary, is often not sufficient. At the bedside, it is, in fact, a frequently inappropriate or at least only minimally helpful concept.[3] Justice, for example, stands, in a sense, opposed to generosity: a generous act is not a just one, and a just act is not a generous one. To be generous is to be more than just; to be just is to be less than generous. And yet beneficence, an essential if not indeed the most essential, historical component of medical practice on a one-to-one basis (and of crucial importance when individuals deal with each other in whatever setting), implies more than mere, cold justice.

Justice, then, plays an important but of necessity different role in both macro and micro-allocation. In macro-allocation it is the fundamental concept underwriting proper distribution of resources: here the groups dealt with are dealt with as groups, and the individuals within the group are unidentified strangers. In micro-allocation issues, in issues in which individuals deal with other individuals, justice acts as perhaps a fundamental consideration but not as a satisfying condition of that interaction. The individuals, far from being strangers, are no longer faceless but are identified and known. Dealing merely justly with our patients leaves that interaction cold, austere, and devoid of its necessary human content. *Prima facie* duties, compounded in part of obligations arising out of individual relationships, deal with notions other than merely those of justice.[4]

Our conception of the standards of justice are rooted in the social context in which men find themselves.[5] Justice as a formal standard—externally applied and neither internalized nor adjusted to its social context—makes justice an immutable and unchanging concept. It, therefore, cannot evolve or adjust to human needs or to human experience. Such justice is empty and therefore no longer justice in the sense that men usually think of it.[6]

Our view of justice conditions our response to what we consider unjust and what unfair.[7] If by justice we mean, by Aristotle's ancient formula, a virtue which gives each his or her due,[8] we are left with the question of what that due is.[9] Justice can, for example, be seen as a Kantian "perfect" duty,[9,10] i.e., that not to be just cannot be universalized and that it essentially violates logic because willing injustice cannot be logically sustained as a "law of nature." To remedy unjust situations thus becomes a very perfect duty. Indeed, according to Kant, justice and law are concerned with "perfect" duties to others, leaving the "imperfect" duties more optional.[11] Unfortunate situations, on the other hand, appeal to a duty of beneficence, a morally "imperfect" duty,[9] i.e., while it is logically possible to conceive a principle of non-beneficence, willing that such a principle everywhere should be a law would represent a contradiction of the will (see also Chapter 2).

Duties of welfare as well as duties of beneficence both concern the welfare of others. If community is a free association of individuals united by more than duties of refraining, then these "others" are members of the community whose welfare is at stake. While justice and, say, beneficence stand in opposition to each other in one sense,[12,13] they both are due members of a community conceived of as such an association. If justice is conceived as a dynamic and evolving concept in communities which hold both freedom and beneficence to be incumbent upon themselves and which view the ethos of such communities as resulting from, among other things, a dialectic between these two principles, then the laws deriving from such a vision of justice cannot be seen to emerge from a regard for freedom alone. Justice and law, in such communities, cannot attend to the perfect duties alone and conform to such communities' vision of themselves.

Duties of justice can be seen in many ways. If viewed consistently in a minimalist way, one model emerges; when, on the other hand, community is seen in a nonminimalist fashion, another model will appear: (1) the individualist view sees in giving what is due purely a duty of noninterference ("autonomy-based justice"); (2) the broader view sees in giving what is due more than merely noninterference with personal freedom. What is due encompasses issues of beneficence ("beneficence-based justice"), and, therefore, such communities see assuring minimal standards of basic needs to at least be an ideal for which they must strive.

Justice, as John Dewey has pointed out, is not an end in itself.[6] It is a means which facilitates communal life as well as personal opportunity. As such the content of justice will vary as history and societies evolve and change. Justice, like all human activities, must be adaptive and must support survival. If justice does not do this, it is inapplicable to the human condition. It will, therefore, wither, die, and in its dying exact a heavy toll. Justice, like all other human activities, is biologically grounded in man's perception of the good.

Our notion of "rights," likewise, is inextricably linked with our vision of the nature of community and justice. "Rights" may be conceived as "natural or "God-given."[14–17] Such "rights," derived from nature or "from nature's God," are immutable, fixed, eternal and, of course, self-evident. Being self-evident, they are not subject to proof or disproof, and, therefore, the concept has an absolutist ring. If one wishes to dispute such "rights" (say, the right of property), one lacks a logical appeal to reason and simply stands in violation of God or nature. Such "rights" are secured to man by God or nature and, therefore, are not man's responsibility. In securing these rights, men are simply the agents of an unquestioned and unquestionable higher power.

The language of "rights" in and of itself is problematic and laden with a baggage of assumed meaning that at times makes it inflexible and unwieldy. In many respects, "rights" seen in an absolutist and contextless fashion become "trump cards" meant to preclude all further discussion.[18] When such "rights" clash, no method of arbitration between two conflicting absolutes, short of force, is possible. One may scoff at the notion of such "rights" and prefer to take a point of view which makes of all "rights" a social construct, promulgated and secured by communities.[5,18] Such "rights" may then be looked at as "interests" to be adjudicated between the individual and the community. Basic and fundamental interests (say, freedom) become a societal good of greater or lesser value in a hierarchy of social considerations. If one adopts such a viewpoint, it is the community's and the individual's duty not only to enunciate but to safeguard such fundamental values. Specific decisions, the product of growth, learning and experience, are not immutably fixed but evolve over time and differ with circumstance. Analogous to freedom as a side constraint or freedom as a value, the view we take conditions our further choices.

"Rights," accepted as God-given, absolute, and inflexible, on the other hand, necessitate a static viewpoint. Eternal concepts adapt poorly to new and unforeseen conditions. If rights are looked upon as interests enunciated and secured by community, fundamental values are not, therefore, taken lightly or easily negotiated away. Rather, such a point of view affirms that what is a fundamental value is not writ large in the stars but is writ small and with much human effort and pain.[5] Persons who not only treasure their fundamental interests but also are held responsible for enunciating and safeguarding such interests will maintain a higher level of vigilance and care in the discharge of their social responsibilities.

WHAT ARE NEEDS?

Inevitably when physicians decide to use or not to use a given intervention or when communities choose whether or not to allocate resources, the language of "needs" is invoked: we do such and such or allocate so and so because it is "needed." Often "need" is the key word, and deciding what to do hinges on its definition.

The concept of "needs," as Daniels has so aptly pointed out, is a slippery one.[19] In popular language a need can be almost anything: a passing fancy (I need to take a look in this store window), a desire (I need to go to concerts), or a condition of my existence (I need air!). In any case, and derived from its root of necessity, a need implies the necessary condition to a predetermined end. My need to look into the shop window can reasonably be expected to satisfy my curiosity as to what it contains; my need to satisfy my love of music is necessarily served by going to (the right kind of) concerts, and my desire to live requires air as a necessary condition.

Using the term "need" does not indicate the importance of that "need" in a hierarchy of values. It merely indicates that having or doing a certain thing is a necessary condition if a given goal is to be attained. In order to attain a goal—no matter how lofty or trivial—a certain thing (or action) is necessary. Its being a necessity depends not on the importance or value of the goal but on the importance of the means (the needed thing) to reach the goal. In that sense the term "need" in and of itself does not indicate anything about the nature of the goal. It is somewhat like the "ought" in a hypothetical: it is an "ought" which must be fulfilled if the indicated goal is to be reached. As such and in and of itself the term need (as the term "ought" when hypothetically used) is essentially value neutral. It can be applied equally to the despicable (if you want to kill Jones you need—ought—to use poison), as it can to the commendable (if you want to save that child you need—ought—to give it food).

If needs are the necessary condition to desired ends, they may still not, by themselves, be sufficient to attain those ends. Food, for example, is only one of the necessary conditions for sustaining life: without it life does not long continue. But food alone does not suffice—other conditions to sustain life are needed and together constitute the sufficient conditions to sustain it. Biological human needs exist in a social setting, and goals are social goals. If modern man is to live in an acceptable manner rather than merely exist in a biological sense, conditions other than those of strict biological need must be met. Such needs are socially defined.

Saying that health care (or basic nutrition) is or is not a "need" demands further definition. In a sense, going to the opera is a "need" for many and having at least a little pleasure in life is a "need" for all. But these are different kinds of "needs." They are different because subserving them satisfies a basic desire to make life worthwhile rather than subserving life itself.

In the vitalist presumption, life itself is a "good" worth pursuing at all costs. Few, as we have seen, would subscribe to this extreme a stand. Those who would subscribe to such a stand are then forced to maintain every spark of organic life no matter what. Those who would not assume the vitalist stance (and, in fact, few of us would) will (provided the content is acceptable) need to maintain life as the basic condition of experience rather than supporting life merely as an end in itself.[20] Life itself is a "first-order presumption," a condition for experience; the things that make such living minimally worthwhile are, in that phraseology, "second-order presumptions."

When we speak of "basic needs," then, we essentially will mean one of two things: (1) a "basic need" may mean a "first-order necessity," something required to sustain primitive biological existence and its goals: air, food, warmth, and shelter are examples; or (2) a "basic need" may mean a "second-order necessity," something required to sustain acceptable existence within a given social context so that its reasonable individual goals can be met: health care and education are examples. In the state of nature (Engelhardt's by now famous Ba Mbuti are an example[21]), "first-order necessities" are the crux of the matter and the "second-order necessities," taken for granted in the modern industrialized world, are either unknown and unimaginable or of little use in realizing the reasonable individual goals peculiar to that society. Other socially structured "second-order necessities" take their place. In modern industrialized societies, for better or worse hardly in a state of nature, "first-order necessities", or the "second-order necessities" of primitive tribes, cannot suffice to permit a realization of reasonable individual goals, and "second-order necessities," far different from those in primitive societies, become essential.

In delineating "needs" beyond first-order needs, then, the social context becomes all important. Even among the Ba Mbuti living their traditional life, there are "needs" beyond those merely sustaining life; but their needs are obviously different from those of highly organized and industrialized societies. To realize access to a normal opportunity range consistent with the pursuit of an array of life plans which reasonable persons are likely to construct for themselves among the Ba Mbuti (or among the ancient Greeks, the medieval peasants, or the 25th-century inhabitants of Greenland) is a different matter than doing so in Moscow, New York, or Tien-tsin today. Although "first-order necessities" remain essentially stable throughout those societies, it is the social context which fashions the things we legitimately may want to call "second-order necessities" and those to which we may deny that standing. Except for the biological needs of "first-order necessities," other needs and their prioritization are a social construct and not one that can be settled for all times or all places.

This leaves unsettled what to include and what to exclude among this category of basic "second-order needs," a category meant to include those things required to sustain at least minimally acceptable existence within a given social context so that reasonable individual goals can be met. The definition hinges on what is acceptable or reasonable as a goal within a given context. And what is or is not acceptable within a given context is ultimately, and in a changing and ongoing fashion, determined by the community.

First-order needs, as we have pointed out, are purely biological. They are needs because they underpin bare biological existence. Unless they are met, biological existence cannot continue and such basic first-order needs are determined by our particular biology. They change from species to species: essential amino acids for one species are not, for example, essential amino acids in another. Basic second-order needs, on the other hand, are basic needs because without them our lives are not acceptable, because without them we are unable to avail ourselves of the legitimate opportunity range prevalent in our particular communities. They are, therefore, socially determined. Like amino acids, which vary from species to species in being or not being essential, the "basic" nature of second-order necessities changes from social structure to social structure. Without meeting "second-order necessities," "first-order necessities" are empty; "second-order necessities," on the other hand, are meaningless without initially satisfying those of the first order. One has to be alive to enjoy a social order and one has to have a fair opportunity within one's social order if life is to be meaningful.

MACRO-ALLOCATION AND THE COMMUNITY'S ROLE

Macro-allocation issues are, as we have said (see Chapter 2) divisible into three parts. (1) The larger community (the state, for example) allocates its funds to segments within it; thus, communities, by whatever means, choose to allocate resources to education, defense, medical care, social services, etc. (2) At the next level, these different enterprises take the funds allocated to them and distribute them to their various subdivisions. Here, for example, the funds allocated for medical care are divided among hospitals, outpatient centers, nursing homes, etc. (3) In the last of these levels, specific institutions—hospitals, for example—decide how much to spend for birthing units, operating rooms, ICUs or outpatient departments. Each of these levels is interconnected with the others so that the higher, in some ways, maintains at least some control over the disbursement at the lower level. Communities may, for example, allocate resources to medical care with an understanding that these funds will be spent in certain but not in other ways. Still, the lower level invariably maintains a certain, even if not complete, autonomy over its own budget. Basically, a utilitarian calculus is followed at all of these levels: communities will allocate funds according to their vision (rightly or wrongly) of what they perceive to be best for the greatest number of their constituents. If they fail to do this, accusations of pandering to special interest groups and of betraying communal interests are sure to be heard.

Communities of various sorts and in various ways make the decisions that ultimately result in macro-distribution at all levels. Decisions here, of necessity, are political in that they are prone to the same decision-making process as other communal decisions. They, therefore, accommodate themselves to prevalent political usage. Decisions made in the Greek *polis*, the Roman Empire, a New England village at the time of the Revolution, or the United States today do not follow the same mechanisms, even though they remain communal decisions arrived at by political means. That is not to say that all political process is equally valid or that all decisions are justly made; it is to claim that decisions, however arrived at, ultimately must be, at the very least, not entirely unacceptable to the community and that they are, in that sense, communal decisions. When communities strongly disagree, decisions within any political construct cannot long endure. Communities, it is true, may make wrong decisions (or decisions perceived to be wrong); that, however, speaks merely to the particular choice and does not invalidate the necessity and the right of communities to make choices.

In granting communities the right to make macro-allocation decisions, the method of arriving at such decisions is crucial. Whatever the political underpinnings, communities in arriving at such decisions will be well advised to employ multifaceted and expert advice. Further, the specifics of communal decisions, like all other judgments, must be adaptive to changing conditions and must vary as technology and communal world views change. Justice, in that sense, evolves and changes.

Physicians' Role in Macro-Allocation and Physicians as Gatekeepers

All this, of course, brings up the question of rationing health care.[22] Like it or not, we are and have been doing just that.[23] Although this statement has been denied,[24] it is, call it what you may, the case. It is not, true enough, overtly done, but it is done, nevertheless. Rationing by ability to pay (be it by private means or by insurance), by race (the Indian Health Service), by disease state (the "end-stage renal disease" funding program), by age (Medicare), or by geographical region (benefits differ from place to place) is very much part of our daily life.[22] We have been rationing health care while often calling that process something else.

Physicians are often charged with two seemingly irreconcilable obligations: on the one hand, they are charged with doing all they can for their patients regardless of other considerations; on the other hand, they are expected to be careful to conserve, as much as possible, the community's resources. I do not have in mind here the performance of unnecessary tests, the giving of useless treatments, or unnecessary lengths of stay in hospitals. Such things are, by definition, useless or unnecessary and therefore are illogical. Rather than being done to serve the patient's "good" (a "good" that can obviously not be served by nonefficacious means), they are done thoughtlessly or are motivated by other considerations. They are, in fact, "bad medicine." When physicians, however, have a fair chance of serving their patients' actual "good," they cannot, within our current vision of the physician-patient relationship, be held back by considerations of costs, societal considerations, or the needs of others.[25]

That is not to say that considerations of cost or societal needs are trivial; indeed, they may in certain situations and under certain circumstances preclude the use of life-saving resources for some. There is no doubt that, from a purely technical point of view, physicians are in the best place to make such decisions. Ought they not, for that reason, be the ones to make and enforce such decisions in the context of their special knowledge of each case? Certainly a strong argument for the physician's role as primary gatekeeper can be made.[26]

To say that physicians caring for individual patients should give preference to the good of society or to the finances of their institution rather than to their patients' "good" is to do violence to our current vision of the physician-patient relationship. Physicians in this situation cannot simultaneously be expected to serve both of these masters. But, somehow, resources must be used wisely, and decisions must be made.

If one accepts the premise that communities are empowered to make macro-allocation decisions, some of these conflicts may be resolved. Physicians can only disburse what is made available to them; resources not made available by the community, or made available only under certain conditions, are not available for distribution by the physician enmeshed in the obligations of the physician-patient relationship. A marginally effective and horrendously expensive modality may, for example, be made unavailable (except, perhaps, under restricted experimental circumstances), or a modality may be precluded for certain groups within a community (for example, communities may decide not to make ventilators available for infants under a given gestational age or may decide to preclude the transplantation of organs into convicted murderers).[27]

Physicians, however, are not only expert at dealing with health and health care. They are citizens of the community (see also Chapter 6) and as such must participate in communal decisions. By virtue of their expertise, when it comes to health care, they are better equipped than most to advise communities. In that role, in which physicians are no longer dealing with identified lives to whom they are directly obligated, they can help give expert advice about such decisions without any fear of violating their and their community's vision of the physician-patient contract. Here they are advisers only, advising on medical efficacy and advisability. Their input is crucial to the final decision, which, however, must be compounded of many other factors and to which experts from many other fields must contribute. The physician, under these circumstances, serves as advisor to the community, which is the ultimate gatekeeper; when it comes to individual decisions made within the context of the physician-patient relationship, physicians are free to treat patients within a recognized framework set by the community. They cannot be expected to make available that which is not.

Other models have been employed. In England, physicians function as primary gatekeepers with individual patients. They have learned to say "no," and usually frame their denial of further treatment under the rubric of "medical advisability."[24] Such models may work if work is defined as saving resources. The ethical dilemma faced by physicians in such situations and the danger that such a method will lead to capricious decisions and ultimately erode our current vision of the physician-patient relationship seem obvious.

Furthermore, physicians in their arrangements with some HMOs stand to profit from work not generated. In some HMOs profit depends on not doing too many procedures, hospitalizing too many patients, or doing too much investigational work. Under some plans the physicians who are responsible for such savings share heavily in the profits which they helped generate. The pressure to do as little as possible—a pressure which may, for that matter, not even be consciously acknowledged—is ever present (see also Chapter 4).

The role of gatekeeper is, however, not always one of limiting access. Hospitals need patients rather than, as was the case a few years ago, being short of beds. Physicians at times own or at least have financial interests in laboratories, free-standing x-ray and surgical units, and other medical installations. They generate the work done and simultaneously stand to gain from the work done by such institutions. In that capacity, physicians serve as positive gatekeepers.[28]

The conflict of interest in which physicians in today's type of practice are inevitably enmeshed is one of the more vexing problems in medical ethics.[28] Inevitably in a fee-for-service situation, physicians are involved in generating their own income, be it by the way in which procedures are scheduled, tests performed, and patients hospitalized or be it merely by regulating the frequency of patient's return visits. Physicians own equipment (be it microscopes, EKGs, or CT scanners) whose use generates considerable income. To claim that the generation of one's own income plays no conscious or subconscious role whatsoever in the way that one uses one's resources is to wear blinders. In non-fee-for-service situations other constraints pitting the physician's own benefit against that of the patient inevitably exist. Even when physicians are entirely on a salary, the ability to regulate the amount of work and, therefore, the ability to regulate one's leisure time inevitably play a role. Often the best that can be done is to minimize the conflicts and, at the very least, to be aware of them.

SOME WAYS OF DISTRIBUTION

When we must decide to allocate resources to individual patients or choose groups of patients to whom resources should or should not be allocated, we have several options of choosing. In general, the choices of macro-allocation will be made prior to micro-allocation; the decision to provide or not provide funds for renal dialysis is an example. There remain decisions that, although individual decisions for identified lives, nevertheless introduce a severe quandary. When, for example, medical conditions have been met, there still may not be enough organs to serve all who may benefit. Decisions made at the communal level (decisions, for example, that would exclude ax murderers from being considered as organ recipients[27]) may not suffice. A residue of eligible candidates clamoring for an individual scarce resource (the famous last bed in the ICU, for example) may persist.

While no firm answers can be given, ways of proceeding with such allocations need to be examined. Briefly speaking, four methods of allocation have been suggested: (1) a market approach; (2) a lottery; (3) first-come, first-served, often (and, I believe, erroneously) lumped together with the lottery; and (4) social value judgments or "judgments of merit." The market approach, in which resources would be for sale to the highest bidder,[29–31] has often been suggested and has lately seemed to gain in popularity. If community is seen as constituted of individuals united merely by a duty of refraining from harm to one another and in which beneficence is not an obligation (see also Chapter 2), an argument for this can certainly be made. Freedom, in such communities, is an absolute condition, and market price alone may control availability. If, however, communities are conceived as cemented by obligations of beneficence, this may not be the case.

A modified market approach (one that makes resources not necessarily available to the highest bidder but precludes them for those who cannot bid at all) is, in fact, largely the way that medical care is distributed today.[32,33] Persons who lack independent funds as well as insurance may have no way of entering the health care system until it is far too late. It is not only the indigent (for often the indigent are at least "covered" with Medicaid) or the elderly who find themselves in this position; it is, above all, the under or minimally employed (the rent-a-cop, check-out clerk, or domestic). In living the fiction that life-saving care is, in fact, available to all and in generally insisting on the truth of this fiction, the community has tacitly expressed its sense of obligation even when it has failed to discharge it.

Intuitively we feel that making vital resources available only as an expression of market forces violates the duty of respect and caring that beneficent communities owe to their members. Introducing an auction approach for resources in which resources are either available to the highest bidder or unavailable to those who cannot bid at all reduces allocation to a "trial by combat" in which the weapons are economic.[27]

The lottery approach has often been suggested as a "fair" method for giving to one what cannot be given to all. It is the method by which occupants of lifeboats traditionally are supposed to choose those who must be jettisoned in order to save the others. Leaving allocation to a lottery may be fair in the sense that choice has randomly fallen and that the decision to choose in this way was made prior to the time that anyone could possibly predict the outcome. Refusing to make a choice prior to exhausting all possible avenues of seeking out entitling differences is, in fact, making a choice. It is a choice which favors caprice over reason and says either that all reason has been exhausted and that no reasonably pertinent or relevant entitling characteristics remain (in which case only a lottery or force remains) or that we have deliberately chosen not to trouble ourselves to make the agonizing choices that we must if we are to live up to morality in the human condition. To hold that all reason has been exhausted and that no relevant entitling characteristics exist in many, if not most, instances violates common sense; to choose not to trouble oneself, denies responsibility.[27]

A first-come, first-served approach, queuing as it were, has often been equated with the lottery.[29] In this approach, allocation decisions for groups have been previously made, and claimants who present themselves are the only eligible ones. Those queuing are within the groups. If physicians must do all they can for the identified lives under their immediate care, they cannot reasonably be asked to defer their present patient's good for the potential good of a possible (or even probable) later one. Objections to queuing which say that the time of queuing is often a social factor (since the more sophisticated and more affluent patient usually presents earlier than the untutored or the poor) are unquestionably true but fail to provide a solution: moving the poor qua poor ahead is just as morally wrong as giving preference to the rich.[27]

Social value judgments, judgments which hold different individuals to be of different social worth, are underwritten by the belief that values can be judged as better or worse by some acceptable standard.[34] Such judgments obviously empower the allocator to superimpose his or her standards on others. On an individual basis and when dealing with identified lives, such judgments are an obvious violation of our current vision of the physician-patient relationship; they are bound to be arbitrary and to lead to capricious abuse. They are, however, quite different from the making of such judgments by communities for groups of their members. Communal judgments of this sort are, at the very least, judgments made for groups of people by communal (rather than by personal) standards, and they are made by communities of which the claimants are a part and in whose values they more or less share. Such communal judgments, while far from being nonproblematic, are less likely to be capricious and arbitrary than are individual decisions. When selecting groups of people entitled or not entitled to receive resources on a communal basis, they are still dangerous[21] and, as it were, should be reserved as, perhaps, a last resort[28] prior to invoking the lottery.

A special case of social value judgment is the judgment that would penalize persons held to have "caused their own illness." These, it is said, do not merit care as much as those not implicated in their own illness. While there can be no doubt that habits and life-style have a profound influence on sickness and health,[36] translating this fact into allocation judgments is quite a different matter. If we hold persons responsible for knowingly choosing their own life-style, we may be left with the conclusion that such persons are largely responsible for their own fate. We may, then, end up blaming the victim and washing our hands of much previously assumed obligation.[37] Our answers here will depend upon the vision of the natural lottery and of community (see Chapter 2) as well as upon our perception that causality is not as simple and as easily defined as one might think. Persons are born into communities and, therefore, into situations not of their own making. Values of their family and of their community, their schooling, and their life experiences condition them to do certain things in certain ways. Free choice in the context of self-causation is a complicated thing. The external forces which tacitly condition our choice of life-style are too complex to be subsumed under "personal choice." Social forces and advertising, to name but two evident forces, are too powerful to ignore. Further, self-causation is too indistinct a concept to be useful. Where do we draw the line: smokers, drinkers, eaters of excess salt or fat, drivers of fast cars, the sedentary, those who fail to air their houses or to

get enough sleep?[38] Social value judgments of this sort, although entic-
ing, seem too complex to be useful.

AGE AND RATIONING

When we speak of rationing health care, we can think of this as
rationing modalities (say limiting the use of extremely expensive, exotic, and marginally effective interventions) or rationing by some other
criterion. Rationing by such other criteria is largely what we do today.
Some have proposed that rationing may be by other means: age, social
utility, etc. have all been evoked not only as a last resort but as a first
line. Age especially has been used.[39,40]

Age has been used because as people live longer they not only
consume more resources but consume resources in whose production
they no longer participate. The amount spent on health care has, in
part, increased because people live longer. Some feel that there is a
"natural life span" beyond which no health care other than the minimal
ought to be provided. They base their argument on a perception of what
is and what is not a "natural" life span and would limit access to
medical care based on an arbitrarily fixed cut-off point.[39] Others who
also are inclined to conclude that age might well serve as a limiting
factor reach this conclusion from a Rawlsian type of argument: they
argue that behind a "veil of ignorance" most of us when given the
alternative would choose to spend our resources earlier in life, thus
assuring for all at least a reasonable life span, rather than providing the
chance of having more life at the end.[10,40]

Many (including myself) are uncomfortable with this argument. In
the first instance those who oppose age as an independent variable in
medical decision making feel that using age in this manner is a statistical artifact and does not speak to the individual and his or her needs.
One 85-year-old is not like another 85-year-old in intellectual or physical capacities. A natural life span for a species is not necessarily a
natural life span for an individual organism within it. The fact that
many persons at age 85 are beyond enjoying their life, are perhaps
senile and bedridden or incapacitated by other illness, does not speak
to the individual. Many at that age live vigorous, enjoyable, and productive lives. Throwing all into one pot merely because an arbitrary
length of time has passed seems capricious. Furthermore, it is impossible (at least at this stage of the game) to say what is and what is not a
"natural life span." Even if this could be determined for the species,
individual variations in all species are profound enough to make one

hesitate in imposing what is again a statistical fact on an individual consideration.

Those who oppose the "veil of ignorance" argument do so for a number of reasons. First of all, the young can and do have little conception of what they would want or not want at a more advanced age. To a 20-year-old person, age 60 is an advanced age and not quite imaginable. The veil of ignorance is, they feel, too thick to allow informed choice. Secondly, it is not at all certain that one would make this choice if given sufficient facts. If health care to prolong life at a more advanced age were to be juxtaposed to having a face-lift at an earlier age, many would hesitate. Health care, it seems to many, is too broad a concept to be easily encompassed under one umbrella: especially an umbrella which would "shield" against it!

To limit access to health care for the elderly—rather than for those of whatever age who can no longer benefit from it—seems an arbitrary decision and one that, among other things, would clearly deny equal protection to an arbitrarily chosen group of people.

HEALTH CARE: RIGHT OR PRIVILEGE?

When we look at health care and health care providers in America today, we are seeing a system and a profession in transition.[41] In former times, physicians and hospitals were far more ready and far more able to offer care to the indigent then they are today. Resources needed to provide care were fewer. Obligations, furthermore, could be met by charging paying patients sufficiently more so that caring for those who could not pay was not as burdensome (sometimes called the "Robin Hood principle"). That is not to say that the poor invariably received proper care or that conditions were better than they are now. Rather, it is to make the obvious statement that society has undergone critical changes and that the delivery of health care is merely one of these.

Poverty in America is one of the realities of life. It is well known that 20% of our people are beneath the poverty level, that one out of six children goes to bed hungry and that one out of seven persons (many of them children and half of them employed) lack access to medical care.[32,42] Under such circumstances, the question of whether communities are obligated to provide a decent minimum of necessities to their members takes on new urgency. Health care is felt by many to be such a need, since without it people cannot "maintain normal species functioning" and therefore maximize the full range of opportunities.[10] Those inclined to this point of view will feel that the provision of health care is a basic necessity in today's world and that the lack of access to such health care constitutes a serious flaw. Others may argue either that health care is not, in today's world, a basic necessity or that communities are not obligated to provide such minimums to their members.

Our viewpoint toward the idea that a decent minimum of health care (or of other necessities) is a human "right" in a just community depends, of course, upon our prior viewpoint of community and of justice (see Chapter 2). If one (1) believes that the "natural lottery" operates in selecting who will and who will not be ill and that it is the working of blind chance, (2) holds that the definition of community entails no necessary duties of beneficence, (3) maintains that "rights" are "natural" or "divine" and are, therefore, to be discovered and not constructed, and (4) sees freedom as the sole necessary condition of communal life and not as a value to be traded on the marketplace of other values, one will hold that communities have no obligations to provide health care.[21]

If, one the other hand, one (1) believes that the results of the "natural lottery" confer obligations on the members of a community because (a) the undeserved misfortune of a member of the community automatically confers such obligation and (b) that the "natural lottery" is, to a significant degree, a social construct, (2) holds that the definition of community entails not only duties of refraining from harm to one another but likewise powerful obligations of aid to one another, (3) maintains that "rights" are not discovered and, therefore, "natural" or "divine" but rather the product of human choices and values, and (4) sees freedom as a fundamental value of a just society but not as the necessary and absolute condition of their existence, then one will affirm that just communities have an obligation to provide a decent minimum of essential needs for their members. They will do this because their view of what is just, what it is to "give each his or her due," is grounded in these assumptions.[5]

Most of us today would want to give at least lip service to a view of obligation and community fashioned on the latter, more generous model. Even those committed to a thoroughly individualist or libertarian philosophy[21,43] will hedge their bets and hold that it would be meritorious or "nice" to help the unfortunate, even though without "creating a straightforward obligation on the part of others to aid those in need."[21] In a sense, we all feel committed not to let our neighbor starve or go without medical care (even though many of our neighbors do, in fact, starve, and even though at least one in seven do, in fact, go without medical care[32]). And having said this, many would feel compelled to provide at least a decent minimum of essential needs to all members of our community. That leaves notions of need, decent, minimum, and essential undefined. Such definitions will vary from society to society and from community to community depending upon time, circumstances, and values. Definitions, therefore, can be seen as evolving and as changing. They, like many of the specifics of ethics, reflect the values of the community by which they are constructed.

REFERENCES

1. Hardin, G., The tragedy of the commons, Science 162:1243–1248, 1968.
2. Hiatt, H.H., Protecting the medical commons: Who is responsible? N. Engl. J. Med. 293(5):235–241, 1975.
3. Cassel, E., Do justice, love mercy: The inappropriateness of the concept of justice applied to bedside decisions, in: Justice and Health Care (E.E. Shelp, ed.), D. Reidel, Dordrecht, The Netherlands, 1981
4. Ross, W.D., The Right and the Good, Clarendon Press, Oxford, 1938.
5. Loewy, E.H., Communities, obligations and health care, Soc. Sci. Med. 25(7):783–791, 1987.
6. Dewey, J., Theory of the Moral Life, Holt, Rhinehart & Winston, New York, 1960.
7. Loewy, E.H., AIDS and the human community, Soc. Sci. Med. 27(4):297–303, 1988.
8. Aristotle, Nichomachean Ethics (M. Ostwald, trans.), Bobbs-Merrill, Indianapolis, 1962.
9. Frankena, W.K., The concept of social justice, in: Social Justice (R.B. Brandt, ed.), Prentice-Hall, Englewood Cliffs, NJ, 1962, pp. 1–29.
10. Kant, I., Foundations of the Metaphysics of Morals (L.W. Beck, trans.), Bobbs-Merrill, Indianapolis, 1978.
11. Kant, I., The Metaphysical Elements of Justice (J. Ladd, trans.), Bobbs-Merrill, Indianapolis, 1965.
12. Loewy, E.H., Presumed consent in organ donation: Values and means in the distribution of a scarce resource, in: Ethical Dilemmas in Modern Medicine: A Physician's Viewpoint (E.H. Loewy, ed.), Edwin Mellen Press, Lewiston, NY, 1986, pp. 133–154.
13. Hunt, L.R., Generosity, Am. Phil. Q. 12:235–244, 1975.
14. Locke, J., Two Treatises of Government (P. Laslett, ed.), Cambridge University Press, Cambridge, 1960.
15. Bown, S.M., Inalienable rights, Phil. Rev. 63:192–211, 1955.
16. Hart, H.L.A., Are there any natural rights? Phil. Rev. 64:175–191, 1955.
17. Frankena, W.K., Natural and inalienable rights, Phil. Rev. 64:212–232, 1955.
18. Churchill, L.R., and Simn, J.J., Abortion and the rhetoric of individual rights, Hastings Center 12:9–12, 1982.
19. Daniels, N., Just Health Care, Cambridge University Press, New York, 1985
20. Loewy, E.H., Treatment decisions in the mentally impaired: Limiting but not abandoning treatment, N. Engl. J. Med. 317:1465–1469, 1987.
21. Engelhardt, H.T., The Foundations of Bioethics, Oxford University Press, New York, 1986.
22. Churchill, L.R., Rationing Health Care in America: Perceptions and Principles of Justice, Notre Dame Press, Notre Dame, 1987.
23. Fuchs, V., The rationing of medical care, N. Engl. J. Med. 311(23):1572–1573, 1984.

24. Schwartz, W.B., and Aaron, H.J., *The Painful Prescription: Rationing Hospital Care*, Brookings Institute, Washington, 1984.
25. Levinsky, N., The doctor's master, *N. Engl. J. Med.* 311(24):1573–1575, 1984.
26. Thurow, L., Learning to say "No," *N. Engl. J. Med.* 311(24):1569–1572, 1984.
27. Loewy, E.H., Drunks, livers and values: Should social value judgments enter into transplant decisions? *J. Clin. Gastroenterol.* 9(4):436–441, 1987.
28. Relman, A.S., Dealing with conflicts of interest, *N. Engl. J. Med.* 313(12):749–751, 1985.
29. Atterbury, C.E., The alcoholic in the lifeboat: Should drinkers be candidates for liver transplants? *J. Clin. Gastroenterol.* 8:1–4, 1986.
30. Perry, C., Human organs and the open market, *Ethics* 91:63–71, 1980.
31. Annas, G.J., Life, liberty and the pursuit of organ sales, *Hastings Center* 14:22–23, 1984.
32. U.S. Bureau of the Census, *1984 Current Population Survey*, U.S. Government Printing Office, Washington, 1985.
33. Blendon, R.J., Altman, D.E., and Kilstein, S., Health insurance for the unemployed and the uninsured, *Nat. J.* 22:1147–1151, 1983.
34. Caplan, A.L., How should values count in the allocation of new technologies? in: *In Search of Equity: Health Needs and the Health Care System* (R. Bayer, A. Caplan, and N. Daniels, eds.), Plenum Press, New York, 1983.
35. Annas, G.J., The prostitute, the playboy and the poet: Rationing schemes for organ transplantation, *Am. J. Public Health* 75:187–189, 1985.
36. Fuchs, V., *Who Shall Live: Health Economics and Social Choice*, Basic Books, New York, 1977.
37. Allegrante, J.P., and Green, L.W., When health policy becomes victim blaming, *N. Engl. J. Med.* 305(25):1528–1529, 1981.
38. Loewy, E.H., Communities, self-causation and the natural lottery, *Soc. Sci. Med.* 26(11):1133–1139, 1988.
39. Callahan, D., *Setting Limits: Medical Goals in an Aging Society*, Simon & Schuster, New York, 1987.
40. Daniels, N., *Am I My Parents' Keeper?* Oxford University Press, New York, 1988.
41. Starr, P., *The Social Transformation of American Medicine*, Basic Books, New York, 1982.
42. Physician's Task Force on Hunger in America, *Hunger in America: The Growing Epidemic*, Wesleyan University Press, Middletown, CT, 1985.
43. Nozick, R., *Anarchy, State and Utopia*, Basic Books, New York, 1974.

CHAPTER 13

"Solving" Ethical Problems

Analyzing and ultimately "solving" ethical problems is not materially differ-
ent from solving problems in any field. The first brief section tries to give a
schema for dealing with simple or complex problems in this field. Then 16
cases are presented for consideration and discussion. They are illustrative of
many of the points raised in the text. Each case is followed by a purposely
incomplete discussion highlighting some, but by no means all, aspects and
issues. Altering the scenario may further enrich the discussion and help raise
other issues. The "what if" phenomenon can, at times, be very fruitful in
illuminating problems: "What if such and such were the case instead of what
is, in fact, the case here?" Discussions of this sort are most fruitful when led by
someone experienced in dealing with such problems.

Introduction to Individual Cases

Medicine is not unique in that every action carries with it an ethical
judgment. To act in other than a reflex manner requires us to have a
base of knowledge, however slim, and a set of values, however dimly
seen. If one concedes, as ultimately one must, that almost every con-
ceivable action in our world impinges on others, every such action
carries, at the least, ethical overtones. Health professionals, in dealing
with their patients or in advising their communities about the allocation and use of resources, must act in ways which critically affect the
weal and woe of others. While not unique in having to deal with ethical
problems, health professionals have to deal with problems which are
often more visible, more immediate, and more emotionally trying.

How does one go about analyzing an "ethical" problem? Problem
solving, in whatever discipline, is, as John Dewey so aptly pointed out,

a system of inquiry whose method is not radically different no matter
what the problem.[1] Health professionals are well acquainted with solving problems. In the process of making a differential diagnosis or determining a course of treatment, the same sifting and sorting process takes
place. It is a dialectic process in which various hypotheses are advanced and tested in relation to the known "facts." As a given hypothesis or "solution" (say, "I think the patient has pneumococcal pneumonia") is advanced, it provokes questions (say, "Was there a shaking
chill?" or "Is there rusty sputum?") which the inquirer asks of the data
base. The answer, then, may confirm or refute the hypothesis: it may
show that the "solution" or "answer" is more or less likely to serve
under existing circumstances. Further, the answer may itself stimulate
the formulation of additional hypotheses, which in turn must be tested
against the data base and against each other.

Values are not neglected in this process. Clinically, we assign different levels of importance to different hypotheses depending, among
other things, on their likelihood and on the necessity for immediate
action. (Say, the hypotheses of a dissecting aneurysm, although unlikely, is examined early because of the threat that such a diagnosis
poses for the patient. Our "value" for preserving life by acting first on
what is most threatening has informed our choice of what to ask and
do.) The questions we ask (be they actual questions or questions we ask
by examination or by ordering laboratory tests) and the criteria we
choose for judging an answer to be acceptable or not are underwritten
by a set of complex and often subconscious values. To the extent possible, the clarification and explication of these subconscious values is
one of the necessary functions of problem solving in general and especially of problem solving in the realm of ethics. Deluding oneself by the
claim that problems are not underwritten by values, is to misunder-
stand the whole enterprise of problem solving.

The solution itself is not static; that is, it is not *the* solution for all
times or all places. It is one of many or several plausible options that,
under existing circumstances, we have chosen to embrace. As such it
serves not as the end point for similar problems but as a starting point
when such problems again need to be examined. It is one point in an
ever-enlarging chain of learning and growth.

To solve problems—in ethics or in anything else—requires a base
of "facts" (knowledge) and a set of criteria in dealing with values.
Deciding, for example, whether a patient should or should not continue
to be treated requires a firm basis in facts as well as an understanding of
the goals ("ends") which such treatment might subserve. It requires a
lot more than merely that, however. Making ethical choices does not

lend itself to a process of decision making in which the likelihoods of various outcomes are simply "cranked" into a formula and whatever outcome is desired by however slim a margin is then chosen. Even here, "the outcome desired" inevitably presupposes values (preferring "cure" to death, which most would, expresses a set of values we take for granted).

Solving problems in medical ethics, then, is similar in its methodology to solving problems in other disciplines. Medical ethics is often seen as different because it must deal with extremely complex subject material and options in a setting charged with emotion.[2] It rarely offers specific solutions for discrete problems and properly tends to raise questions rather than give clear answers. When asked "What shall we do?" the ethicist properly is prone to suggest a variety of options rather than simply saying "do this." Furthermore, "solutions" in ethics are as prone to error as "solutions" are prone to error in more technical endeavors.[3] To ask for certainty is to ask for the impossible in either enterprise. Learning to live with uncertainty and to use error as a prod to further learning is as necessary in ethics as it is in other fields (see also Chapter 3).

Medical ethics raises problems that cannot be "successfully addressed solely within the confines of philosophy or within the confines of medicine."[4] Finding solutions in medical ethics requires an interplay between an understanding of medical facts and philosophical issues and reasoning. Neither, by itself, is sufficient to sort out options in difficult real cases.

An understanding of medicine is crucial to the enterprise. I do not mean by understanding a necessarily detailed knowledge of the field. The clinical ethicist need not be steeped in the intricacies of differential diagnosis nor be versed in the interpretation of blood gases; neither is it necessary for the ethicist to be thoroughly conversant with the subtleties of Hegel or Wittgenstein. But clinical ethicists, if they are to function well, must have an appreciation of the technical complexity of both fields and an understanding and appreciation of both enterprises.[5] Philosophers who wish to function in this capacity must become thoroughly familiar with the medical process and with the setting in which that process occurs. Medicine is a unique enterprise and its workplace is a unique setting, one, which like most specific settings, has its own largely unwritten rules of behavior. Familiarity with medicine, above all, necessitates an understanding of the emotive components of illness: how sick, anxious, and dying persons and their loved ones feel and act as well as what feelings, anxieties, and actions this evokes in health professionals. Physicians who wish to be ethicists need to be familiar with philosophy, with disciplined philosophical reasoning, and with the problems philosophers encounter in their work. The undertaking is a cooperative one: a partnership and a mutual understanding of two enterprises pursuing a common goal.[6]

Moral choices cannot be made without an awareness of the facts of the case. Such facts, first of all, are medical facts: What is the disease? What are the medical options? What is the prognosis? What is the probability that the facts as given are "right"? Ethicists, in analyzing their problems, must first of all be sure of their facts and must seek further facts when the facts in themselves are insufficient. In establishing a basis of medical facts, ethicists do not properly act as judges of the rightness or wrongness of the facts supplied: they are not "superdoctors" capable of evaluating the judgments made by experts in their respective fields. That is not their mission. They are, however, well advised to be certain that the person making the technical judgment is well credentialed and capable of making it. A judgment that a patient is permanently vegetative, for example, is best made by a neurologist experienced in the field. When facts seem insufficient or credentials seem unclear, ethicists are within their right to demand clarification. At the same time, ethicists must realize that the quest for more facts can be a bottomless well postponing essential decisions. Facts must be sufficient to the case in point and to the time available for decision making, and getting further facts must be limited to information that reasonably is essential to the decision that must be made. If one waits for every "i" to be dotted and every "t" to be crossed, one waits forever.

Beyond medical "facts" there are other facts often crucial to dealing with specific problems. These are the "facts" of the patient's personal life, of his or her relationships with others, the "facts" of the patient's prior wishes and worldview, the contextual "facts" of the hospital setting and its myriad of constraints and moral actors, as well as the "facts" of the community and its needs. All of these form the matrix within which the medical facts are embedded. In a very real way these facts are crucial if one is to understand the problem.

Having a sufficient number of "facts," then, is the essential condition for making a moral judgment. The "facts" of the case, furthermore, widen or constrain the possible options. The "facts," however, no matter how complete or accurate, cannot solve the problem. Writing or not writing a DNR order in a patient who is riddled with metastases depends as much on other considerations as it does upon the technical facts; giving or not giving an available organ to one of four possible patients is informed by more than an understanding of HLA loci or even by a knowledge of a given family's circumstances or constellation.

In this process, goals ("ends") must be clearly kept in mind. A DNR order, for example, changes the goals of medicine, and acknowledging such a change of goals should come early in the decision-making process. Means and ends are not fixed: what is an end or goal today may become a means to a further end tomorrow. Tentatively establishing the goals at which our actions should aim and being ready to change the goal in the process of selecting appropriate options is an important step in decision making.

Just as in the technical aspects of clinical medicine, all the while that facts are gathered, options suggest themselves or disappear. In a true hypotheses-forming way, the options suggest a need for further facts, and further facts change the hypotheses entertained. The options we form in sorting out ethical problems are critically dependent upon a background of ethical principles, beliefs, and presumptions (just as the options we form in making a diagnosis depend on clinical "facts," beliefs, and assumptions). The ethicist (just as the clinician in making a diagnosis) must try to sort these out, make them explicit, and establish hierarchies when principles conflict.

The ethicist must analyze the problem, making careful conceptual distinctions (distinguishing, for example, between supplying nutrients and fluids to those burdened by the procedure and those not) and showing that, in some cases, cherished distinctions may not be valid (as, for example, the distinction, under all circumstances, between killing and letting die). As a background to this activity stand the moral theories that we embrace: the principles, beliefs, and presumptions may differ radically when a utilitarian and a deontologist makes these choices. It is surprising, however, how often the conclusions reached are the same no matter what ethical theory or deep underlying belief system is subscribed to. Men of good will often tend to reach the same judgments in concrete problems even when they, at first blush, appear to be informed by widely divergent belief systems.[7,8] The study of specific cases using principles as guideposts rather than as straitjackets and carefully developing one's ethical judgments from the study of a multitude of cases is essential to clinical ethics.[8]

Sorting out ethical problems, then, requires at least the following activities:

1. Get the facts (but do not hide the fear of making a decision behind a never-ending quest for more).
   a. Be sure that the "facts" are given and substantiated by those well credentialed in making such judgments.

     b. Be certain that the "facts" include the socially relevant facts about the patient.

     c. Be sure, ultimately, to examine these "facts" in the context in which they occur.

     d. Entertain tentative options in an ongoing manner and let the options guide the search for further (necessary) facts.

2. Draw clear distinctions. As distinctions are drawn, other options or the need for further facts may become evident. Pursue them.

3. Tentatively determine the goals that are to be pursued. Adjust these goals in accordance with 4.

4. Scrutinize the beliefs and principles motivating the choices.

5. When beliefs and principles clash, examine whether they do so in reality or merely because of a misunderstanding of the concept or its entailments.

6. Establish hierarchies of principles, duties, and obligations.

7. Understand the context in which the problem plays itself out and take differences in moral views into account. Analysis may be useful outside the context, but removing problems from the context changes them.

8. Be aware that any "goal," "solution," "answer," or series of "options" is purely tentative and merely a step in further decision making.

In the last few years, bioethicists have begun to function as medical consultants. Initially skeptical, many physicians have come to be comfortable with discussing difficult problems in ethics with colleagues specializing in that field. In addition, ethics committees on a hospital level and ethics commissions (like the President's Commission for the Study of Ethical Problems) on a community level have been accepted as helpful in the decision-making process.

This book has repeatedly made the claim that ethical factors inevitably enter into medical decisions. If this is true, and if, therefore, physicians and other health professionals in their daily practice must deal with such problems in an ongoing basis, the use of a special consultant to help with ethical problems seems, at first blush, unnecessary. An analogy may help to clear up this confusion: physicians, to function as physicians, must be trained in a variety of disciplines in which they ultimately do not specialize. Nonspecialists deal with a wide variety of problems without calling in specialists. All physicians have been (or should have been) trained to recognize and deal with simple problems in many fields. Above all, physicians have been trained to recognize when problems are not simple and when help is needed. Recognizing that a problem exists is the first step in giving that problem a name and then in solving it. Most physicians will deal, and deal well, with a simple infection, but most physicians not specifically trained in infectious disease would be well advised to call for consultation when an unusual or severe infection exists. Ethics is not different. Most physicians can and do deal well with the everyday ethical problems in their practice; but when difficult problems occur, calling in a consultant is helpful.

Bioethicists, by training, interest, and daily experience, can be most helpful in analyzing problems and, therefore, in providing guidance to the attending physician. Like other consultants, their proper role is not to make decisions but to analyze problems, help guide decision making, outline the pros and cons of various options, and help reach a consensus.[9] They are no more or less infallible than are other consultants, and, ultimately, the decision of how to act must be made by the attending physician. Like other consultants they must be responsible and accountable for the advice they give. When conflicts exist, ethics consultant help search for the shared values which necessarily underwrite the resolution of such conflicts.[4] And above all, ethics consultants are teachers and learners who carry as much or more from their activity as they bring to it.[10]

CASES FOR ANALYSIS AND DISCUSSION

CASE 1

You are a third-year medical student newly arrived on the ward. Your resident informs you that all members of her team (students and otherwise) will be introduced as "doctor" to the patient. After rounds Mr. Jones, who is one of your patients, confides in you that he is happy not to have students to contend with and says that he would not ever permit a student to draw his blood or to do other procedures. At this point your resident asks that you do a necessary test on this patient. You explain your reluctance to her but she insists.

This is a tough one. Medical students are vulnerable for several reasons: they are the lowest on the totem pole, they are the least knowledgeable both about technical facts and about medical protocol, and they are afraid that anything that displeases their attendings or residents may eventuate in a bad grade, which they can ill afford. The pressure to comply is, therefore, great.

But medical students, in part by virtue of their vulnerability, also have several advantages: they have the possibility of appealing to a higher authority and to have their appeal heard, and, because of their inexperience, they can ask questions which might otherwise seem unallowable. Those are slender advantages, but they are, nevertheless, very real.

First of all, there is the question of being introduced as something one is not but is in the process of becoming: doctor. In today's hospital being introduced as something one is not is acknowledged not to be permissible. (In former days, this was different. Students were introduced routinely as "doctor," and the patients knew, understood, and sometimes joked about it. That certainly did not make it "right." But since everyone, or virtually everyone, was aware of the practice and understood it, it was a far different matter.) It is not permissible because, whatever else may be said about it, it is a form of deception and, therefore, an assault on another's dignity. So this matter should have been nipped in the bud at the very beginning when the resident stated that this was the way in which she would introduce her students. Talking to the resident (either the student by him- or herself or a group of students acting together) might have taken care of the matter. When all other appeals fail, the fact that the guidelines issued by the American Association of Medical Colleges is emphatic on this point may be persuasive.

Secondly, after it was regrettably but understandably enough not nipped in the bud (who wants to get off on the wrong foot with one's resident?), it should have been addressed when Mr. Jones made his very pointed comment about students. A simple remark such as "well, Mr. Jones, all students on this team are called 'doctor,' and I am a student" followed by an explanation of the student's role (and supervision) might have done the trick.

Thirdly, the moment of truth comes when you are told to do a procedure on someone whom you know to have been deceived as to your actual role. At this point, you have little choice: either continue the deception or refuse. The initial deception was of the more tacit kind: you permitted another to deceive and you failed to respond when the patient made his statement. But now deception is active: knowing how the patient feels about students, and knowing that he has been deceived, you nevertheless actively participate.

Deceiving persons is considered to be a form of lying, of not giving the truth to someone entitled to it and who asks. If one is to respect others, lying or deceiving persons is at least a *prima facie* wrong: *prima facie* because some would argue that lying or deception under some

very exceptional circumstances is either permissible or at least unavoidable. (Of course, Kant would hold that it is never, and under no
circumstances, permissible.) Deceiving patients under these conditions
is especially unacceptable: the physician-patient relationship as ordinarily perceived is based on trust. Further patients, by virtue of their
being patients, are in a situation of reduced power vis-à-vis the medical
team and are exceptionally vulnerable. That, perhaps, does not give
them any special rights compared to one less vulnerable; but it does
give a special obligation to the one holding power by virtue of such
vulnerability, taking candy from a baby may, strictly speaking, not be
any more wrong than taking it from a trained sumo wrestler, but it is
considerably more reprehensible.

Students do have at least a quasi-physician-patient relationship
with their assigned patients. Learning to accept and to feel comfortable
in dealing with the physician-patient relationship is one of the important (and often forgotten) aspects of the clinical training years. It is part
of the necessary socializing process accompanying training in any field
and it is very much what "becoming a doctor" is all about. The student-
patient relationship is, however, somewhat more complex. First of all,
it involves others on the "physician side" who have considerable
power over the student's fate; secondly, it is an assigned role and one
not chosen by either of the participants; thirdly, it is a transitional one:
transitional because the student is neither quite a lay nor quite a professional person. The transitional role, incidentally, often gives the student a unique opportunity. Not rarely patients, because they too perceive the student as standing between doctor and layman, will turn to
the student with questions and requests they would hesitate to make of
others on the caring team. The student becomes *their* student, one who,
perhaps, can better understand their fears and hopes than can (or do)
the other members of the medical establishment.

The student confronted with such a problem will have little choice
but to solve it either by changing the resident's mind, appealing to
higher authority, or confronting the patient with the truth. Perpetuating
deception, the only other alternative, under almost all circumstances
seems unacceptable.

CASE 2

You are a first-year resident on the surgical service. Your patient is advised by your attending that he urgently needs an operation. In fact you yourself feel that the procedure is not as absolutely necessary (and that a less radical

one might serve equally well) as your attending thinks. Consider two different scenarios:

1. You discuss the matter with your attending, who disagrees with you, maintains that the operation is absolutely needed, and explains his reasoning to you. You are not convinced. On the afternoon before surgery, the patient asks your opinion.
2. You discuss the matter with your attending. He agrees with you that the surgery is not as necessary as he has said but says that he put the matter in the strongest terms because he knows that the patient would otherwise refuse this type of surgical intervention. The surgery, while not absolutely necessary to save the patient's life, is still probably the most advisable in the long run. Your attending asks that, for the ultimate good of the patient, you support him in his stance.

In part, this case again is one which involves deception. Physicians often feel that deception is permissible in "furthering the patient's good." One cannot truly state that this is "always" wrong: scenarios in which deception may be arguable can certainly be constructed. But deception is, at the very least, a *prima facie* wrong: that is, it is wrong unless powerful reasons why it may not be wrong under a given circumstance can be marshaled. And in medical practice instances in which such arguments can be successfully upheld are rare. Deception "for the patient's good" is, even under the best of circumstances, an act of crass paternalism, and acts of paternalism must be justified. In stating that we are doing a given thing "for a patient's good" when the patient him- or herself could consent but has not consented is to say that we either know how the patient would define his or her good (which ordinarily is impossible) or that we think that the patient's definition of his or her own good is plainly "wrong." In the competent patient, this violates all notions of respect.

There are really two problems here: the first, and perhaps most important one, is that of deception; the other is that of the proper functioning of a ward team and the obedience necessary to its proper function. A team, by necessity, must have someone in charge who is both responsible and accountable for what happens.

When the head of a team makes a technical decision (say when he or she decides to operate or to pursue a given course of therapy or not), a decision that by reasons of training and experience he or she is most capable of making is made. In making this decision, the head of the team may be wrong, but he or she is less likely to be wrong than one with less training and less experience. When, however, a moral matter is at stake, things are not quite that simple. The head of the team may have had the most experience with the technical aspects of the problem (he or she may be most aware of the likely outcome of doing or not doing something), but the head of the team, like every other member of the team, is a moral agent who must live according to his or her lights. One may claim that the head of the team knows the patient best and, therefore, knows what the patient "would want," but that is a claim shown to be wrong much of the time. Although one may expect that, in technical matters, the team will ultimately comply with the decision of its head, one, even here, would hope that when time is available discussion and learning will take place. When it comes to matters having a heavy ethical content, discussion becomes all the more important. Members of the team who meekly comply with what they consider to be ethically inappropriate demands of the sovereign are not living up to the demand of their moral agency.

In the first scenario, the resident would be well advised to insist upon discussing the matter with the attending. If unconvinced by the attending's arguments, the resident would have to weigh his or her own ability to make a technical judgment against the technical ability and experience of the attending. When asked by the patient, the resident might well choose to say that while he or she was personally not convinced, the greater experience of the attending inclined him or her to support the decision. The matter here is a predominantly technical one and, therefore, one in which the chance of the attending's being correct is overwhelmingly greater than is that of the inexperienced resident. Supporting the attending seems the reasonable thing to do.

In the second instance, there most probably is no technical dispute. The attending acknowledges that he or she is deceiving the patient (even if that deception is believed by both the resident and the attending to be for the patient's "good"), and the resident has the choice either going along with the deception and, therefore, becoming a party to it, or he or she can refuse to do so. Prior to such a decision, a dialogue with the attending in which both come to state their points of view and search for shared values is essential. Hopefully one may convince the other: the attending may convince the resident either that the patient is not competent to make a meaningful choice (in which case other courses of action rather than deception are possible) or that the technical facts of the case are other than the resident understood them to be and that surgery is, indeed, urgently needed; the resident may convince the attending to do other than deceive the patient. If, however, one cannot convince the other, the resident is left with the original choice: participate in the deception, leave the case once adequate patient care has been assured, or tell the patient the truth.

CASE 3

You are a practicing specialist who is asked to see a patient in consultation. The physician asking you to see the patient is one who refers a large
number of cases to you. The patient is seriously ill. After a careful evaluation of
the case, you conclude that the treatment given by his physician is less than
optimal and that another approach would be more advisable. You write an
explicit consultation note to this effect. When you see the patient the next day,
none of your advice has been followed, and the patient is worse. The family
sees you in the hall and asks about their father and husband. You speak to the
physician, but he or she states that he or she disagrees with you and is not ready
to use your approach.

This case points up a situation that, although not frequent, is by no
means rare. When consultants see patients, a new patient-physician
relationship (that between consultant and patient) is established. The
ethics of referral, however, are not that simple. The relationship is not
purely between consultant and patient: the referring physician also
must be considered.

To make things more complicated, the consultant depends on con-
sultations for his or her living, and the referring physician's continuing
reliance on him or her is economically either essential or, at the very
least, highly desirable. In our fee-for-service entrepreneurial economy,
the decision to have serious disagreement with persons who refer a
large number of cases may have dire consequences. Not only is it likely
that referrals from that particular source may dry up; it is not entirely
unlikely that others who refer patients may turn elsewhere. Serious
economic consequences may attend the consultant who quarrels with
referring physicians. One may say that such considerations are irrelevant to making a moral choice. But choices are composite, and ethical
considerations are only a part of the eventual choice made. It is unrealistic to claim that anyone can be oblivious to his or her own interests.
Loyalties, therefore, tend to be complex.

As usually understood, medical etiquette discourages the washing
of the profession's dirty linen in public. Criticizing a colleague is "not
playing the game." Medical etiquette ought, perhaps, not be a consideration when it comes to making decisions critically affecting a patient's life, but medical etiquette is, nevertheless, a powerful tacit as
well as explicit force. It cannot be entirely ignored. As in a Venn dia-
gram, medical ethics, medical etiquette, economics, personal feelings,
and many other considerations often overlap.

Often, when physicians differ, there is no absolute, or even relative, standard of truth to which one can appeal. Saying that the consul-

tant has, by virtue of his or her being a consultant and a specialist, more intimate knowledge of that which he or she is being consulted about than does the referring physician is usually true. But that statement fails to take into account the fact that more than just expertise in a particular field is involved. The primary care physician who asked for the consultation is, unless he or she withdraws or is dismissed from the case, the physician of record and, therefore, in charge. Furthermore, he or she may know something about the totality of the case and may be more acquainted with the patient's values and wishes. More than just the organ system in which the consultant is expert may be at stake. The referring physician may, for various reasons, disagree with the proposed course of action.

In this case, adequate communication may resolve the problem. One or the other of the physicians may come to understand the problem from an aspect not seen before, and, therefore, disagreement may disappear. When the problem remains unresolved, the consulting physician is left with a variety of choices: in essence, he or she either can continue to try to persuade the attending physician while publicly supporting him or her and showing a "united front," or he or she can inform the patient or the family (if the patient is unable to "think straight") of the disagreement. If time allows (which is by no means always the case), the consultant would be well advised to communicate with the referring physician, and suggest that an additional opinion be obtained. Prior to confronting patient or family and essentially asking them to make a choice and a judgment for which they are ill-prepared, every reasonable avenue must be exhausted.

Coming to terms with this problem requires an examination of a hierarchy of values in which loyalty to one's colleague, self-interest, medical etiquette, and, ultimately, the obligation to a critically ill patient vie with each other and need to be resolved. Consultants who materially disagree with the referring physician's course of action but who, nevertheless, "go along" against what they perceive to be the patient's best interest participate in a form of deception. Consultants who "blow the whistle" in a sense violate etiquette and may do themselves personal harm. Both the consultant and the referring physician are enmeshed in a patient-physician relationship which, under ordinary circumstances takes precedence over all else.

Case 4

Ms. Jones is a 26-year-old unmarried lady who is now about 8 weeks pregnant. She went to see her physician with vague abdominal complaints 5 weeks before. Not knowing that she was pregnant, her physician ordered an abdominal CT scan, which was performed and was negative. The patient is now in the hospital with a urinary tract infection from which she is recovering well. She is being taken care of by two physicians: an internist who is handling her infection and who was her prior physician and an obstetrician who is overseeing her prenatal care. You are an ethicist who is called in to see the patient because the two physicians disagree: one feels that this patient should be aborted because of the exposure to radiation, and the other feels that this should not be done. How do you go about "sorting out" this problem?

This case is one of those in which a technical problem masquerades as an ethical one. There simply are not enough available facts to make a proper decision. How much radiation did the uterus receive, and what is the effect of this amount of radiation on a 3-week fetus? Is the risk of serious fetal malformation 2% or 90%? Answers to these questions are available but may require some research. No rational answer can even be attempted before the facts are established. (If they cannot be, then the absence of factual information has to be dealt with.)

At any rate, abortion is a decision for the patient and not one for the doctor to make. Physicians can give their patients facts, can counsel patients about risks and benefits, but ultimately it is the (rational and competent) patient who must decide her own fate. How the physician personally feels about abortion is not the issue here. Physicians who are morally opposed to abortion cannot, of course, be expected to participate; but by the same token, physicians cannot hold other moral agents hostage to their own belief system. Failing to supply patients with full information (for example, hiding from them the fact that abortion is an option even if an option repugnant to the physician) is deception and makes the patient a hostage of the physician's idiosyncratic belief system.

If the facts are not known and are not obtainable (say, if no information as to the percentage of risk to the fetus from such exposure exists), the patient is entitled to be told about this lack of information. Physicians must learn to share their ignorance as well as their knowledge with patients. Failing to do so is, likewise, withholding pertinent information—information the patient needs to assess risks and benefits in his or her particular case and circumstances.

Case 5

Mr. Smith and his wife have been your patients for some time and you know them well. The marriage has not been a good one. About 7 months ago you found Mr. Smith to have cancer of the colon. The lesion was resected, but metastases to the liver were discovered at surgery. The patient refused further anticancer treatment. In many talks with the patient and his wife, you all agreed that treatment should be limited to promoting the patient's comfort. Specifically, the patient asked that intercurrent illnesses should be treated vigorously only if such treatment would promote his comfort and not merely prolong his life. Some of these conversations were held in front of the patient's wife, and you have recorded the substance of this decision in your records.

You are called to see Mr. Smith in the emergency room where he has been brought after sustaining an inferior wall myocardial infarction. At the time of examination there is complete heart block, the heart rate is 25, and he is unconscious. You explain the circumstances to the wife and state that you will admit the patient to the regular hospital floor, keep him comfortable, and allow him to die. She asks what you would do if he did not have metastatic cancer. You explain that ordinarily one would insert a pacemaker and admit the patient to the coronary care unit and that there would then be a moderately good chance of survival. She insists that you do this. You remind her of the agreement between you and the patient and remind her that she was privy to the agreement. She agrees to the facts as stated by you but says that she has changed her mind and wants "everything done." Furthermore, she threatens to sue you if you do not do "everything possible to save my husband's life."

This is a most disagreeable case. Many factors enter into the decision: factors such as the personal relationship of the actors prior to this event, the fact that the physician inevitably feels empathy and loyalty not only toward the dying patient but also toward the wife, the fear of being sued, and the knowledge that, when all is said and done, the easiest course is to do as the wife wants. The physician knows quite well that the chance of this patient's living, even with a pacemaker and even in the best of hands, is poor. Most likely if the doctor follows the easier course, the outcome will be the same. The patient will die, and no one will be the wiser.

On the other hand, there is the troubling promise and the implicit contract. Even if not formally signed by the patient, the decision is recorded in the chart and not even disputed by the wife. This is not the time to consult a lawyer, and, besides, the lawyer here can only advise as to the legal problem and not as to the ethical question. What if the patient were to live and then challenge the doctor for breach of promise?

The conflict here is not so much one of loyalties (the loyalty to the wife, while existent, is not of the same order as it would be were she the patient herself). Without a doubt the physician's first obligation is to the patient: this can be justified by an appeal to the obligations inherent in the physician-patient relationship or by appealing to fidelity and promise keeping. A utilitarian argument that failure to live up to the obligations of the physician-patient relationship and failure to keep promises eventually dilutes trust in medicine and brings more harm than good can likewise be made.

But that does not settle the practical issue completely. Physicians do not practice in a vacuum. Institutional and other social pressures may be brought to bear and, while puristically speaking not relevant, do play an often crucial role. In doing what they perceive to be "right," physicians must be fully aware of these pressures and must, when possible, learn to cope with them.

In this case, the physician has the option of doing as the wife wishes and treating the patient in a vigorous manner (thereby breaking a promise made to the patient), or the physician may choose to honor the promise and allow the patient to die in comfort (thereby risking the wife's anger and possible suit). The option to pretend to treat but to do so only half-heartedly and ineffectively is, of course, a practical option: practical in the sense of being achievable. It is, however, an option which adds deception to promise breaking and, therefore, one which would be even worse than either of the others.

If at all possible, the physician should attempt to persuade the wife to go along with the patient's wishes and with the promise given to him. This can be done by searching for and appealing to a set of shared values: such values as trying to alleviate suffering, not prolonging dying, and keeping trust with the patient's wishes come to mind. Other shared values, values which may be peculiar to the case in question, likewise must be sought. Enlisting, when time and opportunity allow, others who were, perhaps, close to the patient and his wife should be sought. Here, in persons who are religious, the clergy can be of great help. Ultimately and finally, the promise given to the patient will have to be honored even when doing so may be a risky thing to do.

[Addendum: This is an actual case well known to the author. The patient's wife, after all efforts at persuasion failed, threatened to sue and walked out. With considerable misgivings, the physician did as he had said he would: the patient was admitted to a ward room, kept comfortable, and allowed to die. Mrs. Smith remained the attending's patient and never again mentioned what had occurred. In thinking about the whole affair, one wonders if the wife's action was not an elaborate and undoubtedly unconscious way of alleviating her own sense of guilt. The marriage had been poor, and she may have feared censure (by her own conscience as well as by his relatives) if she acquiesced to what she knew would be her husband's death.]

CASE 6

The parents of 6-year-old Jimmy bring him to you for care. You have taken care of the child for about a year and have noted that the parents are very much devoted to their child. The family are staunch Jehovah's Witnesses of long standing and have informed you of their refusal to take blood or blood products. Consider these different scenarios:

1. Jimmy, who has been entirely healthy, is involved in an accident and is brought to the emergency room. He is bleeding profusely and needs blood. His parents refuse.
2. You find that Jimmy has acute lymphatic leukemia and is severely anemic. The child is in urgent need of blood transfusions and chemotherapy. There is a good chance that with proper treatment this child's life can be prolonged for some years and a fair chance that a long-term remission or cure can be achieved. You know that, should the child be transfused, the parents' attitude towards the child may change dramatically.
3. Jimmy, who is now 15, is involved in a scenario similar to either scenario 1 or 2 (above). You have talked to the child on many occasions and know either that he shares or that he does not share his parents' beliefs when it comes to accepting blood. How would you handle this problem in any of these events?
4. Jimmy has grown up and you continue to take care of him and now of his family. He is 30 years old and in need of surgery. Jimmy is eager to "get it over with" and asks you to schedule him as soon as possible. The surgery is one in which the need for blood could easily come up, and Jimmy again reiterates that he would not accept transfusion even if that refusal should cost him his life.

Let us first consider scenario 1 through 3. There are a number of interesting problems here. The first is the problem of what has and what has not been said by you and by the parents over the year that you have taken care of Jimmy. Did you or did you not know the parents' feelings about blood transfusion? If you did not know this, and if this fact was "sprung" on you at the time of the emergency, it is quite different than if you had known of their refusal right along and had, tacitly, gone along with it.

Let's assume that you didn't know. In the first instance (1), you are suddenly confronted with a dying child who almost certainly could be saved. Your action or inaction will depend upon how you feel toward the "rights" of parents to their child. If you feel that these "rights" are almost absolute (if, in other words, you feel that parents own rather than are stewards of their child), your actions will be far different than if, on the other hand, you feel that children are members of the community given to the parents in stewardship. If you transfuse this child first and then get a court order, the court will undoubtedly back you up (provided, of course, that reasonable grounds for assuming that the child would die without transfusion were indeed present). Whether you could be sued if you failed to transfuse is a moot point and one largely irrelevant to the ethical judgment made (or is it?).

In the second instance, the resolution is far from clear. The child with proper treatment may live, but proper treatment is long term and may require several transfusions distributed over time. Further, the chances of this child's long-term survival are far less sanguine. In many circumstances transfusing the child will distort the relationship between parent and child. That is true in the first example also, but in that example the child would be healthy after transfusion and not in need of prolonged care and support during a critical illness. Is it in the best interest of the child to allow him to live out his time surrounded by the warmth of a loving home, or is it in his best interest not to have the chance of long-term survival denied? (Again assume, as is probably the case, that you can get a court order to proceed.)

In the third instance, the matter is even more problematic. Jimmy is still legally a child but 15-year-olds are not quite the same as 5-year-olds. If the child, when privately spoken to, insists that he shares his parents' belief, then overriding his belief comes dangerously close to the paternalism that would override the belief of an adult. Not all 15-year-olds are the same: some are more, some less mature. Further, the social and parental pressures may be such as to render the decision only questionably autonomous: how much coercion (internal and external) is at play here? After all, Jimmy's worldview has been strongly molded by home and church. Is it, therefore, really *his*? (And could this not, in the final analysis, be said of all of us?) If the child does not share the parent's belief, one can breathe a sigh of relief and transfuse; but one must be aware that coercion can be a multifaceted thing. How coercive is the hospital or you? Inevitably physicians (like all persons) will feel more sympathetic toward those sharing their own system of values (and more sympathetic towards decisions emerging from the same system) than they will toward those with whom they materially differ. Even if physicians cannot help feeling this way, they must be aware of their feelings and take them into account.

If, on the other hand, you were aware of how the parents felt, things are changed. The problem then is largely either one of communication or one of previous agreement. You may, for example, have failed to discuss the matter with the parents, hoping that no reason to give blood would ever present itself. In that case, one might argue, you have tacitly agreed to abide by the parents' wishes, or one might want to argue that no understanding (tacit or otherwise) ever existed. The latter argument might be difficult to uphold, but it is one which has at times been made. If, on the other hand, you have agreed to abide by the parents' wishes, a distinct problem exists.

In the first instance (1), a court order could still be obtained. Some would feel that they might want to turn the case over to a colleague who would transfuse and obtain a court order, but that is not acceptable since, in a sense, it likewise violates the compact and, furthermore, does so in a rather "sneaky" fashion. In a sense, it constitutes moral (even if not legal) abandonment. An argument that saving the child's life under these circumstances is a greater obligation than keeping trust can, of course, be made. Can such an argument be supported? The question of whether failure to transfuse the child is legally troublesome has not been addressed.

In the second instance, arguing on the basis of promise keeping, it seems clear that the physician is "stuck" with the original agreement and bound to respect the parents' wishes. The only argument to the contrary would have to be that in a hierarchy of values, treating the patient (and perhaps, but with no very certain chance for success, saving his life) has primacy over the promise given. In other words, the good brought about by breaking the promise would be greater than the good brought about by keeping it. This utilitarian argument, however, certainly is arguable: it hinges on what is seen, under these circumstances, as the "good" of the patient. Rule utilitarians, furthermore, could still invoke the rule against promise breaking and have us much in the same fix.

If discussions have taken place and promises tacitly or explicitly made between you and the parents, situation (3) still presents a severe problem. If Jimmy continues to share his parents' belief (and if he truly shares their belief and is not simply forced to agree in their presence), he essentially agrees to and becomes a party to the promise. If, however, he does not, then it is difficult to argue that a promise made by one party to another as critically concerns a third is binding. (Promising my wife without my consent that you will not treat me when I become critically ill does not appear to be a binding promise.)

Jimmy grown up (4) is quite a different problem. By now you ought to know that Jimmy and his parents are Jehovah's Witnesses (if you don't, it doesn't say much for the kind of relationship that you have had over the years!). In past conversations you may have agreed to take care of all eventualities and to refrain or not to refrain from blood transfusions. If so (and you have probably agreed to abide by Jimmy's wishes since patients who are Jehovah's Witnesses in general will, if they have another choice, not stay with physicians who do not give this promise), the current situations has merely forced Jimmy to cash in on your promise. Physicians confronted with patients who demand a promise that they are unwilling to give (say, not to give blood should the need arise) either give it against their will (and then are ethically "stuck") or see to it that the patient receives other competent care. Physicians who are "the only doctor" in a reasonable area may then face a difficult choice: they can either make their refusal known early on in the relationship and thus put the ball in the patient's court, or comply with the patient's wish. Hoping that the situation will never come up is whistling in the dark: inevitably the situation does come up.

CASE 7

The patient is a 78-year-old single lady whose only known relative is an 80-year-old sister who, while spry and bright, has had no contact with the patient for over 40 years. The patient has a history of chronic depression and has been in a nursing home for some years. There are no other relatives and no living friends. Two months ago the patient refused any further investigation of a probably cancerous breast mass. At the time, her physician judged her to be competent enough to refuse such investigation and treatment. Following a heart attack, the patient is in an intensive care unit. Attempts to treat her severe heart failure have been unsuccessful. You are called because the question of using more aggressive and invasive means (an intra-aortic balloon pump or angiography and possible angioplasty and/or surgery) has come up. The patient is stuporous and incapable of making any decision. Her sister states that she does not know the patient well enough to participate actively and leaves the decision up to the medical team whom you are called to advise.

This is a difficult case because the physician at first thinks that there is no way of knowing the patient's wishes. If this patient either had not been previously held to be competent to make an important decision or if she had never had to make such a decision, the matter would be much more difficult.

When it came to her breast mass, the patient, despite her psychiatric history, was allowed to refuse further intervention. It seems clear that the patient did not want any invasive or extensive intervention then, and it seems not unreasonable to believe that she would feel the same under existing circumstances. It can, of course, be argued that a breast mass, which may or may not be cancer and which may or may not require surgery, is quite a different thing than an imminently life-threatening occurrence. Perhaps the patient would feel differently about the temporary use of an intra-aortic balloon pump or about angioplasty than she would about having a breast removed. (After all, a mammogram would either mean surgery, which the patient might not want, or would mean that nothing need be done, in which case, and in retrospect, why get it?) Can we really know how the patient would feel about aggressive temporary measures of this sort? And if we can't, on what basis do we choose either to act or not to act?

The question of the patient's competency in the first place is an equally interesting question. Her physician either concluded that she was competent to make the decision (or at least not incompetent enough so that her choice could be easily overridden) or, perhaps, the physician's decision was based on a composite judgment: on the one hand, the physician may have felt that surgical intervention would, for whatever reason, be undesirable and, on the other, that she was competent enough to refrain from challenging her (especially since her refusal coincided with the physician's judgment of the case). Now, however, the physician may feel differently because without intervention, the patient will shortly die. The emotive even if not necessarily the ethical circumstances are different. Should this make a difference?

Was the sister right in refusing to make the choice? What if she had known her sister well but still refused or made the choice that the decision was up to the physician? If the patient was indeed judged to be competent, should her refusal to allow further investigation of her breast lesion have given rise to a frank discussion as to her wishes in other eventualities?

Case 8

The patient is an 86-year-old man, recovering in the hospital after an acute infection. He has been confined to a nursing home for some years, is badly disabled by arthritis so that he can hardly get out of bed, and was taken to hospital when unconscious. Although his infection clears with treatment, he refuses to eat or to take adequate fluids. Unless tied down, he attempts to remove the nasogastric tube. A psychiatrist has seen the patient and has found him to be competent. The patient's physician wishes to insert a gastrostomy tube for feeding, and, when the patient refuses, you are called in to advise the physician. In talking to the patient, you find him to be entirely clear. He states that he has no relatives, is unable to pursue any of his interests, and is miserable. He says that "he has lived long enough, has had a good life, and now does not wish to continue to live."

There is no doubt that unless the patient changes his mind, he will die. Under ordinary circumstances patients who refuse reasonable medical treatment in the hospital can be asked to discharge themselves against medical advice. In a patient completely confined to bed, this is not an option, and nursing homes will not ordinarily accept patients under such circumstances.

The fact that this patient has been judged to be competent and the fact that, deep down, we sympathize with his decision are important. Physicians who feel compelled to support life under all circumstances (and there are not many of those today) and who feel that keeping alive is a "moral duty" will, of course, be inclined to doubt the patient's competence. This is because reasoning in this fashion is part of their particular definition. In the present case, however, competence has been established and therefore is one of the "givens" of the case. Physicians who hold suicide to be immoral likewise will have difficulties with this case and may act quite differently from those more willing to accept suicide or, at least, to look at the matter on a case-by-case basis.

Competent patients are held to be ethically (and legally) free to accept or reject medical intervention. Forcing such patients to undergo a procedure they refuse is coercive and, ultimately, assault and battery. When it comes to fluid and nutrition, we tend to adhere to other standards. Why is this the case, and is it justifiable? Is there a distinction between forcing fluid and nutrition (say, by a nasogastric tube) and doing a gastrostomy for the same purpose? Allowing patients to starve themselves to death in an institution, moreover, may affront both institutional sensibility and the moral views of the health professionals involved. A resolution of such a case, as a resolution of most cases, lies in an attempt to discover an underpinning of shared values among those who would and who would not condone such a practice. What might some of these shared values be? If a decision to allow the patient to have his way is made, does that end the obligations of the health care team? If not, what are these obligations, and why? What if those who must care for the patient (physicians, nurses, and ultimately the institution) are ethically unable to allow a patient to starve before their eyes even when doing so accords with the patient's wishes? If you must advise the health care team, what principles would you invoke?

CASE 9

The patient is a 5-month-old girl. She has one healthy older sister. The parents live in a basement apartment and have a marginal income: the father is disabled after a head injury, and the mother has been caring for the family. The child has been definitely diagnosed as Werdnig-Hoffman disease, a condition in which there is relentless deterioration of motor function so that, ultimately, breathing becomes impossible. Death usually occurs somewhere about 1 year of age. Intellectual and sensory function are preserved; that is, such patients can feel and think in the same way that healthy infants would. The child is comfortable, but her ability to breathe is deteriorating. You are called to advise as to "how far one should go."

What makes this case so very agonizing is that intellectual function and sensation persist intact while muscle power inevitably falters, leaving the patient unable to cough and, eventually, breathe. It is this feature which makes the case critically different from, say, Tay-Sachs or other conditions in which sensory and intellectual function regress. The options are to treat all intercurrent conditions vigorously and to support the infant with parenteral nutrition and the use of a respirator until death inevitably ensues or to abandon some or all of these efforts.

If a decision to treat all intercurrent disease fully and to ventilate and artificially feed as required to sustain life is made, what could it be based on? If, on the other hand, it is decided to forego some or all of these measures, what justification could be invoked? Is there a difference in means or in goals (ends) between these two courses? If a decision to abandon the treatment of intercurrent infections, for example, is made, is there any reason why ventilation might still be appropriate (remember that the patient is able to feel and think and that air hunger is awful)? What about a feeding tube?

What if the parents disagree (with you or between themselves) with your proposed course of action? Are there several or only one acceptable option? If several, how would you rank them and why, and in this particular patient, what would motivate you to choose one over the other? If one is to treat one but not another intercurrent illness (or decide to use one but not another therapeutic modality), on what basis would such choices be made? What shared values could be appealed to?

Do the economic and social circumstances of the parents properly play a role in the decision? If, as is probably the case, the treatment of this case would use up resources so that they were unavailable for other uses (say, continue an immunization program or expand the hospital's outreach to the community), would that have any effect on what might be suggested? Are such considerations ethically permissible ones?

CASE 10

Your hospital asks you to help them formulate a policy for allocating funds. Specifically, the hospital is located in an area in which many automobile accidents occur and, therefore, a fair number of organs become available for transplantation. At the same time, the hospital adjoins a poor area where many are without proper medical care. Limitations in funds have made it necessary to choose between establishing an active transplant program (which would enhance the hospital's prestige) and expanding a completely inadequate outreach program to provide medical care for those without it. The hospital administrator points out that the hospital cannot do both. Further, he points out that, once established, albeit at great cost, a transplant program would begin to "pay for itself," while the outreach program would remain a constant drain.

The "you" who is asked to help formulate this plan is an important consideration. Ideally, the "you" does not have an ax to grind or is one on whom the hospital or its administrator can exert undue pressure. Assume that it is the case that you are a free agent and that you have at least as open a mind about such things as anyone.

What are the considerations here? The economic reality seems to be that starting up a transplant program holds out a very real hope of self-sufficiency in a short time. The transplant program would not be an eternal well into which money would disappear. In addition, the prestige (and, therefore, referrals and eventually money) which would accrue to the hospital might well make this a very real economic asset: one which could even conceivably fund the outreach program!

On the other hand, transplantation is a rather sophisticated need vis-à-vis basic health care. It directly profits only a very few patients as compared to the many that an expanded outreach program would benefit. Does the fact that the outreach program already exists whereas the transplant program has to be newly established give any grounds for preferring one over the other on a moral basis? Does the fact that patients can go elsewhere (even if with some inconvenience) for transplantation, whereas the poor living in the adjacent houses do not, as a practical matter, have this opportunity count? Does the fact that the hospital is near a highway and, therefore, has many potential donors make a difference?

On what basis can this matter be argued? Are there shared values which underwrite the decision to establish either of these programs?

Case 11

The patient is a 56-year-old married lady with long-standing chronic pulmonary disease. She agreed only reluctantly to be placed on a ventilator 6 months ago and then only because she thought that she had a fair chance of "coming off it." Home care was never very successful and was interrupted recently by an intercurrent infection. Since in the hospital (and now with her infection cured), she has persistently asked that the ventilator be discontinued and that she be allowed to die. She has been seen by a psychiatrist and judged to be competent. Were the ventilator to be removed, the patient would inevitably die in the course of 2 or 3 hours. The family, who are very close to the patient, support her in her decision.

The difficulty here, as contrasted to Case 9 for example, is that this patient's death, once the ventilator is discontinued, will be agonizing. It is generally agreed that slowly strangling to death is one of the very worst tortures to befall man. Our 86-year-old gentleman in the example above could at any time decide to start eating; this lady would not have such an option.

What are we, in fact, saying when we refuse to disconnect her ventilator and override her wishes? Are we inappropriately or appropriately exercising our greater power? On the other hand, if we disconnect the ventilator and allow her to strangle, are we demonstrating callousness? Can one moral agent force another (consent or not) to torture him or her? Is the family truly aware of the consequences of either course of action when they "support her decision"?

Is there a resolution in seeking for shared values? If so, what might these be? If a decision to continue ventilating the patient against her wishes is made, how can this be argued for or implemented? If, on the other hand, the decision to discontinue is made, how can this be done? Is the agreement (or at least the absence of strong disagreement) on the part of the rest of the treating team crucial here?

Is a middle road (say, sedating the patient to obtund her) an acceptable option? If not, why not, and if so, how can such a course of action be defended? To what extent would such a course depend on agreement of the entire treating team? of the patient? of the family? What if the physician feels strongly that he or she cannot be a party to discontinuing ventilator support?

CASE 12

Mrs. Jones, who is 18 weeks pregnant, has been in the ICU for 3 days. She was taken to the emergency room after a head-on collision, and over the last few days, brain death has been established. There did not appear to be any abdominal injury and the pregnancy does not appear to have been disturbed. Mr. Jones is a laborer, and there are two other children. You are called to advise about continuing to support Mrs. Jones so that the pregnancy can continue.

First of all, just as in Case 4, we need some more technical information to arrive at a rational decision. The current state of the art is that at

18 weeks a fetus is far from being viable. Many more weeks would have to elapse before viability could even be reasonably possible. Supporting a brain-dead person for that length of time, while possible, is far from easy: it requires the use of sophisticated apparatus in an intensive care setting and is enormously expensive. Furthermore, while one or two cases here and there have used a brain-dead mother as an incubator for her developing fetus, there is not even a moderately reliable track record. Under these circumstances, each such venture is a trip into the unknown.

What are the physician's obligations under these circumstances? If the husband should wish to continue his wife's support under these circumstances, is it proper to continue to use up the resources of a busy ICU (built to take care of critically ill patients for their own good) for such a purpose? On the other hand, if the husband does not wish to continue his wife's support under these circumstances, is it proper to abandon all chances for the fetus' survival and to go along with his wishes?

Would the patient's lacking or possessing insurance coverage be a legitimate consideration? If the patient were maintained, a delivery finally effected, and the infant were severely damaged and required life-long support, what would be the ethically acceptable course: making the father responsible? making the community responsible?

What if the father had not wanted continued support but continued support had been maintained and a damaged infant had resulted? Who should be responsible for the costs and, ultimately, for the infant's ongoing care? If not the father, how does this differ from a "Baby Doe" case in which treatment is given against the parents' will, and the parents are then held responsible for the further care of the child they had not wanted?

Does stopping support here constitute abortion (the deliberate killing of a fetus)? If not, how does it differ? If yes, why? If, the mother starts to abort spontaneously while the issue of brain death is being settled, is there an obligation to try and halt the abortion?

Case 13

Your patient is a 92-year-old gentleman whom you first saw in the ER when he was unconscious with a heart rate of 24. After a pacemaker is inserted, the patient recovers fully, and you find him to be a very pleasant, fully alert man who readily consents to having a permanent pacemaker placed. The pacemaker is placed. All goes well until the second day when the leads become dislodged and the patient's heart rate drops to 32. He is stuporous. You are about to reposition the leads when his 62-year-old daughter who is in the hospital when this occurs, intervenes and states that she does not want "anything more" done. She threatens to sue you should you proceed despite her refusal.

It might be well to review and think about your responses to Case 5 in which the issue hinged about the right of competent patients to make their own decisions and to have their wishes carried out even when they are not conscious. In Case 5 a patient no longer wished to have measures to prolong life taken, and his wife, once he was unconscious, demurred; here a patient presumably wishes to live, and, after he is unconscious, his daughter objects to further treatment.

The case would have been slightly—but not severely—more sticky if the daughter had objected when the patient was first brought into the emergency room. Even here, barring evidence of the patient's stated desire to the contrary, treatment despite the relative's objection would have been given. It would have been given because the patient's relationship to his daughter was unknown and her having the patient's best interest at heart could not be assumed in a situation in which the patient's symptoms could very likely be reversed. At that time, the situation could have been reassessed.

Communication is, once again, essential. Prior conversation with the daughter might or might not have forestalled the situation but, at any rate, should have been attempted. In accepting or not accepting a relative's decision about a patient's care, a decision as to the relative's motives must be made. Even when such motives are almost never entirely clear, are in fact undoubtedly not entirely known to the person him- or herself, a reasonable assessment should be attempted. Situations in which serious doubts remain should be resolved in favor of acting to sustain, rather than in acting not to sustain, life. Is this presumption in favor of life a reasonable one, and if so why?

[Addendum: This is an actual case known to the author. Every attempt to convince the daughter to change her mind was made, but she remained steadfast in her opposition and continued to threaten suit. When all else failed, she was asked to leave the hospital or to stop causing a commotion in the ICU. The pacer was uneventfully repositioned, and the patient left the hospital a few days later. Conversation between him and the physician revealed that the patient and his only daughter had not been the best of friends, that he was rather well-to-do, and that, as the only living relative, she, at least until this time, stood to inherit his entire fortune.]

CASE 14

Mr. and Mrs. Prenkovich have had a good marriage. Mr. Prenkovich was recently found to have an inoperable carcinoma of the pancreas. After biopsy has established the diagnosis, Mrs. Prenkovich informs you that she would "not allow you to tell Mr. Prenkovich." She feels that he could not "take this" and that it would shatter all hope and spoil his last few weeks or months. Mr. Prenkovich has always been the sort of patient who asks little, waits for you to volunteer information, but then seems grateful to you for having done so.

This is a very frequent problem and one that rests on a frequent misunderstanding of a critically ill patient's needs. Mrs. Prenkovich may think that her husband's last weeks or months would be hopelessly darkened if he knew his prognosis, and she wishes to spare the man she loves that pain. In addition, Mrs. Prenkovich may feel that she herself could not cope with her husband once he knew, and she may, often without knowing it, want to spare herself this pain. The motives are complex and generally rest in a misconception. Kübler-Ross, in her book, *On Death and Dying*, has done all of us a great favor by exploding this myth: not only are patients with a fatal disease quite capable of coping with such knowledge, they generally are quite aware of their prognosis (or, what may be worse, terribly afraid of what they surmise but do not know) anyhow. Not telling patients about their true prognosis, furthermore, cuts off communications at the very time that communications are essential: communications between doctor and patient, staff and patient, family and patient, and, above all here, Mrs. Prenkovich and her husband. In his last days on earth, it has been shown, Mr. Prenkovich is likely to be forced to "play games" instead of communicating and receiving what solace he can.

Physicians confronted with this problem often acquiesce to the relative's desire and lie to the patient. Often this is because physicians are most reluctant to discuss the poor prognosis of death with their patients and are only too glad to have an excuse for not doing so. The problem, once again, is one of truth telling. The physician, first of all, is obligated to reason gently with Mrs. Prenkovich and try to convince her that lying and subterfuge are not in her husband's true best interest. A promise to stand by, to help, and not to abandon not only therapy but even more human support is essential. This sort of dialogue takes time: time to hold the dialogue and time for what has been said to be absorbed and digested. There is no rush: the decision does not have to be made today.

If Mrs. Prenkovich (as she well may) persists in her attitude, what is the physician's obligation to his or her patient? If the decision to go along with Mrs. Prenkovich is made, how does the physician deal with the patient? How does he or she handle the unasked question? How the direct one? If the decision to tell the patient the truth is made, how does the physician go about telling the truth, and how can he or she involve Mrs. Prenkovich? Is there a ground of shared values between the physician and Mrs. Prenkovich that might help in the resolution of the problem? Are there others who might help? Are there ever situations in which a Mrs. Prenkovich might be right?

CASE 15

You are taking care of a professional pilot who was brought into the hospital after having sustained a seizure. Work-up has revealed no specific cause, so that a diagnosis of epilepsy is made. Your patient beseeches you not inform his company because this would result in the loss of his job.

This problem has many guises: the husband who refuses to tell his wife about a communicable venereal disease, the psychiatric patient who tells the psychiatrist that he or she plans to harm someone, the patient with any disease that may threaten others but which he or she wishes to hide. The physician is obligated not only to his or her patient but also to the community. Neither of these obligations, however, is absolute, or are they?

Is the obligation of confidentiality an absolute or a prima facie obligation (one that "on the face of it" is binding but which may, under special circumstances, have to be ignored)? What are the circumstances which would permit a physician to breach confidence? Why?

In this case, once again, communication is essential. If at all possible, the pilot must be induced to cooperate, and the physician must undertake to help the pilot reach an equitable agreement with his company. If the pilot is obdurate, what is the physician's obligation? May the physician coerce the pilot and thus obtain a grudgingly given consent? (For example, could the physician inform the patient that come what may he or she will report the condition but offer, if the patient finally consents, to try to mediate so that reassignment to nonflying duties rather than losing a job would result?) Should the physician evade the problem by relinquishing the care of the patient to another physician? If not, why not? What are the limits of communal responsibility today?

If, say, a new law were to require physicians to report the names of all HIV-positive persons so that they could be published in the local paper, should physicians cooperate? If so, what are the grounds on which such a belief could be sustained? If not, what are the grounds for noncooperation? What if drug addicts had to be reported to the authorities so that they could then be jailed? How do you come to terms with such conflicts?

Case 16

PBC is an eventually fatal disease. Current studies show that treating this disease either with steroids or with another immunosuppressive agent prolongs life (but does not cure the disease). A new agent may also be efficacious but has not been tested. It is suggested that a double-blind study comparing this agent to no treatment be set up.

1. You are on an institutional review board (a board which must approve the protocol of all studies in an institution). Do you favor this study as proposed?
2. You are a physician whose patient has PBC. You have the option either of enrolling the patient or of not enrolling this patient in such a study (assume that it has been approved by an IRB). What are your options and obligations?

Testing new drugs is something that needs to be done. When it is done, it must be done with as fully informed consent as possible. The very fact that the venture is experimental means that we are far from certain about the outcome or the possible risks attending. The patient, then, consents to take a trip into the unknown with us in which he or she runs all the risks while we watch. While we are far from certain about the outcome, and while we are unaware of all the risks, we do know some things: we know, for example, what animal or computer models have shown, what experience has been had with similar substances, and what treatment offers or does not offer in the same disease today.

Is it acceptable to compare a treatment with a nontreatment group in a disease in which treatment is known to benefit the patient? Is there an alternative? Are there ways other than such experiments of finding out how patients who receive no treatment will do?

If you have a patient who might be enrolled in such a program and you have no qualms about it, you do not have much of a problem in suggesting enrollment to the patient. If, like me, however, you have serious reservations about a protocol that fails to treat a treatable disease in order to establish a "no treatment" control (and think that a protocol in which one treatment is compared with another would do just as well: after all, finding out how the new stuff works relative to the old stuff is far more useful than finding out how it works as compared to no treatment at all), you have a problem. The new treatment may be far superior, and each patient has a 50% chance of getting it! On the other hand, the patient also may receive no treatment at all when some treatment has been shown to be beneficial. Under these circumstances, should you simply not mention the protocol and treat the patient in the established way? Should you mention it to the patient, not express your opinion so as not to influence the patient and let the patient decide, or should you mention it to the patient, make your recommendations, and then abide by the patient's decision? What arguments might support any of these courses of action?

REFERENCES

1. Dewey, J., *Logic, the Theory of Inquiry*, Henry Holt & Co., New York, 1938.
2. Clouser, K.D., What is medical ethics? *Ann. Intern. Med.* 80:657–660, 1974.
3. Loewy, E.H., The uncertainty of certainty in clinical ethics, *J. Med. Humanities Bioethics* 8(1):26–33, 1987.
4. Gorovoitz, S., Moral conflict and moral choice, in: *Doctors' Dilemmas: Moral Conflict and Medical Care* (S. Gorovitz, ed.), Oxford University Press, New York, 1982.
5. Loewy, E.H., Teaching medical ethics to medical students, *J. Med. Educ.* 61:661–665, 1986.
6. Thomasma, D.C., Medical ethics training: A clinical partnership, *J. Med. Educ.* 54:897–899, 1979.
7. Toulmin, S., The tyranny of principles, *Hastings Center* 11(4):35–39, 1981.
8. Jonsen, A.R., and Toulmin, S., *The Abuse of Casuistry*, University of California Press, Berkeley, 1988.
9. Glover, J.J., Ozar, D.T., and Thomasma, D.C., Teaching ethics on rounds: The ethicist as teacher, consultant, and decision maker, *Theor. Med.* 7:13–32, 1986.
10. Churchill, L.R., and Cross, A.W., Moralist, technician, sophist, teacher/learner: Reflections on the ethicist in the clinical setting, *Theor. Med.* 7:3–12, 1986.

Summary of Sources

Introduction

What follows is a by no means complete listing of available resource material together with a few lines about some of the works listed. After considerable soul-searching, I decided to omit a bibliography specifically listing individual papers. I did this because the extent of such a bibliography would have filled many more pages and produced too unwieldy a book. And even then, the list would be far from complete. The student is referred to the rather extensive bibliography at the end of each chapter. When researching topics of interest, the student might well start with that bibliography and extend the quest both by using a computer search (especially to find the most recent work in the field) and by using each article's bibliography to widen the search.

Neither the bibliography nor the comments are, or are meant to be, complete. Apologies are due to the authors of some of the works which were omitted or given short shrift. Such omissions do not reflect on the merit of the work omitted or upon their authors but rather reflect upon me as the author of this bibliography. The bibliography is meant to serve the student as a handy method of finding more material on topics of interest. Students will find that the bibliographies at the end of some of the works listed can be of additional help in opening up the field. Finally, students are urged to consult their libraries and their librarians for help in researching specific fields.

COMPUTER LISTINGS

The Bioethics File

This is the standard computer index used in doing research in the field of medical ethics. It is quite complete, up to date, readily available and accessible. There are, however, some journals in which ethics occasionally is featured which are not indexed in the *Bioethics File*. It complements, but does not substitute for, *Medline*.

Medline

Medline is the standard reference for computer searches pertaining to all medical matters. It is the first file to consult when looking for technical data (e.g., criteria of brain death, prognosis of coma, etc.). *Medline* lists papers pertaining to medical ethics as they appear in medical journals but misses some of the other journals. For that reason it complements the *Bioethics File*.

The Philosopher's Index

This listing of papers is often helpful and may supply material not listed in the other files. In researching a topic, the student may wish to consult this file when it comes to broader issues (e.g., works pertaining to justice or courage but not specifically justice or courage in the medical setting).

History of Medicine File

If the student feels as I do—that one cannot understand a problem without understanding its history—this will prove to be a very useful tool.

ENCYCLOPEDIAS

The New Encyclopaedia Britannica (15th ed.)

When it comes to searching out a wide variety of topics, this encyclopedium still remains the leader. The *Encyclopedia Americana*, likewise, is a good source of general reference. There is a certain arrogance in those who look down on good encyclopedias when doing research. While they are hardly a source of data for the specific topic being researched (encyclopedias cannot and are not intended to serve the ethicist in understanding deontology or the cardiologist in understanding heart attacks), they, and especially the *Britannica*, are a superb source of ancillary information. The student interested in researching a topic in ethics often has need for looking up less detailed information in areas impinging on his or her research (e.g., the *Britannica* can be most helpful in supplying some historical data or a general understanding of anthropology).

The Encyclopedia of Philosophy

This excellent work, even if badly in need of revision, is an indispensable resource for the student who needs to look up a philosophical point. It is generally well written and readable.

The Encyclopedia of Bioethics

The Encyclopedia of Bioethics is another indispensable tool. It has an excellent review of most topics in the field and a fairly good bibliography at the end of each chapter. The publication date (1978), however, makes it useless for more recent resource material.

Dictionary of the History of Ideas

This reference work may come in handy in looking up source material and in understanding the development of thought as it pertains to a given idea.

It is easy to forget that encyclopedias have indices. The student is urged to utilize the excellent indices available in all of the above works.

STANDARD REFERENCE WORKS (OTHER THAN IN ETHICS)

At times students will wish to look up material other than ethics. The point that it is necessary to have some (accurate) general idea about the technical aspects of medicine has been repeatedly made. There are numerous good standard texts in the field. Review articles are also available and are best found by consulting *Medline*. If, for example, the researcher wishes to know the prognostic features of a given disease or the current indications for a given intervention, a standard text and a recent review article should be consulted. When researching data in the technical aspects of medicine, it is imperative that the books or articles consulted be of the most recent date. This is not necessarily the case in ethics: it would be proper to think of Hippocrates' explanation of fever to be outdated but to continue to read Aristotle for insights into ethical problems.

In addition to medical texts, standard texts in general history and in the history of medicine should be available. The *Encyclopaedia Britannica* is often an excellent resource when it comes to general history. Beyond this there are a number of standard college texts which should be readily available (both Burn and Ralph's *World Civilization* and Ferguson and Bruun's *A Survey of European Civilization* are quite good, but Ferguson and Bruun is confined, as the title says, to European civilization).

There is no single, up-to-date book in English dealing with the history of medicine. Lyons and Pteruzzelli's *Medicine: An Illustrated History* is valuable mainly for its superb illustrations (very useful for making lecture slides), but it lacks more than a rudimentary text. Garrison Fielding's *An Introduction to the History of Medicine* is an encyclopedic work; unfortunately it was published in 1929 and, although still readily available, has not been reedited since. Furthermore, except for the first chapter, which is most readable, it is extremely dry and is useful mainly as a reference work. Ackerknecht's *A Short History of Medicine* (revised 1968) is somewhat more up to date and more readable, as is Major's *A History of Medicine* (1954). Singer and Underwood's *A Short History of Medicine* is readable but it is certainly far from exhaustive or up to date.

The sections on the history of medicine in the *Encyclopaedia Britannica* and the section on the history of medical ethics in the *Encyclopedia of Bioethics* are very well written and a joy to read. Anyone even mildly interested in these topics is urged to read this resource material.

TEXTBOOKS

Rachels, J., *The Elements of Moral Philosophy*, Random House, New York, 1986.

This is a fine and most enjoyable book for the beginner who wishes to get an overview of the general field of ethics as well as to have fun while reading about it. Certainly this is not the book to use if one wishes a detailed or in-depth analysis of ethical theory, but it very much is *the* book to use as a brief introduction. Brevity and clarity are among its chief virtues.

Hospers, J., *Human Conduct: Problems of Ethics*, Harcourt, Brace, Jovanovich, New York, 1972.

This is one of the standard texts in ethics but does not focus on biomedical ethics *per se*. It is more formal, considerably longer, and more detailed than Rachel's book and goes well beyond it. It is well written, useful as a resource, but not as much fun and, therefore, does not serve as a *brief* introduction.

MacIntyre, A., *A Short History of Ethics*, Macmillan, New York, 1966.

This indispensable book can be read on many different levels. It is a book to which one turns again and again. In giving a historical understanding of the field, MacIntyre gives us a critically important dimension and a deeper insight. I have personally read this book on several occasions, each time carrying something new from the reading. Besides these other virtues (if one can use the term virtues as referring to MacIntyre who, after all, is noted for his work in virtue ethics!), it is a most readable book.

Beauchamp, T.L., and Childress, J.F., *Principles of Biomedical Ethics* (2nd ed.), Oxford University Press, New York, 1986.

This is one of the standard works in biomedical ethics and has been much used over the years. Its focus is on the principles of the field.

Harron, F., Burnside, J., and Beauchamp, T., *Health and Human Values*, Yale University Press, New Haven, 1983.

This book covers similar territory as does Beauchamp's (see above). The book has been used in undergraduate schools and is meant to be an introduction to the field.

Jonsen, A.R., Siegler, M., and Winslade, W.J., *Clinical Ethics*, Macmillan, New York, 1986.

Clinical Ethics is a brief book in a purposely "handy" format: it fits readily into a house officer's coat pocket (already loaded with brief books on diagnosis, treatment, EKG analysis, and other reference material). It serves a useful purpose in helping the initial analysis of problems in medical ethics but does not provide a systematic or detailed analysis of a given problem. It may serve as a ready reference in helping to cope with immediate practical problems on the ward.

GOVERNMENT DOCUMENTS

President's Commission for the Study of Ethical Problems in Medicine and Biomedical and Behavioral Research, *Deciding to Forego Life-Sustaining Treatment*, U.S. Government Printing Office, Washington, 1982.

This is the result of a study initiated and supported by the government and involving a number of persons from various disciplines. It has become an important basic resource in bioethical research.

President's Commission for the Study of Ethical Problems in Medicine and Biomedical and Behavioral Research, *Making Health Care Decisions*, U.S. Government Printing Office, Washington, 1982.

This volume deals with issues of informed consent in the health care setting. It is the result of a study supported by the government and involving workers from disparate disciplines.

INDISPENSABLE PRIMARY SOURCES

Aristotle, *Nichomachean Ethics*, Bobbs-Merrill, Indianapolis, 1962.

Kant, I., *Foundations of the Metaphysics of Morals* (L.W. Beck, trans.), Bobbs-Merrill, Indianapolis, 1980.

Mill, J.S., *Utilitarianism*, Bobbs-Merrill, Indianapolis, 1979.

Dewey, J., Ethics, in: *The Middle Works of John Dewey*, Vol.5 (J.A. Boydston, ed.), Southern Illinois University Press, Carbondale, IL, 1983.

Rawls, J., *A Theory of Justice*, Harvard University Press, Cambridge, 1971.

ANTHOLOGIES

Anthologies often are an excellent way of gathering together diverse papers dealing with either the entire field or with selected portions of that field. In putting anthologies together and selecting some but not other papers or some but not other authors, the editor has inevitably expressed his or her values. While this is not necessarily a bad thing, it must be kept in mind. Good anthologies are a most excellent resource in that they bring together the major articles or thoughts in a given area. The student, by consulting the bibliography at the end of each of the papers in an anthology, can significantly widen his or her research. Such bibliographies supplement computer searches since they often list references not included in the search.

Gorovitz, S., et al., *Moral Problems in Medicine*, Prentice-Hall, Englewood Cliffs, NJ, 1976.

This is an excellent anthology not only bringing together the works of some contemporary thinkers in the field but also flashing back and giving excerpts from some of the seminal thinkers in philosophy. Most of the papers have been previously printed but are brought together and juxtaposed here.

Beauchamp, T.L., and Walters, L., *Contemporary Issues in Bioethics*, Wadsworth Publishers, Belmont, CA, 1978.

Brought together here is a fine collection of authors dealing with a variety of topics. There is an attempt to give a balanced view of a variety of problems. Most of the papers have been previously printed in other works.

Hunt, R., and Arras, J., *Ethical Issues in Modern Medicine* (2nd ed.), Mayfield Publishing, Palo Alto, CA, 1983.

After a brief introduction to ethical theory written by the editors, this anthology gives a very useful collection of papers brought together from other journals. Major contemporary topics are dealt with.

Abrams, N., and Buckner, M.D., *Medical Ethics*, MIT Press, Cambridge, 1983.

A wide variety of papers dealing with diverse basic topics are collected here.

Humber, J.M., and Almeder, R.F., *Biomedical Ethics and the Law*, Plenum Press, New York, 1979.

This anthology looks at things from a legal as well as an ethics perspective. It reprints most of these papers from diverse sources and tries (and, I think, succeeds) to give not only the law but the ethical underpinnings motivating the law.

Maypes, T.A., and Zembaty, J.S., *Biomedical Ethics*, McGraw-Hill, New York, 1986.

A brief introduction dealing with theoretical aspects is followed by a collection of papers culled from various sources.

Monagle, J.F., and Thomasma, D.C., *Medical Ethics*, Aspen Publishing, Rockville, MD, 1988.

This work is quite different in that it brings together a number of previously un-published papers specifically written for the current volume. Some of the major contem-porary workers in this field are represented. A good deal of effort has obviously gone into carefully assembling different points of view. It is an excellent work and the papers found here are not generally to be found elsewhere.

Loewy, E.H., *Ethical Dilemmas in Modern Medicine: A Physician's Viewpoint*, Edwin Mellen Press, Lewiston, NY, 1986.

This is a one-author work. While a few of the papers in this book are republished from journals, most are not. Since it is a one-author work, it necessarily has a restricted point of view.

Jonas, H., *Philosophical Essays*, Prentice-Hall, Englewood Cliffs, NJ, 1974.

Written some time ago and encompassing more than medical ethics (there is a fas-cinating chapter about the gnostics, for example) this book includes some works which have become cornerstones of the field. The essays are thoughtful, superbly written, and well worth reading and thinking about. It is a classic.

Steinbock, B., *Killing and Letting Die*, Prentice-Hall, Englewood Cliffs, NJ, 1980.

This is a small book which brings together a diverse number of previously published papers dealing with euthanasia.

Feinberg, J., *The Problem of Abortion*, Wadsworth Publishers, Belmont, Ca, 1973.

A small book bringing together some of the older literature in the field. Despite the fact that much has changed since (notions of viability, for example, have changed) and much has been written about this topic since this book was published, it does bring together some fine papers.

Shelp, E.E., *Beneficence and Health Care*, D. Reidel, Dordrecht, The Netherlands, 1982.

This is an important collection of papers which specifically deals with the problem of beneficence and its application in the health care setting. These largely excellent papers are not published elsewhere.

Shelp, E.E., *Justice and Health Care*, D. Reidel, Dordrecht, The Netherlands, 1981.

As important as the preceding, this collection of original papers deals with the philosophical and practical aspects of justice in a health care setting. It contains excellent papers not available elsewhere.

CASE STUDIES

Veatch, R.M., *Case Studies in Medical Ethics*, Harvard University Press, Cambridge, 1977.

This book attempts to introduce the study of ethics purely by the use of cases. It has been widely used and has become a favorite. The book, I feel, cannot substitute for a more basic approach but can serve to supplement a course dealing with fundamentals in a more systematic way.

Freeman, J.M., and McDonnell, K., *Tough Decisions: A Casebook in Medical Ethics*, Oxford University Press, New York, 1987.

The authors try to introduce ethical decision making by using a unique approach: they give a small number of cases, present discussions among physicians, nurses, and a philosopher and then let the reader choose from a variety of alternatives (rather unrealistically, the philosopher is more often than not presented as well meaning but quite inept). The book is fun to read, perhaps of use to health professionals not deeply interested in the field, but only marginally useful to anyone doing serious work in ethics.

OTHER IMPORTANT BOOKS IN THE FIELD

This listing is neither complete nor exhaustive. There are many other extremely useful works. They are too many to mention, and their omission is in no way meant to reflect criticism. What follows is what I, as one student, found to be most helpful and most enjoyable.

Temkin, O., and Temkin, C.L. (eds.), *Ancient Medicine: Selected Papers of Ludwig Edelstein*, The Johns Hopkins Press, Baltimore, 1967.

This is a collection of one of the most seminal workers in the field. Anyone working with medicine or with the medical ethics of that era cannot do without this collection. Edelstein's research has not generally been superseded. These essays are more than merely seminal: they are beautifully written and a pure joy to read.

Carrick, P., *Medical Ethics in Antiquity: Philosophical Perspectives in Abortion and Euthanasia*, D. Reidel, Dordrecht, The Netherlands, 1985.

This book specifically deals with attitudes toward euthanasia and abortion in the ancient world. In doing this it also gives some insight into other problems and into Greek medicine generally. The book is enjoyable to read.

Daniels, N., *Just Health Care*, Cambridge University Press, New York, 1985.

This critically important book makes a sustained argument for an obligation to meeting health care needs by appealing to equality of opportunity. It suggests that societies have an obligation to see to it that its members have equal access to a fair range of opportunities for realizing an array of life plans persons may reasonably fashion for themselves. To realize this opportunity, persons must have "species-typical" normal function. Daniels' argument is an elegant extension of the Rawlsian argument to health care. Whatever one may think of the obligation to provide health care to individuals within a just society, this is a superb and important argument for doing just that.

Gorowitz, S., *Doctors' Dilemmas: Moral Conflict and Medical Care*, Oxford University Press, New York, 1982.

Gorowitz's book is an excellent and thoughtful analysis of medicine and its ethical problems. Gorowitz gives reasons for feeling that, despite the problems posed by a pluralist society, we do have a rational method of at least beginning to come to terms with troubling moral questions. In this he differs with MacIntyre, who doubts that a rational method for reaching conclusions exists.

MacIntyre, A., *After Virtue*, University of Notre Dame Press, Notre Dame, IN, 1981.

This book does not specifically deal with medical ethics. It is, nevertheless, crucial to anyone who is seriously intent on working in the field. It gives a reasoned account of what has come to be called "virtue ethics." MacIntyre feels that in a pluralist society we lack a rational method of coming to terms with an inevitable divergence of moral views and must, fundamentally, rely on the moral character of the actor.

Churchill, L.R., *Rationing Health Care in America: Perceptions and Principles of Justice*, University of Notre Dame Press, Notre Dame, IN, 1987.

Health care in America and elsewhere is, whether we want to admit it or not, rationed. This book examines some of the philosophical considerations and worldviews that must inevitably underpin our actual approach to rationing. It attempts to start to build a framework in which specific rationing decisions can then be made. It is a readable, brief, and important book and one which anyone interested in issues of macro-allocation would do well to read.

Rachels, J., *The End of Life*, Oxford University Press, New York, 1986.

This thought-provoking and very readable little book is a deeply felt and well-written analysis of euthanasia. Rachels grapples with the philosophical problems underlying the problem. It (like anything we write, whether we want to admit it or not) has a bias: in this case a bias against a blanket opposition to euthanasia. The book, however, deals with a great many more problems than those encompassed by euthanasia and is well worth reading whether one happens to agree with it or not.

Engelhardt, H.T., *The Foundation of Bioethics*, Oxford University Press, New York, 1986.

Engelhardt present a carefully crafted libertarian argument. In a pluralist world which, above all, must insure liberty and peace for all, autonomy and freedom must be the conditions of morality rather than being merely one of several values. We must leave all visions of morality other than those to the individual moral enclaves who are free to pursue or not to pursue any given vision of the moral life. Beneficence in this schema may be "nice" (and it is, Engelhardt states, properly part of medical practice), but it is not enforceable and basically left up to individual discretion. Physicians are bureaucrats of medicine, obligated to be medical functionaries carrying out their patients' wishes provided these wishes are legal. Relationships are regulated by the overarching duty to preserve autonomy and by freely entered contract. The book is beautifully written and gives an excellent exposition of a Nozickian point of view in medical terms. For anyone seriously interested in medical ethics it is essential and often enjoyable reading. Its underlying philosophy is antithetical to the philosophy of this text and it is, therefore, recommended reading.

Pellegrino, E.D., and Thomasma, D.C., *For the Patient's Good: The Restoration of Beneficence in Health Care*, Oxford University Press, New York, 1988.

This is one of the fundamental books of recent years. In steering between the Scylla of autonomy and the Charybdis of beneficence (the one leading to callous noncaring, the other to crass paternalism), it develops an Aristotelean argument finding balanced room for both. It does so by making autonomy and beneficence interdependent on one another. There are important and very specifically spelled-out lessons for health care ethics to be learned from this. This book is an elegant counterpoise to Engelhardt's basically libertarian thesis and deserves a wide and careful reading.

Jonsen, A.R., and Toulmin, S., *The Abuse of Casuistry*, University of California Press, Berkeley, 1988.

This book gives a brief history of "casuistry": the use of cases and case study in ethical understanding and in the understanding of ethical principles. This method— which, the authors argue, had fallen into disrepute because of having been abused and not because the method itself is inherently faulty—is, as the authors show, very much what we tend to do when we address actual—as distinct from merely abstract—ethical problems. It is an excellent book and one, perhaps, best understood after reading MacIntyre's *After Virtue*.

Ramsey, P., *The Patient as Person*, Yale University Press, New Haven, 1979.

This is one of the classics in the field and one of the basic works in the field of medical ethics. As a deeply religious and rather fundamentalist Christian clergyman, Paul Ramsey brings an admittedly biased point of view, which, however, he often transcends. It is a point of view well worth pondering even if the present book far from agrees with many of the views expressed.

Cassel, E., *The Healer's Art: A New Approach to the Physician-Patient Relationship*, J.B. Lippincott, Philadelphia, 1976.

A well-written and most worthwhile book by a seasoned, thoughtful, and philosophically knowledgeable internist. It combines a unique wisdom of approach to practical problems with a thorough understanding of the nuances of the relationship.

Starr, P., *The Social Transformation of American Medicine*, Basic Books, New York, 1982.

While this book does not deal with medical ethics, it deals with an aspect of medicine which anyone working in the field of macro-allocation needs to understand. In the field indicated by the title, it is the fundamental work in the field.

Callahan, D., *Setting Limits: Medical Goals in an Aging Society*, Simon and Schuster, New York, 1987.

If only because of the attention it has received in the press, and even if one does not agree with the author's thesis (that there is a "natural life span" beyond which no health care needs ought to be met), this is an important book. It should be read by those interested in geriatric care and those dealing with the just allocation of medical resources.

Daniels, N., *Am I My Parents' Keeper?* Oxford University Press, New York, 1988.

This is essentially an expansion of Chapter 5 in Daniels' book *Just Health Care*. He here makes a largely Rawlsian argument as to why age should be an independent variable in allocating resources for health care. Even if one does not agree with this proposition (and I certainly do not), it is a well-structured argument and one that is more persuasive than is Callahan's.

Kübler-Ross, E., *On Death and Dying*, Macmillan, New York, 1969.

This was the pace-setting book in opening up the field of how to deal with dying patients. Although much work has been done since, the book remains of more than historical interest. The stages of dying which the author sketches are meant to be descriptive of a general process and not prescriptive for individual patients (as they have, unfortunately, sometimes been taken to be).

Index